Bracebridge!
- A MUSKOKA HERITAGE
THE WAY I SEE ITS CHARACTERS, ITS HISTORY AND THINGS WE SHOULD REMEMBER

By KENNETH CARMAN VEITCH

2013 Kenneth Carman Veitch

IBSN #978-0-9918864-0-1 Electronic book text #978-0-9918864-1-8

Publish date- July 2013

Publisher- CreateSpace –An AMAZON Company

Cover artistry by Paul Bennett Photography.

The front cover setting is the parlour room at the Inn at the Falls, Bracebridge, Ontario, Canada. The image reflected in the mirror is a picture of the west side of Manitoba Street, Bracebridge, Ontario, Canada circa 1905 provided to Robert J. Boyer by Mrs. Zaida Corrigan and included in *A Good Town Grew Here.*

The back cover features a section of Forrest Jacob's Bracebridge mural, on display in its entirety at the Bracebridge Sportsplex.

Editors Note…

The reader will notice that some subjects are described more than once in **Bracebridge!** A MUSKOKA HERITAGE. This is not by accident or a result of careless editing. They are intended to be there because they are relative to the focus of those chapters in which they appear. To exclude them would be wrong.

For example, **Chapter 42. AN INTERESTING CORNER – DOMINION AND MANITOBA** would not be complete without mentioning the *circuses* held there in the 1800s after railway service arrived in Bracebridge, nor would **Chapter 9. THE RAILWAY** be complete without mentioning the *circuses* the rail service brought to the pioneer community.

There are other examples, all intended to give the reader a more complete picture of that particular part of our interesting heritage.

ACKNOWLEDGEMENTS

I am forever grateful…..

…..to all those in our past, right back to the very first explorers and surveyors, that took the time to write about their experience here. The numerous books, manuals, newspapers and articles in our Bracebridge and Muskoka collection must surely make us the envy of every other municipality. Without them, present day writers, including myself, would find it very difficult if not impossible to produce the work we do so that those of the future may know and appreciate our past. I have no doubt those writers knew their work would be forever important and appreciated.

KENNETH CARMAN VEITCH

CONTENTS	PAGE
FOREWORD…	11
INTRODUCTION…	13
1. IN THE BEGINNING…	15
2. SURVEYORS-"LINING UP" MUSKOKA…	17
3. IT DIDN'T TAKE LONG…	19
4. BOOMING EARLY DAYS…	21
5. EARLY BUSINESS'S AND BAILEY'S GRIST MILL…	23
6. EARLY HOTELS IN BRACEBRIDGE…	25
7. TEVIOTDALES DISTRICT EXCHANGE…	29
8. MUSKOKA ROAD AND THE NEW ROAD TO GRAVENHURST…	31
9. THE RAILWAY…	33
10. THE NORTHERN ADVOCATE AND THOMAS McMURRAY…	37
11. THE BIGGEST AND BEST EARLY BUSINESS…	39
12. HOTELS GET BIGGER AND BETTER…	43
13. DIFFERENT POINTS OF VIEW ON EARLY BRACEBRIDGE…	47
14. PROHIBITION…	53
15. EARLY BRIDGES…	61
16. HER MAJESTY'S OLD RELIABLE SHAVING SALOON…	67
17. WILLIAM HOLDITCH'S TWO HORSEPOWER BOAT…	69
18. HOUSE OF COMMERCE…	71
19. DOWLER MATCH FACTORY…	71
20. BRACEBRIDGE BRILLIANT LIGHT COMPANY…	73

21. BRACEBRIDGE MARBLE AND GRANITE WORKS… 73

22. DUFFERIN HALL… 75

23. NEW YORK HORSE SHOEING EMPORIUM… 75

24. THE GOLDEN BEAVER STORE… 77

25. THE OLD ESTABLISHED WAGGON SHOP… 79

26. THE BRACEBRIDGE LIQUOR COMPANY… 79

27. CHANCERY LANE… 81

28. DOBBIN'S TOWN PUMP… 81

29. CRYSTAL PALACE… 83

30. BRACEBRIDGE CHEESE FACTORY… 85

31. THE PALACE RINK… 87

32. MEMORIAL PARK… 91

33. FLORA BARNES… 95

34. STONE COTTAGE, CASTLE DUNC AND LOCK-UPS… 97

35. AUBREY WHITE… 101

36. RENE M. CAISSE AND ESSIAC… 105

37. THE TANNERIES… 107

38. THE RIVER… 113

39. DR. JAMES FRANCIS WILLIAMS MD… 119

40. PAWSON HARNESS SHOP… 123

41. THE "OLD" POST OFFICE… 123

42. AN INTERESTING CORNER - DOMINION AND MANITOBA… 125

43. AUBREY STREET… 127

44. THE "TOWN" HALL WAS REALLY THE "VILLAGE" HALL… 137

45. VIOLA (HUGGARD) MACMILLAN… 141

46. ARNOTTS NURSING HOME/GOGGINS PRIVATE HOSPITAL?......143

47. BRACEBRIDGE'S ABANDONED BABY…...............................145

48. GEORGE RICHARDSON (VC)…..147

49. HOWARD VINCENT (DCM)… ………………………………… 149

50. ORGANIZATIONS WE HAVE KNOWN…...............................153

    SONS OF ENGLAND… 153

    SONS OF SCOTLAND…..154

    TORONTO-BRACEBRIDGE OLD BOYS AND OLD GIRLS ASSOC….155

    BLACK HAND… 156

    ORDER OF THE KNIGHTS OF THE MACABEES…....................157

    INDEPENDENT ORDER OF FORESTERS….............................157

    ANCIENT ORDER OF UNITED WORKMEN… 158

    KALAMITY CLUB…...158

    CLEF CLUB…...159

    BRACEBRIDGE CITIZENS BAND… 160

    BRACEBRIDGE CHORAL SOCIETY… 161

    TOC-H… 162

    CANADIAN CLUB OF BRACEBRIDGE… 162

    CANADIAN PATRIOTIC FUND…...162

    WOMEN'S PATRIOTIC LEAGUE…..163

    EIGHTEEN KNITTING CLUB…..163

    KNIT KNUTS CLUB… 164

    BRACEBRIDGE CRICKET CLUB…...164

    98 CLUB… 164

    BRACEBRIDGE CLUB..165

    MOTHERS PENSION BOARD…...165

WOMENS INSTITUTE… 165

LOYAL ORANGE LODGE… 165

CATHOLIC ORDER OF FORRESTERS… 165

SHEIKS… 165

GAME PROTECTION SOCIETY… 166

CATHOLIC MENS SOCIETY… 166

CHOSEN FRIENDS LODGE… 166

WOMENS CHRISTIAN TEMPERANCE UNION… 166

BAND OF HOPE… 167

HARMONY CLUB… 167

BRACEBRIDGE LITERACY SOCIETY… 167

BRACEBRIDGE LADIES AID SOCIETY… 167

BLUE GLASS CLUB… 167

367 CLUB… 168

WINTER EVENING AMUSEMENT SOCIETY… 168

51. CHARACTERS WE HAVE KNOWN… 169

JOHNNY MOON… 169

OSCEOLA GLADIATOR… 173

CARL PILGER… 174

BILLY THE PIG… 175

"GATLIN GUN" SPENCER… 175

MORLEY CROCKFORD 176

ALF "SHORTY" CONNERS… 177

"RAS" JERMAN… 178

CECIL MCNEICE… 178

TOM HOLLIDAY… 178

FRED "BING" CROSBY………………………………………………………180

LARRY MAURO…………………………………………………………………181

BONEY……………………………………………………………………………182

"MAW" FORTH…………………………………………………………………183

"LITTLE" JIMMY………………………………………………………………183

52. STRANGE THINGS ARE DONE……………………………………………185

BLACK SQUIRRELS AND RACCOONS…………………………………185

TANNERIES AND THEIR EFFECT ON THE RIVER……………………185

THE MUSKOKA GOLD RUSH……………………………………………186

THE TEDDY BEAR……………………………………………………………187

MUSKOKA LAMB……………………………………………………………187

53. BUSINESS -THE FOUNDATION OF BRACEBRIDGE……………………189

MUSKOKA PUBLISHING COMPANY……………………………………189

MEDLEY BROS…………………………………………………………………189

NORTHERN PLANING MILLS……………………………………………190

WAITE'S BAKERY……………………………………………………………190

WES FINCH & SONS EXCAVATING LTD………………………………190

MacNAUGHTAN HARDWARE……………………………………………191

ECCLESTONE HARDWARE/ECCLESTONE & BATES………………191

HAMMOND TRANSPORTATION/MUSKOKA TRANSPORT………192

MUSKOKA GARAGE…………………………………………………………193

P.J. MARRIN WHOLESALERS………………………………………………194

H.J.BROOKS & SONS…………………………………………………………194

THE THOMAS COMPANY…………………………………………………195

ELLIOTTS 5 TO $1.00 STORE………………………………………………196

STONE'S MENS AND LADIES WEAR……………………………………197

MUSKOKA TRADING COMPANY	197
UPTOWN SERVICE STATION	197
RIDLEY CLEANERS	198
SHIER'S INSURANCE	198
DOWNTOWN GARAGE	199
MUSKOKA FOUNDRY	199
J.D.SHIER LUMBER	200
NORWOOD THEATRE	201
REYNOLDS FUNERAL HOME	202
THE BIG BUSY STORE (T.J. ANDERSON AND SONS)	204
FOWLER CONSTRUCTION COMPANY LTD	204
MUSKOKA CONTAINERIZED SERVICES	205
BB AUTO AND SPORTS SUPPLY	206
W.J. LANG AND SONS	206
HOLIDAY HOUSE	206
CATHCART'S GARAGE	207
NEWARK BOAT FENDERS	208
SANTA'S VILLAGE	208
DAWSON'S ELECTRIC	210
KNOWLES PLUMBING	210
54. HOW HOT IS HOT?	213
55. THE LAST WORD	217

FOREWORD...

Bracebridge is located in the geographic heart of Muskoka and recorded history clearly indicates that it quickly evolved into the centre of political, economic, judicial, and social life in the region. Unsurprisingly, it has a long and rich heritage that's apparent as soon as one enters town.

I can think of no one better to chronicle this history than Kenneth Carman Veitch, a near-lifelong resident who for many years has been referred to as its local historian, a title that he hesitatingly accepts. He would rather simply be known as one who refuses to allow Bracebridge's interesting past be forgotten. Whether it is an event that took place or someone who has been a part of Bracebridge history, Ken will either know about it or know where to find information on it in his extensive reference system. Indeed, I like to think I know Muskoka pretty well-- having written about its history in local publications for more than a decade and co-authored five books on the subject-- and yet often I've have to turn to Ken for his expertise and knowledge. He has never disappointed me.

And therein lays the reason I felt compelled, honored even, to write a Forward for this book, Ken's second. He believes that history belongs to all of us. Whereas some historians are protective of their work and jealously hoard it, Ken is the exact opposite. A true gentleman and scholar, he willingly extends his assistance and encouragement; his sole reward being the knowledge that the history of the town he loves so dearly is being perpetuated.

Being familiar with Ken's work in the past I eagerly agreed to write this Forward even before having seen the completed manuscript. Now that I have and read its richly detailed and remarkably entertaining text, I am more than happy that I did. Simply put, ***Bracebridge!*** – *A MUSKOKA HERITAGE* is a wonderful tribute to Bracebridge and is a remarkably compelling story. I read it with a new appreciation for the community and indeed for the man who has devoted a number of years chronicling its past.

If you're lucky enough to live in Bracebridge, embrace it. Ken has, and it shows on each and every page of this walk down memory's lane.

Andrew Hind, author (Ghost Towns of Muskoka, etc.)

INTRODUCTION…

My interest in local history started as a child growing up in the small settlement of Ufford, just north-west of Bracebridge, with my grandparents. They were born into pioneer Muskoka families during difficult years when *their* parents were trying to clear land and create farms, (my grandfather was born in 1876, my grandmother 1881), and were well qualified to relate to me many intriguing and interesting tales about early settlers. Those stories have stuck with me ever since; many of which I have related in my recent book ***My early days as a boy in UFFORD …and stories people tell me.*** Because of the success of that effort I am encouraged to write about my larger community in ***BRACEBRIDGE! –A MUSKOKA HERITAGE.***

A number of great books have been written about the courageous adventurers and struggles of early pioneer settlers in this area. Gary Long told about many in his very informative book ***This River the Muskoka*** and Florence Murray provided an incredible collection of documents and reports in her book ***Muskoka and Haliburton 1615 to 1875***. The ***Guide Book & Atlas of Muskoka and Parry Sound Districts 1879*** by W.E. Hamilton, the Robert J. Boyer books ***Early Exploration in Muskoka, A Good Town Grew Here,*** and others, are a very valuable account of early excursions and pioneer Bracebridge. Very interesting historical information is contained in ***Reminiscences*** by Redmond Thomas, ***BRACEBRIDGE FIFTY YEARS AGO*** by G.H.O. Thomas, ***A Good Town Continues*** written for Bracebridge's 125th anniversary, other valuable works by George Boyer, James Boyer, Gary Denniss and my own miscellaneous files.

I greatly enjoy these books and documents that focus on the Bracebridge /central Muskoka area and the glorious Muskoka River. The 26 publications in my collection form the foundation of my ***Veitch Index*** which I use daily in responding to enquiries from the public about our past. Because of that I'm often referred to as the ***"local historian"***. As far as I'm concerned that's pushing it. If I am to be recognized because of this work I prefer to be known as a dedicated collector of interesting information regarding the people and events in the history of this wonderful part of Muskoka; ***"a source of information"***, and nothing more. As the ***"Bard of the Yukon"***, the famous Robert W. Service said about his enchanting rhymes, ***"For God's sake don't call me a poet, I've never been guilty of that"***. What I write about here is for the most part gleaned from my treasured collection or my own experience, but it should not be forgotten that it often involves *my* interpretation of the way things happened.

So consider it an interesting story about the history of Bracebridge and my way of telling it in an entertaining way. History written in great detail can be dreadfully boring so I have endeavoured to summarize it in a way that makes it a little more fun and easier to read while still informing the reader of some basic facts about our rich heritage. Some personal experiences and tales of little known but interesting characters and situations provide an additional bit of fun.

I hope you enjoy reading it as much as I have enjoyed writing it.

Kenneth Carman Veitch

1. IN THE BEGINNING...

Starting at the beginning is a pretty good place to start, the way I see it, and the story of Bracebridge as a settlement, then a community, then a post office, then a Township, then a Village and finally a Town seems to have begun in 1859 when the first white settler built his log shack here and made this place his home.

Prior to that though a number of explorers travelled this country, directed at first by the British Military, and thoroughly explored the rivers of the area apparently trying to find a water access between Georgian Bay and the Ottawa River. It is said it was a strategic attempt to bolster the defence system for this new land prompted by the fear of attack from the United States. Bracebridge was front and centre for this exploration which actually started on the Black River which runs from its headwaters in the County of Haliburton through the Township of Oakley (now Oakley Ward of the Town of Bracebridge) to the Severn River in Simcoe County. The focus though quickly became the much larger Muskoka River where travel was so much easier and with its two branches seemed to possess a greater promise of success.

That all started in the 1700s and continued until the mid-1800s. A list of adventurers can be compiled from the many well written books and collections on early Muskoka. As early as 1611 there are references made to Norsemen possibly travelling through Muskoka. Samuel Champlain, Recollet missionaries, Francois Joseph Bressani and others all indicate that in those early days there were many who had an interest in this part of Ontario. The rudimentary maps they prepared made little specific reference to the geographic details of Muskoka, although they did attempt to show lakes and rivers in rough form. The land was sometimes shown as trapping and hunting ground, indicating that they recognized it as being occupied by a native population. Many of those native tribes travelled through Bracebridge on the Muskoka River as did the explorers and adventurers that came after them.

In pursuit of that elusive access to the Ottawa River, the Royal Engineers sent W. B. Marlow and W. M. Smith to, in part, explore the Black River, followed later by Lieutenant Briscoe. They may have been the first non-natives to travel through Muskoka. It was Briscoe who in 1826 changed the focus of the exploration from the winding and difficult Black River to the Muskoka River. Their findings were not well received however and further expeditions were dispatched to explore both these routes the following year.

Into that early interest in this area came the Shirreff family. Entrepreneur father Charles who was impressed with the economic opportunities that would be provided by a water connection between the Ottawa River and Georgian Bay, son Robert who was interested in development of that vast highland known as the Algonquin Dome (Algonquin Park), and son Alexander who in 1829 conducted an exploration of the Muskoka River system. His work exploring the rivers was an improvement and like others before him, suggested the healthy tree growth in Muskoka indicated good soil, therefore very suitable for settlement. That conclusion produced untold suffering for many of those who took up the offer of free land under the Free Grant Land and Homestead Act many years later. He was unable to ascertain whether or not a reasonable and practical water access existed across that part of north-eastern Ontario with the result that the search, (along with a convoluted plan for a complicated canal system), was abandoned, including any development along the way.

Nevertheless, the government of Upper Canada wanted more and in 1835 John Carthew of the Royal Navy and Frederick Baddeley of the Royal Engineers were charged with producing an exploratory survey of the area adjacent to the Georgian Bay. Baddeley was the first to provide a *record* of visiting Bracebridge Falls, although others had obviously been there, known then as North Falls because of its location on the North Branch of the Muskoka River, while Carthew was the first to record accessing the Dee Bank River, Three Mile Lake and Skeleton Lake. They provided accurate records of their travels, particularly important to Bracebridge because much of their work focused directly on this area of Muskoka. They clearly stated their disagreement with Shirreff about the quality of the soil but were impressed with the water power potential of the many waterfalls.

Never satisfied though, the government commissioned a further study in 1837 by the famous David Thompson who explored and mapped Lakes Muskoka, Rosseau and Joseph. His records show that he travelled the Musquash River, the Muskoka River South Branch, Lake of Bays, the Oxtongue River, and a chain of lakes until he reached the Madawaska River system.

His instructions, as well as requiring him to map the lakes of this area, apparently (and incredibly, in spite of all the previous negative reports), asked that he also look into the practicality of a system of canals linking Georgian Bay with the Ottawa River; all of which he did in 1837. His report was negative, no doubt due to the multitude of waterfalls and rough terrain that would be encountered in any such construction. His positive comments about the hardwood and pine trees and the land generally may have given support for the later settlement of Muskoka, but many of his observations proved to be far too positive, especially his estimate of there being over a *million* acres of land fit for cultivation along the Muskoka River.

The second and last exploration was ordered by the Geological Survey of Canada in 1853 who contracted with Alexander Murray to study the geology of the area between Georgian Bay and the Ottawa River. In this venture Murray chose to ascend the North Branch of the Muskoka River, (most others had used the South Branch), and in doing so recorded visits to Mary Lake, Fairy Lake and Peninsula Lake.

Obviously there was a great deal of earlier travel over these rivers by First Nations and fur traders because some explorers reported the existence of encampments and trading posts. One of these Trading Posts was located on Lake of Bays possibly belonging to the Hudson Bay Company or the North West Company, which no doubt gave rise to its first name ***"Trading Lake"***. Even though some of these explorer/adventurers did not seem to have the advantage of knowing the work of those who went before them, their records did provide a great advantage to the next wave of activity -the surveyors, which are the subject of another chapter in **BRACEBRIDGE! -A MUSKOKA HERITAGE.**

There is one indisputable *constant* in the records of the early adventurers that we should all remember; every one of them travelled through some part of what we now know as Bracebridge. They paddled our rivers and camped on our shores when this area was a vast wilderness. Standing on the shore of the river in Bracebridge Bay Park it is nice to reflect for a moment and picture those ancient explorers camping there as they must have done in those early days.

2. SURVEYORS-"LINING UP" MUSKOKA...

The hired explorers and adventurers had hardly finished their work when along came the surveyors; in fact they overlapped in some cases. When explorers John Carthew and F. H. Baddeley carried out their exploration of the lakes and rivers of Muskoka they were accompanied by two surveyors- William Hawkins and Samuel Richardson. They were charged with extending the survey line northwest from the already surveyed Rama Township. Their work was completed in 1835 and was the first survey line in Muskoka, today easily identified today as the road allowance upon which parts of Keith Road, Ecclestone Drive, Wellington Street and the north part of Manitoba Street are located.

That line forever established what would later be the boundary between the geographic townships of Ryde and Morrison, Draper and Muskoka, Monck and Macaulay, Stephenson and Watt, Stisted and Cardwell, and so on further north into Parry Sound District and beyond. These townships are today designated as *"wards"* in various amalgamated municipalities of Muskoka.

This historically became known as Hawkins Line and it is not written why Samuel Richardson, his survey partner, was not included in that title. Perhaps he was an assistant with Hawkins having been designated the chief surveyor in charge of the work.

A need to accommodate the tide of immigration from Britain, the ongoing concern over reports of the United States eyeing territorial expansion, and positive comments from the explorers regarding the good conditions for settlement in Muskoka, gave rise to a decision to push back the borders of the wilderness in this part of the province, sometimes referred to as the *"waste land"*, and encourage its development.

The implementation of this settlement decision required another survey line, this time running in an east-west direction from the Madawaska River to intersect with the north-south line completed by Hawkins in 1835. Hired to complete this survey was Robert Bell who started the difficult task in 1847 and, after experiencing great hardship struggling through rugged wilderness, completed it several months later. Like the north-south line this survey was also very important to Bracebridge and Muskoka because it formed the boundary line between what would later become the geographic townships of Draper and Macaulay, Oakley and McLean, and the southerly boundary of Ridout.

Of particular interest to Bracebridge was the fact that these two survey lines, the first legal move to establish property lines and boundaries in all of Muskoka, intersected very close to downtown Bracebridge, in fact, directly underneath what is now the location of the south end of the Wellington Street bridge adjacent to the present Riverside Inn.

This was a very significant occurrence because it was from this point that all the townships of Muskoka were created by later surveyors charged with the responsibility of setting the numerous township boundaries and the surveying and marking of the concessions and lots that would eventually be placed in ownership. In recent times a member of the Bracebridge Economic Development Committee, Robert Dolphin, suggested and encouraged the use of a slogan for Bracebridge designating it ***"The Heart of Muskoka"***. It was a good suggestion because in fact it was from this intersection of Muskoka's first two survey lines in Bracebridge that all other Muskoka municipalities were created, making it truly "***The Heart of Muskoka"***.

3. IT DIDN'T TAKE LONG…

It was only twelve years after those surveys were completed that things started happening. No doubt the reports of the many explorers and surveyors about the abundance of hardwoods and pine in Muskoka, and in the case of Bracebridge the multitude of waterfalls that could provide hydraulic power for the wheels of industry, resulted in entrepreneurs taking notice of the economic possibilities.

John Beal apparently paddled or rowed across Lake Muskoka and up the Muskoka River until he came to what he no doubt knew, if he was following the information provided by those who came before him, was North Falls. This may have been his destination or perhaps he decided to settle here because he recognized the importance of the unimpeded access from these falls to the *"big"* lake, sensed the power available in the waterfalls, or maybe he just liked the lay of the land, who knows. It is not clear what he did for a living or whether or not there was a family involved. He clearly had to be quite determined to settle here or he would not have climbed over deadfalls and up steep ravines looking for some flat land, which he found a few hundred meters north of the river near where in 2013 we have Oliver's Coffee Shop in the north end of the downtown business area. There is little record of Beal's origin, when he left North Falls or where he went.

The location of his log shanty set forever the location of the road which we now know as Manitoba Street. After the Muskoka Colonization Road arrived in North Falls in 1861 it continued northward following the laid out survey line of J. S. Dennis in anticipation of eventually reaching Huntsville and Parry Sound. In surveying this route the policy was to avoid difficult terrain but also to place it near existing residences, in this case it was that of Mr. Beal, Bracebridge's first settler.

Mr. Beal was not here alone very long. In short order David Leith settled in North Falls and the Coopers, having completed building the Muskoka Colonization Road from Muskoka Falls, known then as South Falls, also decided to stay. Joseph Cooper (son of James Cooper) claimed to have built the first bridge over the North Branch of the Muskoka River at the top end of North Falls. Prior to that bridge being constructed, the only way of crossing the river was on a pine tree that had been dropped to span the river to serve that purpose.

Some clarification concerning the Cooper family, (if it is possible), is required here. Many members of that family settled in North Falls in the first days of the community, but our historical books and documents vary a bit on which one did what. In those records, as listed in the *"Veitch Index",* there are *167* entries for the name *"Cooper".* In an attempt to identify those who were part of the fabric of *early* Bracebridge and at the risk of missing some, included in the records and various books under the surname *"Cooper"* are references to – Alex, Andrew, Arthur, Edward, Ernest, George, Gordon, Harold, Bob, Hugh, James, Joseph, Robert, John, Thomas, Cooper Bros. and some that just show Cooper. There is nothing to say they were all related but some certainly were.

Early days in Muskoka names James Cooper as *"…one of the road contractors,…"* and had two sons Joseph and John, noting that Joseph *"…was old enough to have worked on the* *construction of the first bridge..."* although it does not confirm that he actually did. In *Bracebridge Around 1930* it states that *"...Joseph, had worked with his father James Cooper in the colonization road work at Bracebridge and also built the Dominion Hotel."* It also states that in 1863 the first boy baby to be born in Bracebridge was Thomas, Joseph's son, and the *Guidebook & Atlas of Muskoka Parry Sound Districts 1879* records that a Thomas S. Cooper owned property in Macaulay Township in that year.

A handwritten letter said to be written by Joseph Cooper at the age of 94 states that he and his father (James Cooper) felled the pine tree across the Muskoka River at the top of North Falls to gain access to the north side and that his father took the contract to cut the road from Washago in 1861. It also states that he (Joseph), since he was a carpenter, had to build bridges, *"...one where we cut the Pine tree and one where the station now stands."* He also states that his oldest son was the first white *child* to be born in Bracebridge and that the Liddard family had a daughter born about the same time.

However, in *A Good Town Grew Here,* regarding the building of the colonization road it states that, -*"...and by 1861 was on its way through Bracebridge. The contractors were Joseph and Robert Cooper,...".* Another version appeared in a newspaper article in the *Muskoka Sun* on June 30th, 1988 where it states that *John* Cooper assisted his father (James) in opening the (colonization) road *"...which reached Bracebridge in 1861, and it was in that year that Joseph Cooper, another member of the family, built the first bridge across the river."*

Regardless of whether it was James, James and Robert, Joseph and Robert or James and John, the Cooper family along with John Beal and David Leith, were founders of Bracebridge. They are to be admired as adventurers, entrepreneurs and for their courage in plunging into the rugged Muskoka wilderness of the 1860s.

An *"...amusing circumstance.."* as described by W.E.Hamilton in *Guide Book & Atlas of Muskoka and Parry Sound Districts 1879* about that pine tree bridge involved a fellow that was somewhat inebriated attempting to cross the river on it when he slipped and was about to plunge into the raging rapids of the falls. To his good fortune though, the demijohn that he carried dropped on the opposite side of the pine log and he hung suspended there until he was rescued.

4. BOOMING EARLY DAYS…

It was the immense stands of timber and the glorious opportunity to harness the hydraulic power from the water falls that brought great prosperity to the pioneer settlement of North Falls. A first-hand description of the settlement is contained in **Muskoka and Haliburton 1615-1875** where it is stated-

> *"Bracebridge in 1861, according to W. E. Hamilton, 'consisted of the log huts and potato patches of Messrs. John Beal and David Leith, James Cooper's log house, and a small brick tavern and store, built on the south side of the river (there being no bridge save a large pine tree, which spanned the falls) by Hiram Macdonald.' But with its strategic position on the Muskoka Road, and River, with an abundance of water power, and above all with a number of active, determined promoters, Bracebridge grew rapidly in population and importance."*

and later-

> *"By 1870 Bracebridge had free schools, several churches, at least three hotels, stores, sawmills, a newspaper, and a developing tourist trade. That year Charles Marshall found the 'little town' romantic and picturesque, but also bustling and prosperous."*

Imagine. By 1870, just 11 years after John Beal pulled his canoe onto the shore below the falls and found a place he liked for his log shanty, all this had happened in a frontier town in an era when nothing happened quickly. Fast *anything* hadn't arrived yet.

Because of the rapidly increasing population and commercial operations, post offices were being established in Muskoka. At the encouragement of boating czar A.P. Cockburn, North Falls was designated a post office in 1864 with the name of Bracebridge, so named, according to George W. Boyer in **"Early Days in Muskoka"**, by William Dawson LaSuer, a secretary in Canada's Postmaster-General's Department. The name was derived from the Washington Irving book **"Bracebridge Hall"**, (one elderly gentleman disagreed, saying it was named Bracebridge because it was the location of a **"well braced"** bridge). Around the same time McCabes Landing was designated Gravenhurst. It has been said that the name Gravenhurst also came from Irving's book, but again that has been disputed by others. The ever observant and entrepreneurial Cockburn understood the importance of these two busy centres on the Muskoka Lakes water system.

It was the burst of energy and enthusiasm of the pioneers and entrepreneurs that gave rise to governmental organization and, since the community of North Falls was situated in the geographical township of Macaulay, it is not surprising that Macaulay and the adjoining townships of Draper, Stephenson and Ryde were formed into a United Township for municipal jurisdiction in 1868. It was not the first though; Muskoka and Morrison Townships formed a United Township in 1865. Interestingly, Draper was considered the senior municipality and the first Clerks Office was established in Uffington.

Few of the United Township municipalities lasted very long however because their immense size made communication difficult. Macaulay in 1869 is recorded as having 481 residents, no doubt most of them in the immediate area of the Bracebridge Post Office.

With the ever growing importance of the Bracebridge area it was becoming more and more obvious that law and order needed to be developed. Through the M.P.P. of the day, again A. P. Cockburn, a petition was presented to the Provincial Government in 1868 to form a Division Court District, constitute the District for registration purposes and designate Bracebridge as the District centre because of its easy access from all quarters. The petition was signed by many residents from the developing townships around Bracebridge, even as far away as Ufford in Watt Township. It got immediate results and Charles E. Lount was appointed Stipendiary Magistrate to conduct court, act as land agent and establish a registry office.

This resulted in the Provincial government buying the land on Dominion Street and in 1870 building the first registry office and a lock-up, which became the District Jail. This property continues to this date in 2013 to be the site of various Provincial offices.

Some things never change apparently. In 1888 there were a number of jurisdictional changes taking place in central Ontario including the boundaries of Victoria and Simcoe Counties and there was a move afoot to elevate Muskoka from a Divisional Court District to a full Judicial District. Since Bracebridge had been the location of Provincial Government offices since 1870, coupled with the fact that it was strategically located in the centre of everything, it was suggested, logically enough, that it would be named the government seat for Muskoka.

However, in a fit of jealous rage, the Reeve of Huntsville called a meeting with representatives from Huntsville, Gravenhurst and Parry Sound to oppose the formation of a county government for Muskoka if Bracebridge was to be the government seat. There had been requests made to the province by the Simcoe and Victoria County Councils that Muskoka be given its own county status, (obviously Muskoka was a burden to them), but there isn't that much evidence that the people of Muskoka *wanted* county status. Their interest was to get their own *judicial district* to save residents of Muskoka having to travel to Barrie for court cases. Unquestionably, it was the people of Bracebridge who worked to establish the judicial district and were no doubt well aware that they were in a very favourable position to be designated the government seat.

Incredibly, even in 1888 Huntsville, Gravenhurst and Parry Sound didn't want Bracebridge to be designated as the government seat of any kind, no matter that it was by far the most appropriate location, and tried to do whatever they could to stop it. But their devious plan failed in spite of deputations being sent to Toronto to discuss the matter with Provincial authorities. The **Muskoka Herald** of the day reported that **"those from Huntsville and Gravenhurst went away sorrowful"**. Some things never change, did I already say that?

5. EARLY BUSINESS'S AND BAILEY'S GRIST MILL...

The kick start for the Bracebridge economy obviously came from the logging industry and for a number of good reasons, not the least of which were the advantages provided by the Muskoka River. The unimpeded access provided by the Muskoka River to the big lakes of Muskoka, Rosseau and Joseph made it easy to get to North Falls and South Falls, although North Falls (Bracebridge now) was the more attractive destination for business activities. The South Branch upstream from its intersection with the North Branch to the dynamic South Falls was inaccessible for the big lake boats because it was shallower and quite twisty, besides being a much greater distance from Muskoka Lake.

The two branches of the river were like highways in the early days of the developing logging industry, providing access to the vast stands of timber upstream and a convenient facility for floating logs downstream on their way to the mills that popped up everywhere, especially in Bracebridge and Gravenhurst. Stores, service industries and hotels appeared rapidly. Because much of the population at any given time was transient as men moved between the logging camps and the mills, hotels and taverns were very popular. At one time, by a simple calculation, it could be determined that there was a tavern for every 75 permanent residents, but in reality it was the transient workers that kept them in business.

The logging industry played a huge part in Muskoka development but it wasn't just the timber that brought entrepreneurs here. It was the waterfalls, and there were lots of them. In fact, activity around them began right along with the surge of logging companies. Within a few miles of North Falls, what would be considered easy walking distance in those days, there were seven other significant drops in the two branches of the river. Not necessarily known by these names back then, today we recognize them as Muskoka (South) Falls, Hannah Chute, Wilson's Falls, High Falls, Balsam Chute, Trethewey Falls and an active water flow in Flynn's Rapids. Some of these falls will be described in greater detail in later chapters.

They were attractive because of the hydraulic power the flow of water produced. It was invaluable to early industry. That is what spun the waterwheels that in turn powered the saw blades, pumps, grinding wheels and machinery; and it was free for the taking. Little wonder North Falls became the centre of industry in Muskoka in a hurry.

One of the first industries to make use of water power was the grist mill built by Alexander Bailey at the bottom of North Falls. He had previously owned and operated a fur trading post on the bank of the river near Muskoka Lake. Aside from the logging and waterfalls based manufacturing operations, early rural Muskoka developed a modest farm based economy that existed for many years. Bailey's mill produced flour from the grain grown by the fledgling farms in the vicinity. Early settlers would get together with their neighbours and bring their summer production to town with their oxen and wagons, wait while the mill processed it into flour, and return to their farms with, they hoped, a sufficient supply of flour for the winter. Often the quantity of grain required the mill to keep running for many hours and the settlers would find it necessary to stay over in Bracebridge and take advantage of the hospitality provided by one of the many hotels. It often became more of a celebration than anything else and hotel and tavern owners were more than willing to accommodate the visitors.

One group that organized this type of annual event consisted of a number of farmers from the settlement of Ufford strung along the south shore of Three Mile Lake, northwest of Bracebridge. A vivid description of one such occasion was provided by Bert Shea in his excellent book on the history of Muskoka, *"History of the Sheas and the Paths of Adventure"* wherein he quotes from a discussion he had with an elderly man whose father was an unidentified pioneer shopkeeper in Bracebridge in that era. It reads in part:

"Any time in December before Christmas we in the town looked for the day when the Three Mile Lake Wolves with their ox team would come to town loaded with wheat. Their coming needed no help to announce them for we could hear them coming for miles. Their howls and shouts carried on the frosty air and as they passed through town, it was a parade worth watching and even the dogs were filled with fear and went into hiding. Woe betide any who got fresh with THEM-'tis little wonder they were known as the Three Mile Lake Wolves….."

and later:

"…After one of these grand celebrations, before they left town the following morning, as a challenge to their adversaries of the night before, they joined hands at the top of Higgins Hill and marched abreast down the main street, through the village, clearing all obstructions before them."

There are a number of great stories about those pioneers and how they acquired the name of the *"Three Mile Lake Wolves"* and, while this particular event occurred well after the earliest days, it does give an insight into the way things happened as Muskoka progressed. A lot of work to produce your crops but a little fun was in order at the end of the day.

The mill was strategically placed to gain access to the main water flow, part of which was directed into a channel leading to a large water wheel. Thus activated by the flow, the wheel turned a shaft that entered the building and spun the large stone grinding wheels that ground the grain into flour. The details of how that process produced flour was never fully described but it must have worked because it was used for that purpose for a number of years. It was later converted to a saw mill once the Northern Railway and steamships began bringing better flour and farmers started using their grain more for feeding livestock.

Access to the mill was by Mill Street leading from Muskoka Road at Birds Bridge down the steep south side of the falls; used in 2013 as a walking path. The location of the mill resulted in a wharf, shown as *"Steamship Landing"* on early maps, being built in the small bay just to the south of the foot of the falls. It was here where A. P Cockburn's first steamship *"Wenonah"* docked on its maiden voyage to Bracebridge in 1866. That wharf was replaced by a much larger one on the north side of the river at the foot of Dominion Street and Kimberley Avenue in 1871 which in turn was replaced by the present massive concrete wharf in 1905.

In the development of Bracebridge Bay Park in the 1980s, a water wheel to emulate the original of the grist mill was constructed in approximately the same location as the one Bailey created and the original concrete wall built to direct water into the channel was retained; another praiseworthy example of the effort put forth by the Town of Bracebridge to preserve the historic features of a pioneer settlement. It was clear that whoever Alexander Bailey hired to build his waterwheel (or perhaps he built it himself) knew a lot more about how to do it correctly than those that built the modern day version. It would seem Bailey's ran for years while the modern day version has been totally replaced once and requires regular maintenance to remove floating branches and an occasional beaver caught in the raceway leading to the blades of the wheel.

The mill had various owners and rebuilds during its existence and finally burned in 1909, a fate not uncommon to many early sawmills.

Alexander Bailey's 1864 Saw Mill/Flour and Grist Mill

6. EARLY HOTELS IN BRACEBRIDGE…

The hotels in the frontier town were no doubt a thing of beauty, probably in line with one's vision of what a frontier hotel in a western movie would be; rough-cut lumber siding, wooden cots, an outhouse stuck in a corner or in a backyard, an iron woodstove with exposed metal stove pipes running through the house to retain heat, a long shanty type table for feeding guests, a large pot on the stove containing warm water for washing, etc.. How could they be much considering what they had to work with? The Cooper Hotel at the bottom of the present day downtown business section, reported by one source to be in the location where the Dominion Hotel would later be built, was one of the earliest. As stated in the last chapter, it was a combination of members of that family that built the part of the colonization road leading to North Falls and were among the first settlers. According to maps of the day, Cooper's property seems to have consisted of the land along the side of the falls including that occupied in 2013 by the Northern Buildal retail outlet.

Hiram James MacDonald (often spelled *McDonald*) played a huge role in early Bracebridge. As referenced earlier, W. E. Hamilton recorded that he (MacDonald), and presumably his family, was here in 1861 and operated a tavern and a store on the south side of the river adjacent to the large pine tree that spanned the river at the top of the falls. Once built, the bridge that replaced the pine tree quickly became known as ***"Bird's Bridge"*** because it was at the north end of the bridge on the north bank of the river where Henry J Bird established his woollen mill in 1872. Part of the stone foundation of his building still remains at the water's edge of the river.

Charles Marshal in ***Muskoka & Haliburton 1615 to 1875*** stated that in 1870 there were three hotels in the settlement of North Falls, the Victoria, the Royal and Dominion; the names obviously reflecting the owner's British heritage. Some early records refer to the Dominion as the ***"Dominion House"*** while others say ***"Dominion Hotel"***. He gives no reference to Coopers Hotel, which may have ceased to operate by that time. Marshall provides a further insight into the community when he describes the quality of the accommodation facilities in the settlement where guests would sleep in rows upon the floor, how the ***"Northern Advocate"*** local newspaper has a circulation of 1,100 and how the emigration agent (should he have said immigration agent?) had disposed of *60,000 acres* of land within the last two months! Even with the Free Grant Land and Homestead Act of 1868 at the peak of its operations it is very difficult to imagine how that much land could possibly be processed for development in such a short period of time.

No doubt MacDonald's hotel ***"The Royal"*** was an integral component of his tavern, or vice-versa, and, according to Redmond Thomas's March 9, 1944 ***"Comment"*** column in the Bracebridge Gazette, was located adjacent to the south end and east side of Bird's Bridge where in 2013 there exists two residential buildings, one housing the office of Muskoka Family Focus Children's Place the other a private residence, immediately across the river from the present water reservoir. Robert J. Boyer wrote in ***"A Good Town Grew Here"*** that the hotel building was built in 1868 and burned in 1904, sadly taking the life of the infant child of Mr. and Mrs. John Warlow, while Mr. Warlow was away working in a logging camp. The property was owned then by a Mrs. Pelletier and had been converted into two residences. The Royal Hotel, according to G.H.O. Thomas, was the first hotel in the settlement although Coopers Hotel must have existed around the same time. A Mr. Ross is shown as ***"running"*** the Royal Hotel in one reference but is shown as ***"owning"*** the Dominion House in another.

The Dominion Hotel (or House) burned, was rebuilt and renovated many times over the years; the brick building that it became at last continues to stand in 2013 on the east side and at the south end of Manitoba Street. The hotel ceased operating as such in the 1920s but the building still remains as one of the larger structures in the downtown business area; in 2013 housing a number of retails outlets and the relocated Bracebridge Dairy Bar. It is pleasing to note that the upper stories still show the intricate brick work forming the shape of the windows, the openings where balconies were set into the building and a decorative brick coping along the top of the front wall.

The Dominion Hotel, also known as Dominion House, in its heyday

The Victoria Hotel, in 1868 owned by Alexander Bailey, was located on the west side of Muskoka Road at the top of *"Free Methodist Hill"*, so named because the Free Methodist Church at that time, according the G.H.O. Thomas, was also located there. Muskoka Road was the main and busy entrance to Bracebridge at that time and included a very steep hill adjacent to the west side of Woodchester (the *"Bird House"*) property, (Henry J. Bird's proud home overlooking his Bird Woollen Mill), as it approached the south end of Bird's Bridge. The Free Methodist Church in 2013, at the intersection of Queen Street and Entrance Drive remains not far from the top of the hill that was named after it, just to the south and west of its original location.

It was probably an excellent location for a hotel and tavern in the earliest days because it was from the Muskoka Road here, prior to the building of the first Free Methodist church, that a road existed leading to the east side of the community and north-east Muskoka as described fully in a later chapter. It was also the location of the first church structure in the community -a Presbyterian Church built on King Street in 1868 which they shared with the Methodists.

Hiram James MacDonald did not stop at hotels and taverns when it came to doing business in the pioneer settlement. He acquired a large tract of land adjacent to the Muskoka Road not far from Mr. Beal's log shanty and in due time subdivided it into building lots. His family will be forever remembered because he named the streets after himself, his wife and his children; hence the streets of today known as Hiram Street, James Street, MacDonald Street, Mary Street, Ida Street, Jane Street, and Ann Street, according to a fine summary of the origin of Bracebridge street names written by **Robert J. Boyer** as a newspaper article. However, in *A Good Town Continues* Margaret Street is added as another street named after a child of MacDonald, substantiated by the fact that a Miss Margaret Stewart of Los Angeles whose father was Hiram James MacDonald visited Bracebridge in 1947. Why she was named as a *"Miss"* yet bearing *"Stewart"* as a surname is not explained. Although nothing to do with his family, he also named two streets running north from Liddard Street, according to a *Thomas 1944* article, one being Algoma Street after the Anglican Diocese of which Bracebridge was a part, and Serepta Street, in honour of Right Reverend Monsignor Jamot, the Roman Catholic Bishop of Serepta. Those two streets were never opened for use but still appear on old maps of the Town. MacDonald was also active in early municipal affairs of his time, serving as treasurer of the United Townships in 1868 then as a councillor for the Village of Bracebridge when in 1875 it became its own municipality and the first municipal jurisdiction in Canada to bear that name.

Incredibly, as Mr. Boyer points out, that was the last evidence of Mr. MacDonald ever being in Bracebridge in spite of his significant contribution to the young and growing Village. His ventures after Bracebridge are unknown, unfortunate to be sure, but his legacy lives on in the names of many of the popular streets of today.

7. TEVIOTDALES DISTRICT EXCHANGE…

Another early business that deserves mention because of its size and contribution to all of early Muskoka was the ***District Exchange.*** John Teviotdale came to Canada from Scotland in 1846. After spending some time in business in other parts of Ontario he arrived in Bracebridge in 1867, bought the small store of Gilman Willson and immediately went to work to build a significantly larger and better stocked store. He obviously had a good deal of experience in that type of business because the ***District Exchange*** quickly became one of the most substantial retail establishments in Muskoka and operated from a building that was one of the most architecturally pleasing. It was located in a building which many years later was the location of Ecclestones Hardware known in 2013 as the Giaschi Building.

The ***District Exchange*** played an important role in bringing people to the Bracebridge business street.

He was politically active and elected as Reeve of the United Townships (which included Bracebridge as part of Macaulay Township) in 1870, the year that the County of Victoria passed a bylaw to separate Macaulay from Draper and Stephenson. It is unclear whether that move was politically motivated but probably so.

It seems he did not operate the store for long. He sold everything to Perry and Myers, an entrepreneurial partnership that had also purchased the Grist Mill of Alexander Bailey at the bottom of the falls. The Teviotdales must have come to Bracebridge with a lot of money or they did extremely well in the general store because they certainly wound up owning a lot of property. The ***Guide Book & Atlas of Muskoka and Parry Sound Districts 1879*** shows many properties held by Ann (or Mrs.) Teviotdale. It is possible that they advanced the first settlers of those properties credit at the District Exchange who, after struggling to make a farm out of their difficult free grant land property, gave up and handed it over the Teviotdales under a settlement arrangement. We will never know, but how else would they have acquired so many township lots spread throughout the various townships surrounding Bracebridge?

Regardless, the Teviotdales helped the pioneer community thrive. Their home was on River Street leading to Wilson's Falls, a house lived in by the Speck family in more recent years, now a vacant lot after the house was demolished. In the backyard of that house was a spring where fresh water ***"bubbled out of the rocks"*** and was used for drinking water by many residents of that area of town. It was also used in later years by the Bracebridge Liquor Company for watering down raw liquor, although initially thought to be used in the manufacture of spirits from original ingredients.

The spring will always be better remembered though for its contribution to Confederation Day, July 1st 1867. As discussed elsewhere but worth repeating here, at the large celebration held in honour of that glorious event, lemonade was made for all those in attendance, using water from ***"Teviotdales spring"***. A claim to fame, not unlike William Holditch organizing the naming of many of our streets on that same occasion.

Unfortunately, Mr. Teviotdale died suddenly in 1875 at the young age of 42. He had made an unsuccessful bid to represent Muskoka Parry Sound in the federal election of 1872 as the candidate for the Conservative Party. He lost to a worthy opponent though, none other than A. P. Cockburn who was in the process of developing the Muskoka Navigation Company and who, like Thomas McMurray, was a great promoter of everything and anything to do with Muskoka.

John Teviotdale's District Exchange later owned by Perry & Myers with their post office addition on the right side. This was one of the earliest and best general stores in all Muskoka and a life saver for pioneer settlers.

8. MUSKOKA ROAD AND THE NEW ROAD TO GRAVENHURST...

So much has been written about the *Muskoka Colonization Road* it only needs to be summarized here. As touched on in Chapter 3, James, Joseph, John and Robert Cooper or some combination thereof, (texts differ in this regard), had the job of building it from South Falls (Muskoka Falls) to North Falls (Bracebridge). As noted earlier, Joseph claimed it was he and his father James who felled the pine tree at the top of North Falls to provide access across the river, and that he was the one who built the first wooden structure bridge there and later the one linking the present day Taylor Road with the downtown.

The *Muskoka Colonization Road*, developed for the purpose of opening Muskoka for settlement by the Government of Upper Canada, provided the first road access to Bracebridge when it was extended north in 1861. In some records, the description of the Muskoka area was less than complimentary.

Because its development continued beyond North Falls the Muskoka Road designation included the downtown business section of the new settlement until it was named Manitoba Street on Confederation Day July 1st, 1867. From the south end of present day Manitoba Street going south it crossed the North Branch of the Muskoka River on Joseph Cooper's (Bird's) bridge straight up the steep hill (for many years but now a sidewalk) adjacent to Woodchester, down the other side past the property where the Royal Canadian Legion is now located, crossed present day Cedar Lane, wound up the hill on Fraserburg Road, straight through the Finch gravel pit area, down the south side of that hill where it crossed Sharpe's Creek on a wooden bridge, turned to the south across the farm of Gerry Fox and on to South Falls where it crossed a bridge over the river at the top of the falls and on south to Gravenhurst. The main street and downtown business section of Gravenhurst still bears the name Muskoka Road.

This was a busy road as soon as it was completed in spite of the fact it was incredibly rough; understandable considering the limited ability of the road building equipment of the day and the total lack of any kind of shock absorbers on the carriages and wagons that used it. Mud and quagmire in the low areas, rocks and roots on the high ones, dominated. A number of diaries and documents tell of the horror of the ride on the Muskoka Road from Severn River to Bracebridge.

Nevertheless, hundreds, if not thousands, of pioneers trudged and fought their way up this road. Families on foot carrying their belongings, towing a cow or two, buckboards, sleighs, wagons, surreys, and stages bounced along this road. Many, after finding their free grant land property unable to fulfill their dream of a new life in Canada, ended their experience in Muskoka by going back down this road in dismay; dreams shattered, their savings gone and another unknown future ahead of them.

But many of them struggled through and successfully created their Muskoka homestead. Some would be the ancestors of many of our friends and neighbours. The Harvie Stage Company, whose office and stables were located on part of the property now Memorial Park in downtown Bracebridge, was the main passenger carrier between Bracebridge, Orillia and all places between.

Over the years visible evidence of this very significant part of our heritage has been eroded and, in fact, removed. In addition to it becoming Manitoba Street in the downtown area, the part of Muskoka Road from the end of Manitoba Street to Birds Bridge has been renamed Entrance Drive. The section from Bird's Bridge up the hill past Woodchester was closed as a road many years ago when the travelled road was realigned around the hill and that section of Muskoka Road became a pedestrian walkway. On the south side of Cedar Lane it was renamed Fraserburg Road. Where it crosses the Finch property it is closed to public access as it is across the Fox property to the south and in both cases it's designation as Muskoka Road lost. The abutments of the bridge over Sharpe's Creek are still evident.

As a result of all that, the only part of Upper Canada's Muskoka Colonization Road that remains so named in Bracebridge is the section between Cedar Lane and King Street; not much, considering the huge part this trail played in the development of Bracebridge as the economic centre of Muskoka.

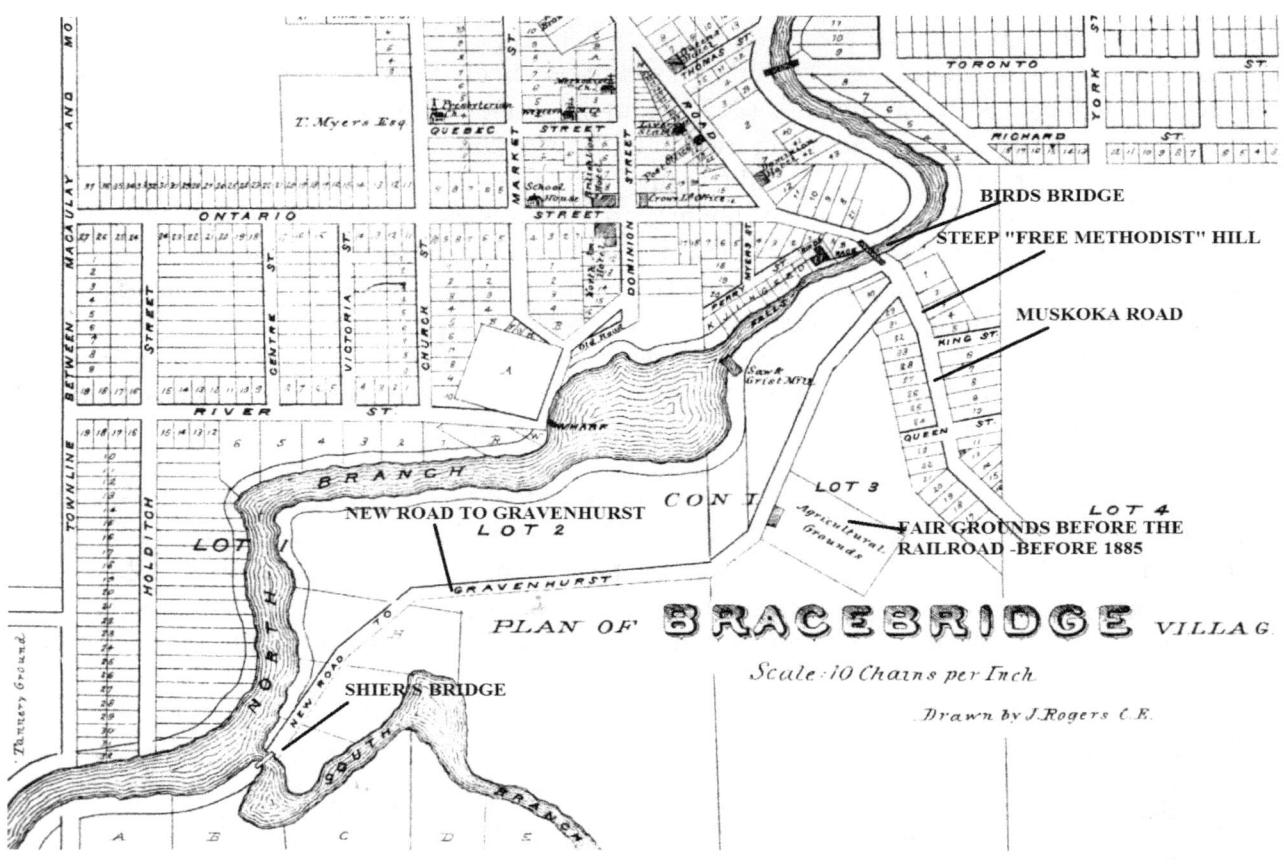

The "New road to Gravenhurst" as shown on the map of Bracebridge in the Guide Book & Atlas of Muskoka and Parry Sound Districts 1879, (amended with my name inserts) linked Muskoka Road with a new bridge (Shier's Bridge) over the South Branch of the Muskoka River. It enabled traffic to avoid that section of Muskoka Road on the steep north side of "Free Methodist" Hill. A part of that "New Road to Gravenhurst" became the north end of Entrance Drive many years later.

It had to be a godsend although most of the books about our history refer for the most part to the more memorable Muskoka Road. The **"new road"** had to be an easier route, at least on the north end. In addition to avoiding *"Free Methodist Hill"*, it also bypassed the treacherous Sharpes Hills with its steep descent down to Sharpes Creek and the climb up the hills on its way south to Gravenhurst. Nevertheless, Muskoka Road continued to be a busy route no doubt because its southerly end over level property near the Muskoka Airport was enticing enough to lure travellers there as opposed to the new route, or maybe the enchantment of Muskoka Road carried more promise.

As the Muskoka Navigation Company developed its fleet settlers must have considered the Muskoka Road a dismal second choice for travel. Ironic, because as roads improved and railways pushed north, use of the majestic steamships themselves came to be considered the secondary way to travel around Muskoka. As a result, they gradually evolved into a delightful recreational event that thrilled thousands of passengers for decades with a variety of excursions including the popular *"100 Mile Cruise"*; eventually becoming an unviable operation as automobile travel and the private cottage industry blossomed.

9. THE RAILWAY…

It was a determined initiative by Muskoka people that brought the first railway line to Muskoka. It was reported in the August 20, 1869 edition of the **Orillia Expositor** that a meeting of Muskoka ratepayers was held in Gravenhurst on August 18 where a number of resolutions were passed extolling the virtues of the area and potential benefits available to the Northern Railway if they were to extend rail service into the *"…vast tracts of agricultural, mineral and pine timbered lands contained in and to the north of the District of Muskoka."* A number of influential people attended that meeting including A. P. Cockburn M.P.P., A. J. Alport, Reeve of Muskoka Township and other names common to Bracebridge history, like Davis, Browning, Piercy, Fuller and Kirkpatrick, all of whom were appointed to a committee to confer with F. W. Cumberland, managing director of the Northern Railway in an attempt to further the cause. An invitation was extended to company executives *"…to visit our principal Lakes, Rivers and Colonization roads…."*

The **Weekly Globe** reported on September 19th, 1869 that the company directors accepted the invitation and participated in the excursion. Regardless of this interest exhibited by the Northern Railway Company, in what may have been political posturing, a petition was lodged with the Legislature asking for an Act of Incorporation to form a new company to be named The Toronto, Simcoe and Muskoka Junction Railway Company. Its objective, however unclearly defined, was to construct a rail line from the Northern Railway of Canada somewhere in Simcoe County to unite the waters of Lake Simcoe with those of Muskoka lakes.

That request was granted and the resulting legislation creating that company was passed and assented to on December 24th, 1869. On January 27th, 1871 The Northern Advocate reported that the company had commenced operations to build a rail line from Barrie to Washago, noting what a great advantage it was going to be to the settlers to have a rail service within just 25 miles, rather than the 65 miles to Barrie. It also suggested that should the line be extended to Bracebridge it would be a great boost to settlement because newcomers *"…would not be subjected to seeing the country from Washago to Gravenhurst which was so uninviting that*

multitudes became discouraged, turned around and left in disgust", presumably before they got anywhere close to Bracebridge.

The money needed to build this line became a problem. The estimate of the cost was $565,224.00 for the section from Barrie to Washago and $412,800.00 from there to Bracebridge. Enormous numbers for those days. There are reports that the municipalities of Muskoka did not commit themselves sufficiently to cover enough of the cost and numerous requests were made for governmental support.

Even though the *Northern Railway Company* was the first to be contacted about building this line and that it was the new *Toronto, Simcoe and Muskoka Junction Railway Company* that had started the construction, the *Northern Extension Railway* in their 1873 annual report claimed *they* were involved and had the contract for extending the line from Washago to Gravenhurst. Regardless, when the rail line arrived in Gravenhurst in 1875 the Orillia Times reported that the people of Gravenhurst celebrated the opening of the *Northern Railway* to the water of Muskoka Lake.

Puzzling to say the least, but clearly explained in ***MUSKOKA AND HALIBURTON 1615-1875,*** where it states, ***"Some confusion in the names applied to this company results from a series of amalgamations. On December 27, 1871, the Toronto, Simcoe and Muskoka Junction Railway united with the North Grey Railway to form the Northern Extension Railways Company, and on June 3, 1875, the Northern Extension Railways Company was absorbed by the Northern Railway Company, which became part, at a later date, of the Grand Trunk Railway, and still later of the Canadian National Railways."***

Well, maybe it was not so clearly explained because in spite of all that, and to add a little more confusion, one source reported that it was the *Northern & Pacific Junction Railway* that extended the rail lines to Bracebridge in the mid 1880's.

No wonder we were confused. These corporate manipulations all took place in a relatively short period of time in an era when nothing happened quickly. It seems to me the big rail firms of the day stood back and let the local people do the work to get it all started, then when they saw it was going to happen jumped in to grab the business. Whether one bailed the other out, bullied them out or bought them out is not reported. Regardless, extending the railway, any railway, to small pioneer communities was a glorious and blessed event. It put them in easy communication with the rest of the world compared to what they had. It was the lifeblood that gave sustainability to every community in its path.

When the rail line entered Bracebridge it crossed the *"New road to Gravenhurst"* and cut right through the community fair grounds of the day resulting in the fair officials having to search for a new location. To their aid came Alfred Hunt, entrepreneur and the owner of the first bank in Muskoka, the *"Hunt's Bank"*, who allowed them to use his property later to be designated *"Jubilee Park"*, where the annual fall fair was held for over 100 years. The remainder of the former fairground property then became the home of Muskoka Linen Mill and after its demise the Muskoka Foundry of Mungo Park McKay. In 2013 the location of the delightful Simply Cottage retail outlet.

The rail line's intersection with the *"New Road to Gravenhurst"* created a dangerous level crossing at the south end of a lengthy rock cut and it was eventually closed to traffic. An alternative route to the downtown for residents of the area was provided later by the placing of a bridge over the rock cut, far above the rail line, linking Shier Street (which part of the New Road to Gravenhurst had become) with Queen Street and connecting again with the new road on the east side of the bridge. It is written that the steel bridge was started in 1929 and *"finished"* in 1933. The absence of a bridge there in 1921 is noted in *"Reminiscences"*.

A well-circulated picture of the rock cut includes a flatbed railroad car loaded with large rocks and a work crew working on a rock removal project. Some confusion circulated about the date that picture was taken and as a result of further investigation and a few phone calls it became clear that the picture was probably captured during a widening of the rock cut sometime after 1933 to accommodate newly enlarged engines and freight cars.

Rail service introduced an exciting new way of life to Bracebridge. A tale related to the writer in the 1970s by a favourite elderly historian described one of the great pleasures experienced by pioneer communities when rail service arrived –circuses. Prior to train transportation, they had no way of transporting themselves to remote areas, due to the rough and sometimes impassable colonization roads. With rail service that all changed. Sometime after 1885 circuses came to Bracebridge. It is reported that they were held in various locations, mostly in farm fields or other open areas. On each occasion, the circus company would unload their equipment and immediately dispatch clowns and an animal or two to tour around the streets accompanied by a barker who would shout out the location, time, features and price of this glorious event. They were very happily received.

Part of this tale involved one occasion when the animal in the parade was an elephant and as they turned onto Kimberley Avenue (called Market Street prior to 1900) from Manitoba Street, the unfortunate beast died and fell in the middle of the dirt road. Since power excavator and loaders were still waiting to be invented, the only way of dealing with this awkward problem was to summon all the available sturdy men from the community who proceeded to dig a huge hole in the road beside the elephant. It was then rolled it into it, given a good layer of quicklime, and buried. Thus, Bracebridge became the location of an elephant burial ground.

The circus is in Town! A joyous event for pioneer communities made possible by rail travel.

There is no written evidence of that happening, however, Redmond Thomas wrote in *"**Reminiscences**"* of a circus that took place in a field across from the Bracebridge Public School on McMurray Street in early days whose feature entertainment was a hippopotamus. It was a female and, unknown to her handlers, was pregnant and chose Bracebridge to give birth. Her natural instinct to roll the little one in mud to protect it from parasites and predators, which would have worked fine had she been in her natural environment, failed in this situation because she was in a cage, and the little one died. Again it is not known for sure, but time and circumstances would certainly lead one to believe that it was buried near the circus grounds in the immediate vicinity of the Bracebridge Public School.

While the Northern Railway served the central corridor of Muskoka, it wasn't until around the turn of the century when the Canadian Pacific Railway moved into western Muskoka, making Bala their distribution centre for Muskoka, and the little known James Bay Railway endeavoured to serve the area of Lake Joseph.

The "Rock Cut", originally created by manual labour in the early 1880s, is being widened in this picture taken in the 1930s to accommodate larger engines and rail cars.

10. THE NORTHERN ADVOCATE AND THOMAS McMURRAY...

No book telling of the early history of the settlement of Bracebridge would be complete if it failed to mention Thomas McMurray. He was a pillar of strength in the central Muskoka business community, political affairs and promotion. There has been a lot written about him and the best description of him and his activities was recorded by Robert J Boyer in *"A Good Town Grew Here"*. Without him, today's very picturesque McMurray Street would be known by some other name.

McMurray, like many of the Boyer and Thomas families of a later date, was a newspaperman and like the others provided great insight into the early affairs of Muskoka through his work. He was of Irish descent and immigrated to Canada in 1861, ventured north where he rented a rowboat at McCabe's Landing (Gravenhurst) and crossed Muskoka Lake to the Muskoka River. After spending a night at North Falls he rowed his boat to South Falls, eventually staking claim to 400 acres of property in Draper Township and proceeded to establish a homestead with his family.

McMurray was elected the first Reeve of the United Townships of Draper, Macaulay, Stephenson and Ryde in 1868, served as a preacher and, while it is not clear whether or not he was the prime instigator of it, in 1863 submitted a petition signed by Draper residents to the Provincial Government of the day asking that a town site be surveyed at South Falls. The resulting lots were designated the Muskokaville Plan and an active and vibrant community has existed there ever since. Considering McMurray's status in that area of Draper it is reasonable to suspect that he had a big hand in collecting the names on that petition, perhaps with his friend Richard Hanna.

His entrepreneurial spirit knew no bounds and in 1869 he sold his Draper holdings and moved to Parry Sound thinking that the Great Lakes Harbour would be an advantage to his next venture, the newspaper business. He created the Northern Advocate there but must have quickly became discouraged with his reception because by 1870 he had moved back to Bracebridge; a location that he now recognized as being more central. Boyer presents a list of businesses in *"A Good Town Grew Here"* who had advertised in the October 21, 1870 edition of the Northern Advocate. Most of those companies were domiciled in Bracebridge clearly indicating that it was being published in Bracebridge at that time. It is also clear when reading through the list that Mr. McMurray had a very wide influence because some of the advertisers were located well outside the immediate area of Bracebridge and some were key players far beyond Muskoka, including the Federal Government and Northern Railway.

The Northern Advocate did not last long however. McMurray decided to move on to bigger things, erecting a building, (some say buildings), for rentals and sold his paper to David Courtney who unfortunately died by drowning in the Muskoka River in 1875. Apparently that was the end of the Advocate, a demise perhaps aided by a competitor, the Free Grant Gazette of E. F. Stephenson that appeared in Bracebridge in 1872. In 1878 the Herald newspaper was introduced into Bracebridge by Graffe & Co. and apparently purchased some of the Northern Advocates former equipment.

An excellent picture of Bracebridge in 1871 clearly shows a sign advertising The Northern Advocate painted along the top edge of the Loyal Orange Lodge building on Manitoba Street. It is also interesting that James Boyer, grandfather of Robert J. Boyer, was employed as the

Northern Advocate editor at the same time as he was the Village Clerk, starting a distinguished record of the Boyer family in Muskoka newspaper history.

It was shortly after the sale of the Advocate that Mr. McMurray's business empire started to crumble, literally. His new building, the first brick structure in Bracebridge often referred to as the *"Brick Block"*, was located on the property upon which the St. Thomas Anglican Church years later would be constructed and where it remains in 2013. Making use of a new brick manufacturing business that opened in Bracebridge was a good community thing, however, the *"Brick Block"* builders used brick that had not properly cured with the result that the brick absorbed moisture from the mortar and within a very few years started to disintegrate.

G.H.O. Thomas recalled living in the upstairs rooms in that building during those few years as member of the *"Kalamity Club"*, an organization described elsewhere as a group of young working men who could not afford to live anywhere else. Every night they could hear bricks falling and finally the exterior walls were so decimated they felt uncomfortable getting dressed in their rooms. The building was finally demolished and the sound components of the structure were used in the construction of the building just to the south on Manitoba Street.

In 1999, while excavating for a building project in the back yard of a Shier Street property, a concrete block was brought to the surface. Once cleaned up, it was found there was an inscription on the block reading *"McMurray's Block 1873"* and after some study it was concluded that it had served as the cornerstone of his building, confirming that the term *"Brick Block"* was a light-hearted nick name for Mr. McMurray's efforts.

Probably the cornerstone had been dumped there many years before when the remnants of the crumbling brick building were being disposed of and to the credit of all involved, it was placed on a pedestal in the front yard of the St. Thomas Anglican Church to commemorate the pioneer effort that created one of the most modern buildings of the day in Bracebridge.

Another building of note created by Mr. McMurray was his residence called *"The Grove"* on McMurray Street where in 1925, after a number of different owners, the Bracebridge High School was located. It was a large, beautiful building with carefully terraced lawns on the westerly downhill side.

Always the entrepreneur, and with printers ink still in his blood, Thomas McMurray then returned to Parry Sound where he founded another weekly newspaper, the North Star.

The cornerstone of the "Brick Block", 140 years old in 2013

11. THE BIGGEST AND BEST EARLY BUSINESS…

With great respect to all early businesses, by far the biggest and best in entrepreneurship, creativity, impact and longevity was the Bird Woollen Mill. What courage it must have taken for Henry J. Bird Sr. to travel to this pioneer community in 1871 and select it as the place for his new business.

Like many of the early pioneer entrepreneurs, he chose to come to Muskoka because he had heard or read about the abundance of waterfalls of the area from early explorer's reports. That caught his interest because hydraulic power was essential for his operation. He no doubt was aware of the land ownership incentive and advantages provided by the Free Grant Land and Homestead Act but he was also of the opinion that Muskoka would be a good sheep-raising district because the average rainfall (and perhaps colder weather) appeared to favour the growth of wool, and he was proved right. He knew what he wanted to do.

Once again we see the importance of our waterfalls and the significant roll they have played in the development of this area. Without them we would never have heard of Henry J. Bird. He served Bracebridge in a multitude of ways including allowing his river flow operated pump to be used to fill the wooden holding tanks buried in the streets that provided fire protection for the business area of the pioneer community. As beneficial as that was at the time, the Town was growing so fast a more extensive water system had to be developed and in due time a multiple use water main to Barron Springs was installed.

Henry J. Bird Sr. was born in the Village of Woodchester in England in 1842. He worked in his father's weaving mills where he learned the skills of the trade, then travelled to Australia, United States and finally Canada where in 1871 he arrived in Bracebridge and started building his own woollen mill. He had previously purchased a mill in Glen Allen, Ontario but suffered disappointment there as a result of flooding. For 82 years the Bird Woollen Mill was the foundation of the Muskoka economy. During that time it employed hundreds of people, donated to community activities, supported sports teams and gave the Town incredible status as a manufacturing centre. Its contribution to Bracebridge, financially and psychologically, would be absolutely immeasurable.

Henry J. Bird Sr.'s first woollen mill building. To the left in the distance can be seen the upper story and roof of Alexander Bailey's grist mill at the bottom of Bracebridge Falls.

The first building was located on the north bank of the river at the top of the falls and is clearly shown in an 1873 picture of downtown Bracebridge. Part of the stone foundation and wall are still visible there in 2013. Picture the workers trying to build that wall on the very brink of the raging rapids above the falls in 1872. It had to be located there to take advantage of the flowing water needed to activate the machinery of the mill. Over the years many additions would be made to the Mill structures as the business grew but it would always continue to use the original building as part of its operations, perhaps for sentimental reasons because part of that building was also the Bird's family home until they built the house of their dreams on the hill overlooking the mill in 1882.

Woodchester, the Henry J. Bird Sr. home built in 1882

He called his new home, *"Woodchester"*, after his home village in England. The octagonal concrete structure built following the theoretical design of Orson H. Fowler, an American author, was one of very few such structures in all of North America. Although badly in need of repair it stands in 2013 as the museum of Bracebridge after its purchase and restoration by the Bracebridge Rotary Club in 1980. It was very revolutionary with its octagonal design, concrete walls, central water system fed from a rainwater collection tank on the roof, ventilation shafts that brought fresh air into the different levels of the building and a *"dead-waiter"*, a central elevator system that lifted and lowered a box with shelves operated by a pulley system designed to carry prepared meals from the kitchen on the bottom floor to the upper dining areas. It was way ahead of its time.

For over 80 years the Mill was a successful operation, building a reputation across Canada with its highly regarded *"Bird's Blankets"* and *"Bird's Mackinaw coats"*. This writer can recall, as a boy growing up in the small community of Ufford, just northwest of Bracebridge, his grandparents collecting every worn out piece of woollen cloth and stuffing it into a large flower sack. Once a year they delivered this bag to the Bird Woollen Mill and in return would receive a supply of Bird's Blankets. No doubt there was a cost for these new products although if I remember correctly, there was a credit provided for the wool that was provided. How the used wool would be processed for reuse is unknown, but this service offered up for Muskoka residents clearly makes Bird Woollen Mill by a long shot the first bona-fide recycling manufacturer in Muskoka.

In spite of the good management and success of the Mill however, financial difficulties arose; all due to matters over which the company had little or no control. The 1929 stock market crash, the great depression of the 1930's, the Federal Government's expropriation of all their products following the breakout of the Second World War (purchased at a fixed cost which was actually less than production costs), and the final blow -the War Measures Act, which forced all raw wool purchases to be made through Government warehouses in Toronto. Up to that point, the Mill had used Muskoka grown wool which, as Henry J Bird had correctly predicted in 1872, was of a different (and better), texture than that grown elsewhere. Increased cost of wool and shipping fees, neither of which were taken into consideration in the imposed fixed price, and the reduction of tariffs on competing products after the war brought about the decision to quietly close operations. The financial losses of many years were too much to bear.

It must have been a sad, sad day in Bracebridge.

Henry J. Bird Sr. was the creator and founder of the Bird Woollen Mill but a long line of family members continued to direct the company operations. He was President for 40 years, his eldest son Henry J Bird Jr. for 37 years, his youngest son Thomas N. Bird briefly in 1949 and John H. Bird, Thomas' eldest son, for 5 years. Peter Bird, John's son, who provided a great deal of information on his family history for this publication, would have been the 5th president had the Mill continued in business.

Entrepreneurs abounded in Bracebridge during pioneer days and while many businesses' came into being none came even close to having the longevity, economic benefit and positive impact on the community like the Bird Woollen Mill. There are a number of things in Bracebridge in 2013 to remind us of this great heritage, The Woodchester home, Bird's Bridge, Bird Parking Lot, Woodchester Parking Lot, Bird Lane, Bird Mill Mews, Bird Grove Park and a number of descendants of Henry J. Bird Sr. that remain residents to this day.

The Bird Woollen Mill was, and is still, a survivor.

12. HOTELS GET BIGGER AND BETTER…

Early pioneer entrepreneurs like MacDonald, Cooper and others recognized an opportunity and quickly got into the hospitality business with their hotels and taverns to take advantage of the rapidly growing lumber industry economy. It didn't take long however, for the rapidly growing community to reject the rustic and rugged facilities created and a need for better accommodations became clear. With the advent of Bird Woollen Mill, the grist and saw mills and a burgeoning retail area, many of the visitors and travellers to Bracebridge became a little more dignified than the rough and tough workers of the lumber camps who didn't mind frontier hotel type conditions. After all, they were no doubt a lot better than what they knew in the wilderness logging camps. As a result the more rustic accommodation facilities faded away and in the 1870s Bracebridge became the home of quality hotels with the Queens, North American, British Lion, and in 1885 with the first train service, the Railway Hotel.

The pioneer Dominion Hotel, or Dominion House as it was sometimes called as described in **Chapter 6**. *EARLY HOTELS IN BRACEBRIDGE…*, did survive into the new era of better service, but it did so after a number of rebuilds, necessitated to some extent, by fires. As noted earlier, the building in the last form of its existence still stands on the east side and south end of Manitoba Street near *Apple Tree Park*; in 2013 housing a number of retail businesses. Evidence of the beautiful facade on the street side still remains although the upper floors are no longer put to any use.

The new version of hotels in Bracebridge was glorious indeed. The North American Hotel, situated where the Inn at the Falls parking lot is located at the corner of Dominion and Ontario Streets, was in business in 1871 and popular because of its location on the route to the wharf down the steep hill at the end of Dominion Street. It eventually became a boarding house. As an aside, in the 1990s I received a call from the Inn at the Falls manager who asked me to help them solve a problem because a huge depression suddenly appeared in the middle of their parking lot and a large wooden structure could be seen in the cavity. They thought it might be some sort of tunnel or secret chamber and that perhaps a beautiful mystery could be developed to add to the mystique of their Inn, which already had a reputation of being haunted.

I knew there had been no buildings on this property for many years and after inspecting this strange structure I turned to my *Veitch Index* for a solution. A lengthy search resulted in finding a story about the North American Hotel. After it had become a boarding house, (that reportedly had a reputation of accommodating less than savoury tenants), one of their residents who had a habit of getting inebriated quite regularly came stumbling home from a nearby tavern and while crossing the yard stepped into a sagging area in the soil. The unfortunate fellow broke through into a cavity and a large wooden vat that served as a holding tank for the sewage of the boarding house.

The tank was situated in an inconspicuous place on the lot and because it was several feet below the surface he was unable to crawl out, nor could he get a response to his calls for help. When his absence was noticed the next morning he was reporting missing to the local police who organized a search party. Finally he was rescued, covered with sewage and humbled indeed, having spent his night deep underground soaking up the contents of the tank.

A study of the North American Hotel building location from old maps would indicate that the tank that was discovered and thought to be a secret chamber was no doubt the same sewage tank that was involved in that mishap, to the great disappointment of all.

The Railway Hotel, later becoming the Albion Hotel, came with the construction of the Northern Railway to Bracebridge in 1885. Without question it was an immediate success; how could it not when the impressive new railroad service that every small community across Canada craved with a passion went right by the front door? The railway in your community meant instant prestige, recognition and success and everyone wanted it to come right into the middle of town. To have it a distance away meant your area was discredited and unworthy of the service the railway provided. A good example of that is when the railroad extended further north from Bracebridge there was great expectation that it would go through the settlement of Hoodstown, already a well-established community, but to their dismay it went further to the east. Huntsville was created and Hoodstown disappeared into oblivion.

One historical document sites a problem experienced at the **"Higgins"** Hotel (Queens Hotel -at that time owned by Jack Higgins) that involved a patron bringing his faithful dog, named **"Old Ring"** who never left his side, into the eating area to which a waiter took exception, kicking at it to get it out of the way. The patron was so upset that his dog was mistreated a physical altercation occurred resulting in him and his group taking their business thereafter to the Albion Hotel.

The British Lion Hotel, by its very name smacking of royalty and prestige, played a huge role in establishing Bracebridge as an important destination for good accommodation beyond anything else in Muskoka. It was built around 1870, and was in its prime when the 1871 picture of Bracebridge showed it with its name proudly displayed across the entire upper façade of the building. It was also situated in a very opportune location on the west side of Dominion Street, at the top of the hill on the road leading to the wharf and across Ontario Street from the North American Hotel. The class and dignity it conveyed made it much more popular than the North American Hotel. The British Lion Hotel went through a number of rebuilds, renovations and demolitions to the extent that the present building identified in 2013 as the Lee, Roche and Kelly Building bears similar perimeter recognition but little else of the old British Lion Hotel. It was dearly loved by the English immigrants because it had so much relevance to their homeland.

Another important historical note regarding the British Lion Hotel is its involvement with the Rene Caisse Cancer Clinic; better described in a later chapter in this book. Actually the involvement was with the structure only because the hotel had gone out of business in the 1930s and been seized by the town for arrears of taxes. It had to be an ignominious era in Bracebridge when one of its most elegant pioneer facilities had to be taken over for the debt it owed to the very people it served for so many years. It had housed Royalty, namely, the Governor General of Canada and his wife Lord and Lady Dufferin in 1874, the Duke of Manchester, thousands of visitors and early settlers. For years it was likely the first visible evidence of the Bracebridge business section to those walking up the steep Dominion Street hill from the wharf after disembarking from the big lake boats.

Another grand facility that exuded prestige and royalty by its very name was the Queens Hotel. It occupied a prominent place in the downtown business area of Bracebridge and was close enough to the railroad to benefit from the thousands of travellers who used this new comfortable way of travelling when it arrived in 1885. Like all buildings it went through many renovations, fires, rebuilds and expansions and still remains as an important business property in Bracebridge. It also forever gave the steep hill on which it fronted the name *"Queens Hill"*.

While it had a number of different owners, it thrived in the good times and survived the tough times mainly because its owners for the most part gave it the care it deserved. It did not suffer from the great loss of business resulting from the decline of the big lake boats that brought about the demise of the British Lion and North American Hotel.

The original building had been *"...in the hands of the Higgins family since the early 1870's"* Robert J. Boyer wrote in his 1997 *"Muskoka memories"* newspaper article but it is not identified in the 1871 picture of downtown Bracebridge. Presumably then, in its earliest form it was a modest structure compared to what we see in later pictures and perhaps hidden behind the other buildings that had popped up Manitoba Street.

The "Queens Hotel" one of the great hotels in the history of Bracebridge

In fact that must have been the case because in another document it states that in 1868 five tavern licences were issued, one of them to the Queens Hotel. Obviously then it competed for the very early transient trade with the rustic pioneer hotels of Bailey, McDonald and Cooper. It is likely that it outlived them because it presented a more sophisticated approach to hospitality. The Higgins family were hotel people and they stayed in that business for close to 40 years, selling it to Thomas J. Woods in 1908. Because of the successful *"Local option"* liquor prohibition vote of 1911 the tavern business abruptly ended and the Queens Hotel was sold to John and Mrs. Thomson who headed up an active temperance group of local citizens. It stayed in responsible ownership successfully and was purchased by the Patterson Brothers who operated it as the Patterson Hotel.

That ended the wonderful era of the famous Queens Hotel. When the Patterson Brothers sold the property the use changed dramatically. A variety of subsequent owners created bars (including mud wrestling), entertainment halls and restaurants, until Al Beverly bought the property and relocated his decorating centre from a building at the intersection of Chancery Lane and Manitoba Street to its main floor. Other stores and offices in the upper and lower floors of the building were developed and again the property became a valuable asset to the Bracebridge Downtown area.

When Don and Jen Skinner purchased the property in 2007 there was a rebirth of the Queens Hotel building. With loving care and attention many of the original features are being restored. It may never be a hotel in its former glory again but hopefully its famous name will not be lost in time.

An interesting story related to the writer many years ago regarding the Queens Hotel tells of an event that took place during, or just before, the Second World War.

Two young men, obviously of foreign birth, came to the hotel and asked for accommodation, explaining that they had no money but would be willing to work for the hotel or do something significant for its improvement to pay for their stay. That apparently was alright with management and since they claimed to have some related ability, the young men were challenged to provide something of an artistic nature for the hotel. That being agreed upon, they decided to paint a mural on a wall in the hotel.

That was done and the young men went on their way. Not long after however the same two young men were apprehended, some say in Gravenhurst, others say Winnipeg, and placed in custody because it was found they were German spies under orders to provide details of the railroad system across Canada. There is neither written record of that nor evidence of resulting confinement, if any, that the writer has ever found; however, there is always some truth in anecdotal reports, however possibly exaggerated or altered with the passage of time.

To some degree, this story was proven to have creditability when during part of the restoration of the Queens a painting was discovered under many layers of paint on one of the walls above a covered over, long forgotten fireplace. It is slowly and carefully being uncovered and is indeed an impressive work of art depicting a Muskoka scene.

Compared to the other prestigious hotels of that era, the Queens Hotel was a survivor that managed to retain its character, is still with us in its heritage, and would appear to be blossoming into a new and enriched life in Bracebridge.

13. DIFFERENT POINTS OF VIEW ON EARLY BRACEBRIDGE…

There has been a lot written about those who first travelled through Muskoka and those who later had the courage to clear a bit of land and make it their home. The explorers/surveyors dispatched by Britain to venture into the **"Muskoka Frontier wasteland"** to try and find a water route from Georgian Bay to the Ottawa River in an attempt to bolster their defence against invasion and later to settle the land, expressed their view of the landscape of Muskoka in the reports they filed upon return. As expressed earlier, there were many who travelled through the area and it would seem that as each proceeded to fulfill their obligation to their employer none had the benefit of the information contained in the report filed by those before them. The reports often varied widely.

A number portrayed the District in glowing terms; claiming it to be the land of opportunity consisting of great forests and potential farmland while others saw nothing but rock, swamp and diseased trees.

Those who later ventured to Muskoka to settle the land, whether it was to take advantage of the hydraulic power provided by the many waterfalls, to harvest the huge stands of pine and hardwoods or to develop farm homesteads, also reported to the outside world on their experience often boasting about how it was growing rapidly into a successful, modern and burgeoning society. In the larger central areas, especially North Falls (Bracebridge) and McCabe's Landing (Gravenhurst), there *was* a lot of activity and growth. However, reading between the lines, it appears that some of the writers of those positive comments were either promoting the District for the sole purpose of getting more people here to further their *own* interests or trying to justify to the world how wise and brave they were in moving to the Muskoka frontier.

Those living in the larger settlements no doubt had a right to be proud of their new place and obviously worked hard at making things work. It is when you step away from those larger places and into the rural areas that were the focus of the Free Grant Land Act that a different picture emerges.

For the most part, the early settlers of the land were fine, hardworking and determined individuals. Some were very successful and saw their dream of a place in the new world come to fruition, mostly because they had been fortunate enough to settle on a rare piece of fertile land. The work of clearing the land of the massive trees that covered it and building a log house and barn was difficult but when they accomplished that they no doubt had a reasonable existence and were proud of their success.

Many however, worked just as hard to do the same thing but the result was not the same. Their land turned out to be virtually useless as a farm because of the absence of good soil. After they had cleared the land of trees, the rain and snow washed what soil there was into the swamps and valleys and they were left with an abundance of rock. To make a living from the land was impossible. They could only exist by the man of the house getting hired on with a logging crew and spending the winters in a bush camp far from his family, working dawn to dusk six or seven days a week. This provided enough money to sustain them and they would spend their summers on their free grant land, working long hours to continue the development of their property. After 2 or 3 years of that they often gave up in despair, their hopes dashed, their health suffering and their dream of making their fortune in this promised land of opportunity long gone.

They would move into nearby communities and try to sell their property (which in many cases they could not, having no title to it because they had not completed the terms of the purchase agreement under the Free Grant Lands Act), or abandoning it completely and leaving the area to start over somewhere else.

Those who came to the established communities of the District usually did so with different intentions. They were entrepreneurs attracted by the waterfalls that could produce hydraulic power for manufacturing, business created by the harvesting of the vast stands of trees, the possibility of lumber milling, retail and service opportunities. There were many related economic benefits that evolved from all that; many found employment transporting freight on land and water and later in the promising tourism industry.

The ***Guide Book & Atlas of Muskoka and Parry Sound Districts 1879*** by W. E. Hamilton is a great resource for providing information on how Muskoka was promoted during that era.

It is an extensive and detailed description of the two Districts with a lengthy focus on Bracebridge. Muskoka's attributes are described in glowing language while just briefly touching on the negatives to the point they appear so insignificant as to be of little or no concern. It proved to be, and still is, a valuable source of information on Muskoka. The description of the quality of the land, however, was misleading. Many that would have read it were those seeking to overcome a hopeless situation in their homeland abroad; possibly living in a ramshackle tenement complex with little or no possibility of ever owning their own property, let alone one hundred acres of good farmland that was claimed to be available in Canada under the Free Grant Land Act. They would have been incredibly impressed by what they read and many were quick to seize the opportunity.

As an example, the Atlas reads in part ***"It is difficult to give an average of the proportion of good land in the districts, but we are not over-shooting the mark in calling it 60 per cent."***

Those of us who love Muskoka know that it is *all* good land, but since this section generally makes reference to soil conditions one suspects ***"good land"*** is meant to infer that it is good *farmland*. A quick tour around the District quickly shows that if they had said 6 per cent they would have been a lot closer to the truth. In another place, using a somewhat obscure description, they said the level plain beyond the intersection of Dominion and Manitoba Streets, (yes, the streets were named at the time the Atlas was published in 1879, having been so named on Confederation Day in 1867), was 40 feet deep, very largely consisting of rich clay loam eighteen inches or two feet deep, *without a stone or pebble*. How they were able to measure that depth of the soil with the limited equipment available in the 1870s is not explained. Maybe they did it somehow, but knowing how unpredictable the rock formations are everywhere else in Bracebridge, there could not have been any consistency in depth of the soil at that location, certainly not 40 feet. In fact, rock is probably why there is a hill at that intersection in the first place. Certainly the west side of Manitoba Street in the downtown area has bedrock that forms the hill behind the stores and in some cases it is exposed in the building basements.

It states that the remaining 40 per cent of the District includes swamps, *"..many of which, at a trifling cost, could be reclaimed so as to make the most valuable portions of the farm."* They fail to say where the material to fill those swamps would come from, or the difficulties that would be encountered in getting it there.

It goes on to describe the *rocky* portion of the 40 per cent as a *"..wonderful store-house for heat, and a reservoir of moisture.."* and *"..serves to break the winds in all directions,.."* It seems to me the one writing all that was breaking a lot wind themselves when they made these observations.

Nevertheless, the Atlas is a wonderful document that provides a valuable insight into many aspects of the two districts. No doubt Muskoka's most active promoter Thomas McMurray and Crown Land Agent of the day Aubrey White played a large part in assembling the information.

Another very valuable publication shedding great insight into the early struggles of Muskoka is **MUSKOKA AND HALIBURTON 1615-1875 A Collection of Documents** Edited by Florence B Murray and produced by THE CHAMPLAIN SOCIETY FOR THE GOVERNMENT OF ONTARIO UNIVERSITY OF TORONTO PRESS 1963. It is a collection of actual government documents, letters, reports, opinions etc., of the missionaries, earliest explorers and surveyors up to the time when much of Muskoka was being settled.

That publication contains reports of some who took a very different, and often conflicting, view of Muskoka. In his 1869 letter to the Editor of the Montreal Daily Witness Thomas McMurray took issue with an article in that publication entitled *"Cruelty of sending newly arrived Immigrants to worthless Free Grant Lands".* He spoke about the success experienced by the immigrants, couching it with some recommendations that would help them, (which in itself indicates that things weren't so great), suggesting that too many immigrants chose to select properties near the road (presumably meaning the Muskoka Road that led from the Severn River into the heart of Muskoka) and had they gone a mile or two into the bush they may have found good soil for their farms.

A *Toronto, Mail*, July 20, 1872 correspondent, following a visit to Muskoka wrote an article entitled *"Farming in Muskoka"* where he reported that the general character of the country *"…is bold, picturesque, diversified with hill and dale, well-watered, almost devoid of swamp, and contains from 70 to 75 per cent. of good farmland,…"* One has to wonder just where in Muskoka he visited. He later pronounced Muskoka's agricultural capabilities rich and varied.

That isn't the way Joseph Dale saw it when he wrote his *"Warning To English Immigrants"* in 1874, prefaced *"London, June, 1875"* as quoted in Florence Murray's work. He reported that he had recently returned from the Free Grant District of Ontario and stated that *"…it occurred to me that the few following pages might be of some assistance to those who are about to take such an important step as to emigrate".*

He said *"…we took the mail carts to a place called Gravenhurst, through a most dismal, rocky and wild country… …on all sides are great masses of granite... …it is a wonder how anything, even a birch tree can grow; here and there are to be seen a few poverty stricken shanties and attempts at settlements, most of them deserted,…".* He described Gravenhurst as *"…a very languishing village which but for the summer tourists, would probably soon have to put the shutters up."*

He indicates that he rode by steamboat up the Muskoka River to Bracebridge, noting some clearings on the sides of the lake and river but that *"…some of them are nothing but patches of rock."* He said that many of the immigrants who were required to clear their land had never used a *"…backwoods-man's axe…"* and whose acreage *"… which by desperate labour have been cleared by hand, reveal to the emigrant nothing but rock, rock, rock, …"*

He was not impressed with Bracebridge as a community either, saying it *"…is not a flourishing village, the two or three small hotels in the place being the only houses doing any good business."*

Did he not see the popular retail store the *"District Exchange"* of John Teviotdale that was founded in 1868? or Perry & Myers saw mill that in 1864 under Alexander Bailey's ownership cut 1000 board feet of lumber a day? or his grist mill that ground grain into flour for Muskoka settlers? How could he miss the Bird Woollen Mill production facility sitting on the north bank of the Muskoka River in the middle of the Bracebridge Falls that commenced operation in 1872? In fact, in the October 21st 1870 edition of Thomas McMurray's Northern Advocate, there were 3 hotels, 6 transportation/stables, 15 stores, 3 legal offices, 2 doctors, 4 builders and 2 mills in Bracebridge and area advertising their services. No doubt there were other businesses as well in the area that chose not to advertise in his newspaper.

Dale did give some credit to the business resulting from visitors to the *sporting regions* of Muskoka, which in his opinion was in response to a promotion contained in a railway guide, but he was relentless regarding the difficulties and hardships endured by the emigrants who he felt were often misled by existing residents of the area.

What a difference there is in reading Mr. Dales observations compared to those of Thomas McMurray who claimed that *"…most of those who have arrived are well adapted for the settlement."* It would seem that Dale didn't *want* to see anything good. He did not see the huge logging operations in process, the active steamship service, and failed to recognize the potential of the waterfalls to turn the wheels of industry. He must not have spent much time in the area or talked to the people and he certainly didn't come in contact with any of the active promoters of the day. In many ways he was correct when he talked about the hardships, the quality of the soil and the unfair treatment experienced by the immigrants. But there were many who met those challenges of their situation and fought on to success.

Another contrast with Dale's negative view of Muskoka in 1875 is the report contained in Robert J. Boyer's *"A Good Town Grew Here"*. It states that Lady Dufferin, wife of His Excellency Lord Dufferin, Governor General of Canada, on their visit to Bracebridge in 1874, made a number of positive comments about the area.

Her comments, in part, referred to the Muskoka River as *"…a most curious narrow river…"* and later, *" … this brought us to Bracebridge. Bracebridge is an entirely new town, …it has grown wonderfully in the past eight years…the houses are remarkably neat and finished-looking…"*. One has to wonder what Dale was looking at around the same time when he filed his dismal report on Muskoka. He must have had a preconceived negative vision of the area.

Long before those reports were compiled though, the early explorers and surveyors had some conflicting opinions about Muskoka. The great explorer and cartographer David Thompson during his search for a canal route from Muskoka to the Ottawa River in 1843 noted that, *"Although the examination of the Muskako* (sic) *River for a canal was a failure; yet it brought us acquainted with a valuable tract of Country for settlement."* and *"…Forests of a very fine growth of Maple, Ash, Elm, Bass* (sic)*, Beach and a few Oaks, which always indicate a rich soil. The side of the Rivers and Lakes have a border of stately Firs, from 50 to 100 yards in depth, behind which all is hard wood as above."*

On the other hand, J. W. Bridgland who was contracted, in part, to survey a road line from the Eldon Portage to the mouth of the Muskako (sic) river as directed by the Crown Lands office in Quebec, filed a report in 1853 that contained the following comments, *"…not a portion, sufficient for a small township, could be obtained in any one locality, of a generally cultivatable nature. The country northward of Black River, may be described as one vast field of granite rock…"* and describing the land toward Muskako (sic) Lake *"…in general, still more barren, and uncompromising…"* and after rounding the south end of the lake, *"…the agricultural prospect is still worse;…"* he also said the water is blackish and bitter and that, *"The pine is however inferior, frequently forked, crooked, and punkey, consequently not very valuable for lumber."* Too bad he hadn't stuck around for a few years to witness the thousands of logs, mostly high-grade pine, that were cut from that land and floated down that *"blackish and bitter"* water of the Black River and the two branches of the Muskoka River.

Of all the written word on early Bracebridge the most dramatic and honest appraisal of conditions back then would come from the personal accounts of those who actually *lived* through them. There is such a record in the form of a diary, hand written by Mrs. John Adair, as a memoir to her children so that they would be aware of the struggles of their parents in coming to the new world. John Adair was a builder; therefore probably one of the more affluent and successful residents of Bracebridge in that era, although it would seem he didn't start off that way. Among others, he built the original stone building that at one time was the home of William Cosby Mahaffy who came to Bracebridge to set up his law practice, later becoming the first District Judge for Muskoka, and after a number of different owners was converted to the Holiday House Inn of Ernie and Timmie Allchin. After their ownership it again evolved through other owners and continues in 2013 as the Inn at the Falls.

She wrote about riding with two children up the Muskoka Road from Washago to Gravenhurst aboard a stage that was driven recklessly and on a trail that was so rough that she had to prop herself up against the side of the stage with her umbrella so that she wouldn't get thrown out of her seat. The stage was no doubt one of the *Harvie Line of Stages* who, once the trails were cut through the bush to the various settlements, had a scheduled route from Washago to many parts of Muskoka. They boarded a steamboat at Gravenhurst and were met at the Bracebridge wharf by her husband who had come to Muskoka earlier and *"…fell in love with Bracebridge."* They had a very welcome dinner at McDonald's Hotel (Hiram James McDonald) and stayed there a few days waiting for their freight to arrive. She spoke highly of the McDonald family and the good care they received there.

Her husband had arranged for them to stay in part of a house that was the residence of Mr. and Mrs. Gow, (probably George F. Gow who was the first Reeve of Macaulay Township in 1871), and said she was shocked when she saw the condition of the house. It was a frame house with no paint and no plaster, yet they appreciated the generosity and kindness of the Gows in letting them stay there because there was no other place. She glued newspapers over the rough boards that formed the walls and put wallpaper on top. They had to install two stoves for heat and during the coldest times sat between them to be comfortable. For a place for her two girls to sleep, she put wallpaper on a packing box, inside and out, and that became their bed.

Sickness was a constant companion. One of the little girls became sick with a disease the Doctor (probably Dr. J. N. Byers) called *"continued"* fever, (Mrs. Adair was sure it was typhoid fever), and became so wasted that they carried her around on a pillow. They would hold a glass of water to her face to see if she was still breathing. Just as she was recovering their other little girl got scarlet fever which then spread to her sister and the struggle to keep them alive continued. Throughout her memoirs Mrs. Adair makes reference to the kindness of the people of the community in times of need and that Bracebridge was a *"...lively little place always quite up to date."* Although she doesn't mention what year, she makes reference to starting their public library. No doubt she was referring to the Mechanics Institute and if so that sets the date at 1874.

John Adair built many houses and shops in Bracebridge and they often lived in them as he completed the interior finishing work. One location was on property he later sold to the Beardmore Tannery Co. on the north side of the Muskoka River opposite the mouth of the South Branch of the Muskoka River where in 2013 *The Waterways* condominium is situated.

The most poignant section of her memoirs comes where she describes the sadder moments of their stay in Bracebridge. She tells a story about her neighbour…

"One day in this respect; just after breakfast an old man, whom we knew, Mr. Vincent was his name, came just after breakfast, he and his wife were a strange old couple, and all alone, as far as relatives were concerned, and had come from London, England, very poor but the most cheerful and optimistic folks I ever knew. Well, he came in to ask me to help him, his wife had died and he all alone with her, he just left her and came over for me. I went with him hoping he would get another neighbour to come to, they lived half a mile from anyone else and were very poor and proud – but he did not want to ask another…only I went with the old man and found her just lying there dead…I straightened out the little body, and washed and dressed it ready for the coffin; there were no undertakers, Dad (her husband John; this memoir was being written to their children) *may have made the coffin…I have always been glad I did not let my natural cowardice hinder me from helping the old man, as he and his wife had planned for me to do. I certainly learned from these same old friends that we can be happy even when circumstances are trying.*

I could tell many strange things, but will not, of old country people, mostly English, who came to Bracebridge, and had no friends, and little money, and no knowledge of the new country, in the kind of work that had to be done. Some of them like the above old couple suffered hardships…"

Quite a story, from one who lived through those early times and thought it important enough to write about it. The Adairs eventually left Bracebridge and moved to Winnipeg but in recent years two descendants of the Adairs, Jane (Little) Loftus and John Little, have had a positive influence on Bracebridge. It was Jane who provided me with a copy of that part of the memoirs telling about the experience of her family in Bracebridge. Jane's interest in our heritage and the importance of not forgetting the struggles of our ancestors is greatly appreciated.

14. PROHIBITION...

Of all the controversial events described in the various histories of Bracebridge, nothing compares to the longevity, determination and deep-seated stubbornness of the two sides of the prohibition debate. It has been stated earlier that at one point in early Bracebridge there was a tavern for every 75 citizens. That of course is an indication of the large number of transients moving back and forth through Bracebridge to the lumber camps; the permanent residents would never have been able to support such a large number of watering holes, in fact, many residents didn't want *any* in the community.

They were, after all, a God fearing lot for the most part, confirmed to some extent by the number of churches that quickly popped up throughout Bracebridge; the first being the Presbyterian Church that was built on King Street, roughly in the area of the property that in 2013 is the parking lot for Woodchester and the Chapel Gallery. The Gallery building itself, built in recent years, was designed to emulate that original church. It has been previously noted that the first church services here were held by the Presbyterians in a trading post on the Muskoka River near Muskoka Lake.

There were a number of dedicated groups promoting prohibition. W. E. Hamilton in the ***Atlas of Muskoka Parry Sound Districts 1879*** spoke about the existence of the Beaver Temple Lodge of the Independent Order of Good Templars and a Temperance Association. He completes his comments with his observation that the Templars lodge ***"...has been in existence for several years, but seems now to be torpid, if not defunct."*** I suspect he inserted that caveat for fear the existence of such organizations might interfere with development of the area.

The Women's Christian Temperance Union (W.C.T.U.), the Committee of 100, churches and many individuals supported the effort put forward to eliminate the sale of alcoholic beverages in Bracebridge. Of course, the hotel and tavern owners were dead-set against any interference with their livelihood, and why wouldn't they be? Because they were active in the community they brought a great deal of business to the area and everyone benefited; at least that is the way they saw it. But the demon rum had to go according to the prohibitionists and they left no stone unturned to get their way.

The result was that the people of the community were asked to make a decision through numerous referendums (officially known as ***"local Option"*** votes) conducted by the Municipal Councils of the day. The Council would have been extensively badgered by groups who wanted prohibition or, if it had been previously voted in, by those who wanted it removed.

The electors were bombarded over the years with door to door lobbyists that resulted in the public demanding a referendum be held asking that the sale of liquor be prohibited. One of the first votes resulted in a victory for the prohibitionists. Robert J. Boyer in ***A Good Town Grew Here*** wrote that in 1874 the Council of the Township of Macaulay, of which the area served by the Bracebridge Post Office was a part at the time, in response to a positive result on a special vote of the electors passed a bylaw under the Temperance Act 1874 to prohibit the sale of intoxicating liquors in *"..shops and places other than taverns"*, although it is not mentioned where else liquor was being sold. No doubt the hotel and tavern owners were OK with that, since it left them as the only place where one could purchase liquor. In fact, the 1874 bylaw of the township was more likely passed under the Dunkin Act of 1864 passed by the *"Province"* of Canada. The Canada Temperance Act, also known as the Scott Act and named after its sponsor, was not enacted until 1878 by the Parliament of Canada.

It is an interesting aside that in the same year the bylaw was passed, the residents of the area surrounding North Falls and generally those served by the Bracebridge Post Office, petitioned the government and were granted their own status as a municipality. This resulted in separation from the Township of Macaulay and in an historic move that will be remembered forever; ***the municipality of Bracebridge was created***.

Was the timing of the separation a co-incidence? I doubt it. The busy Bracebridge settlement was obviously more business minded than their rural neighbours and therefore more aware of the need for a well-developed retail economy; and that included selling liquor. As a result of that separation, although there is no comment in this regard, it would seem that the former Township bylaw governing the sale of liquor did not apply and it was up to the newly formed municipality to make its own rules.

So the battle continued. G.H.O.Thomas in his booklet ***Bracebridge Fifty Years Ago,*** (which would make it 1884 since it was written in 1934), makes reference to the existence of a number of temperance organizations including the Beaver Lodge Independent Order of Good Templars, known by the acronym I.O.G.T.

The more determined promoters of prohibition must not have been included in the geographical boundaries of the newly formed Village of Bracebridge in 1875 because silence seems to have prevailed, at least on the surface, for a few years. As a result, as described in more detail in ***Chapter 26. THE BRACEBRIDGE LIQUOR COMPANY…***, in 1894 George W. Sibbett seized the opportunity to open his own liquor store in the building immediately to the north of the Independent Order of Odd Fellows building on Manitoba Street

Maybe this new liquor store stirred the prohibition pot because just a year later the Women's Christian Temperance Union asked the Municipal Council to limit the number of hotels that could do business in Bracebridge. Council did not agree and refused to introduce such a restriction, instead leaving that decision up to the Liquor Commissioner.

But the ball had started to roll and the prohibition movement was growing right across Canada. In *A Good Town Grew Here* Boyer explains that in 1898 a Dominion plebiscite was held and every province except Quebec voted in favour of eliminating liquor sales. However, no legislation or regulation evolved as a result of that vote and it wasn't until 1908 that any further action is noted.

In the meantime though, evidence of skulduggery appeared following a 1902 fire that destroyed a large part of the west side of Manitoba Street. In the burnt out attic of one of the older buildings an extensive piece of machinery was discovered. After a lengthy inspection by the liquor commissioners it was concluded that it was a moonshine still, no doubt a relic from the era of the 1874 Macaulay Township bylaw.

In 1908, in response to pressure from prohibitionist organizations, a referendum was held as part of the annual election. Although it is quoted that this was the *first* local option vote, in fact it was the second for those in the Bracebridge community. Since the first was that of the Township of Macaulay, this then became the first one that bore the Bracebridge name. This vote was negative for prohibition and there were those in the community that proudly stated that the reason for its defeat was that the local hotels were such good operations, **"...we doubt if there is another municipality in the Province where the law is better observed"**.

Well, not so fast! This fight was not over; in fact it was just beginning. That decision put all the temperance forces to work. The lobbying got more intense and in 1910 another petition was presented to the Municipal Council signed by 193 names and preparation was made for another *local option* vote as part of the 1911 election. The campaigning was furious. Guest speakers for both sides beseeched the electorate to support their side; never had there been such dedicated volunteers. In the end, the prohibitionists won, achieving the necessary margin for victory and the bars in the four hotels and the Sibbett Liquor Store were closed.

However, Bracebridge was all alone with its **"dry"** society. Both Huntsville and Gravenhurst referendums went against prohibition and the sale of liquor continued; so did most municipalities in Ontario. What was the difference? The logging industry brought many workers to the community because Bracebridge was such a central **"stopping-off"** place in the District; were the Bracebridge people fed up with these transients, the lifeblood of the local hotels and taverns, hanging around the community? We will never know.

No different than present day politics, there were those who thought it a conflict of interest for anyone in the liquor business to come out in opposition to prohibition but there was also a suspicion that some supporting it had inappropriate motives. Everyone knew that it was just a matter of time before the provincial government assumed control of the sale of liquor and it was suspected that one local druggist, a strong supporter of prohibition, was lining up to have his drugstore selected as the local government liquor store. G.H.O. Thomas wrote in **Bracebridge Fifty Years Ago** that the morning after the successful vote for prohibition, the following sign was posted on the front door of the suspect's drugstore:

GOOD-BYE LITTLE DRUGSTORE

DON'T YOU CRY,

YOU'LL BE A BOOZE SHOP

BYE AND BYE!

If that in fact was the devious plan, it didn't work because it would be many years before Bracebridge would have a government liquor store.

And the battle continued. In 1913 the Municipal Council received a petition asking for a vote to have prohibition removed, resulting in another referendum on that question being put to the electorate at the 1914 election. But the previous decision prevailed and prohibition on the sale of liquor in the community continued. Perhaps as a peace offering to those who opposed prohibition, the Women's Christian Temperance union, when the Federal Building with its new post office (the first of its kind in Muskoka) was built in 1914, contributed a drinking fountain which was placed in front of the new building. It was a beautiful addition to the downtown business area with a streetlight on top and a connection to a town water main that automatically filled large openings on three of the sides for horses to drink, a small bowl at the bottom for dogs and cats and a tap on the back that residents could use to fill water jugs. The suggestion was clear -drink water instead of liquor. After a number of relocations in the downtown area, it was finally placed in *"apple tree park"* at the south end of Manitoba Street where it remains in 2013.

Women's Christian Temperance Union drinking fountain in its original location...

...and here in its 2013 location in "Apple Tree" Park

In 1915 a new organization was formed called The Committee of 100 whose focus was to eliminate the sale of liquor *totally* across Canada. Supported by a central committee, each area developed their own local group and in 1916 a petition of 300 signatures was assembled. It is not stated to whom the petition was presented but it must have been to the provincial authorities supporting a request for a province wide vote on prohibition since Bracebridge already had such a bylaw in affect.

The difference in this request was that importation of liquor would apparently become illegal. Up to that point, while you couldn't buy liquor in Bracebridge there was nothing to stop you from getting it elsewhere and bringing it into the community, as long as you didn't try and sell it. No doubt bootleggers (referred to as **"blind pigs"** by Redmond Thomas in **Reminiscences**) did a roaring business.

The request received a favourable response and in the 1919 provincial election a referendum on prohibition was held. It was approved by a large majority and Ontario became a *"dry"* province. This was the first election where women were given the opportunity to vote. As a result of this province wide ban all local option bylaws became null and void.

It must have taken a while to implement the new regulations and put in place measures to stop the importation of alcohol. It was an awkward if not impossible task and in 1924 another vote approved the creation of government controlled liquor stores. In 1927 the Ontario Temperance Act was replaced by the Liquor Licence (Ontario) Act and the former local option bylaws were reinstated.

It didn't take long for the liquor proponents to take action. A referendum to place a Government Liquor Store in Bracebridge was held in 1928 and was defeated. It was defeated again in 1933.

Persistence paid off however and in 1938 a similar referendum was approved by a vote of 798 to 510 and in 1939 a liquor store opened beside Muskoka Garage on Manitoba Street and a Brewers Warehouse on Main Street.

It took a lot longer for the public to approve the serving of liquor anywhere else though and Bracebridge was *"high and dry"* for many years. In 1955 a referendum to issue *"dining lounges"* licences and *"lounges"* licences were both soundly defeated. It was not until 1962 that a referendum approved the sale of alcohol with meals. Some adjoining townships in the Bracebridge area still did not have that approval and many took until 1970 to pass similar bylaws. The referendum procedure for controlling the sale of alcohol was archaic and new regulations were in due time introduced to deal with applications for new liquor sales outlets in Ontario communities.

No doubt the prohibitionists of 1900 would shiver in their graves if they knew the content of our present-day liquor rules.

It is reported that the owner of the Albion Hotel, the day after the success of the 1962 referendum was announced, immediately bought a brand new Cadillac -something he could never afford previously- and hired a chauffeur to drive it. He knew, like the tavern owners of old knew, there was a lot of money to be made selling beer and liquor.

There are many interesting, often humorous, stories describing the two sides of the prohibition debate as related by Redmond Thomas in ***Reminiscences***. During the heated campaigns there were fiery speeches, lectures, sermons, advertisements, door to door campaigns, and slogans. The most active were the prohibitionists. There were buttons that read, *"DADDY VOTE FOR ME"*, *"THE BARREL OR THE BOY"* and *"A DOLLAR MAY BE SPENT ON BOOZE RATHER THAN BREAD OR BOOTS"*.

One of the more determined of the prohibition organizations was the ***Independent Order of Good Templars*** who quite properly referred to themselves by the acronym ***I. O. G. T.***, and advertised themselves as such…

I. O. G. T.

INDEPENDENT ORDER OF GOOD TEMPLARS

…however, their opponents irreverently mimicked them by using the same acronym as it applied to themselves or perhaps to infer that the prohibitionists weren't quite as pure as what they wanted the public to believe…

I. O. G. T.

I OFTEN GET TIGHT

Public posters were also used; some that left little doubt as to how the women were going to treat their husband if they dared to touch that **"demon rum"**,

-for example, an unmistakable message!

Not to be outdone, the anti-prohibitionists could have retaliated in a meaningful way with *their* version of the same picture,

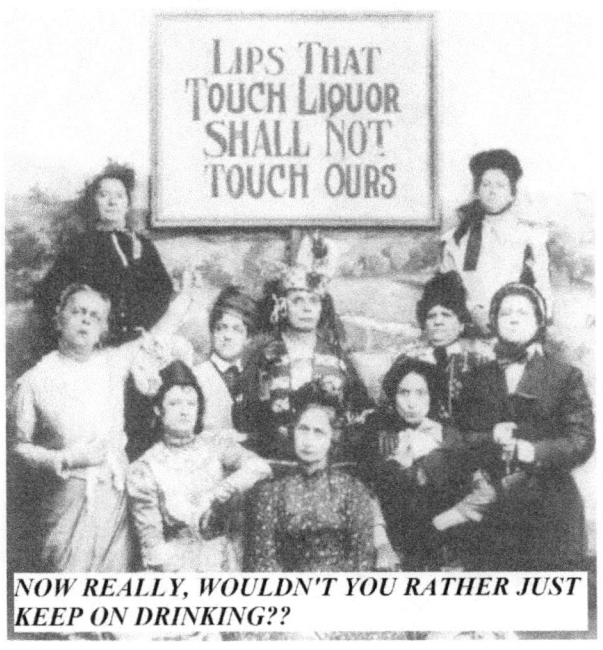

-but added words below the picture to convey a completely different message.

So ends the story of prohibition. There is a lot more to that story in official journals than what I have listed here, but this chapter has focused on it as it directly related to Bracebridge. To dig into it beyond what we know was the experience of those who lived here through that era would become very boring. It does however, shed light on the questionable legitimacy of petitions that are wildly promoted by the enthusiastic pressure of activists who may, or may not, have the broader interests of the community in mind. It would take many years before liquor products were allowed to be sold to the public in Bracebridge and many, many more years before there was a production of any alcohol products *produced* here; that being when the Lakes of Muskoka Cottage Brewery opened their doors in 1996.

15. EARLY BRIDGES...

The Muskoka River North Branch and the Muskoka River South Branch, while they both have their headwaters in Algonquin Park, are two separate watersheds. The North Branch starts with streams and lakes feeding the Big East River which winds it way to Lake Vernon in Huntsville and from there becomes the Muskoka River. The South Branch similarly starts with the Oxtongue River which flows into Lake of Bays and its outlet at Baysville becomes the Muskoka River.

When the logging industry was at its peak these rivers were busy places. Thousands of logs floated down these rivers and, while the North Branch is the larger of the two, it seems the South Branch carried more logs over its rapids and log slides than did the North Branch.

The significant part of these two branches however is that they meet in downtown Bracebridge where they combine to form the Muskoka River which then flows through Muskoka Lake and on into Georgian Bay. The river is so taken for granted that most residents of Muskoka have no idea what an important role it has played in our history and what benefit it continues to play in the balance of our environment and lifestyle.

The intersection of these two branches of the river added to the attractiveness of Bracebridge as a choice area for settlement. The two entirely different watersheds were each filled with huge stands of virgin timber and the rivers provided ready access. Add to that a few reasonably good patches of land for farming, the waterfalls so necessary for industry, and it is no wonder that **"North Falls"** quickly became the heart of Muskoka.

However, while the two branches of the river added greatly to the economy of the area, they were also a disadvantage in that they created a need for numerous bridges to provide access to the different parts of the new settlement.

In fact, in present day Bracebridge there are 8 bridges in the business area alone. They are:

1. Birds Bridge, the first, built to replace a large pine tree used for crossing the river

2. Hunts Hill Bridge, now Taylor Rd. Bridge, dates back to 1870s

3. Shier's Bridge, built in 1874 to connect the **"new road to Gravenhurst"**

4. CNR Rail Bridge, built by Northern Railway in 1880s

5. Rock Cut Bridge, built in the 1920s to provide better access to downtown

6. Silver Bridge, built in the early 1930s as part of the Ferguson Highway later Hwy 11

7. Kelvin Grove Bridge, the stream now flows through a large buried storm drain

8. Wellington Street Bridge opened in 1984 to relieve traffic congestion on Manitoba St.

In the past there were other bridges, all long forgotten. Pioneers were a shrewd bunch. They knew where they wanted to go and rose to the challenge. Because there were those who wanted to travel beyond Bracebridge to areas in north Muskoka and Lake of Bays, (known then as Trading Lake), in response to a petition signed by 30 ratepayers, the Township of Macaulay and the Crown Lands Department in the early 1870s built a bridge just upstream from Wilson's Falls where Gilman Willson had built and operated his Norwood Mills sawmill.

Gilman Willson, (those who wrote about him differed regarding the spelling of his name, both first and last; in some places it was Gillman in others Gilman, in some it was Willson and in others Wilson, in reference to the falls it is almost always called Wilson's Falls), had come to Bracebridge as a Methodist Episcopal minister, the first minister to take up residence here. It seems after a while he found that there was a better living to be made sawing lumber than there was saving souls, so he and partner William Holditch built the Norwood Mills sawmill. His daughter Elizabeth's 1866 marriage to William Holditch was the first marriage in Bracebridge.

Prior to the Wilson's Falls Bridge though, as noted by Redmond Thomas and G.H.O. Thomas, there was bridge at a shallow section of the Muskoka River North Branch above the rapids near Bass Rock Park. At first the rapids were called Cooper's Rapids, then Hallstead's Rapids, and in later days, Flynn's Rapids; to me they are best named Bass Rock Rapids. This bridge, on the upstream side of the Bass Rock Park area, was difficult to stabilize because it kept getting washed away by the force of the spring floods. It led on the east side of the river to a very steep hill and a difficult trail along the edge of the river to Wilson's Falls.

It is interesting to note that this bridge is shown on the map of Bracebridge contained in the ***Guide Book & Atlas of Muskoka Parry Sound Districts 1879***, and in fact the road leading down to it is called "***Bridge Street***", an indication of the importance placed on that crossing of the Muskoka River. Another indication is that one of the first orders given by the newly formed Village of Bracebridge in 1875 was to shovel the snow off that bridge. The bridge and Bridge Street, both the name and the road, have long ago disappeared into the mists of time.

Halstead and McNicol constructed and operated a sawmill in these rapids powered by its rapid flow of water, that is, when the flow of water in the river was high enough to permit it, and when it wasn't they would activate a dam that raised the river level to redirect water into their machinery.

It was quite likely the difficulties experienced with that bridge and dam that gave rise to the petition submitted to the Township of Macaulay asking for a better one at Wilson's Falls. G.H.O. Thomas states that in 1884 all traffic bound for Baysville and Dorset crossed the river at Wilson's Falls and continued to do so until around 1900. By that time the bridge was falling into disrepair and was condemned. In 1902 it was removed by the Township for fear of liability in the case of an accident. The Township had no interest in footing the bill for a new bridge because, in their rather short-sighted opinion, it was more for the use of the residents of Bracebridge than those of their Township. No doubt the bitterness felt by the Township Council when the Village of Bracebridge separating in 1875 had not yet disappeared.

As a result all traffic was forced to use what G.H.O. Thomas described as a *"frail bridge"* leading to Hunts Hill, fit only for pedestrians and light loads. A reference is made to it in a newspaper article of 1888. It states that due to flooding on River Street (possibly caused by the dam at the Halstead and McNicol sawmill),

"…road traffic to Baysville was diverted to the new road built in the Hunts Hill section."

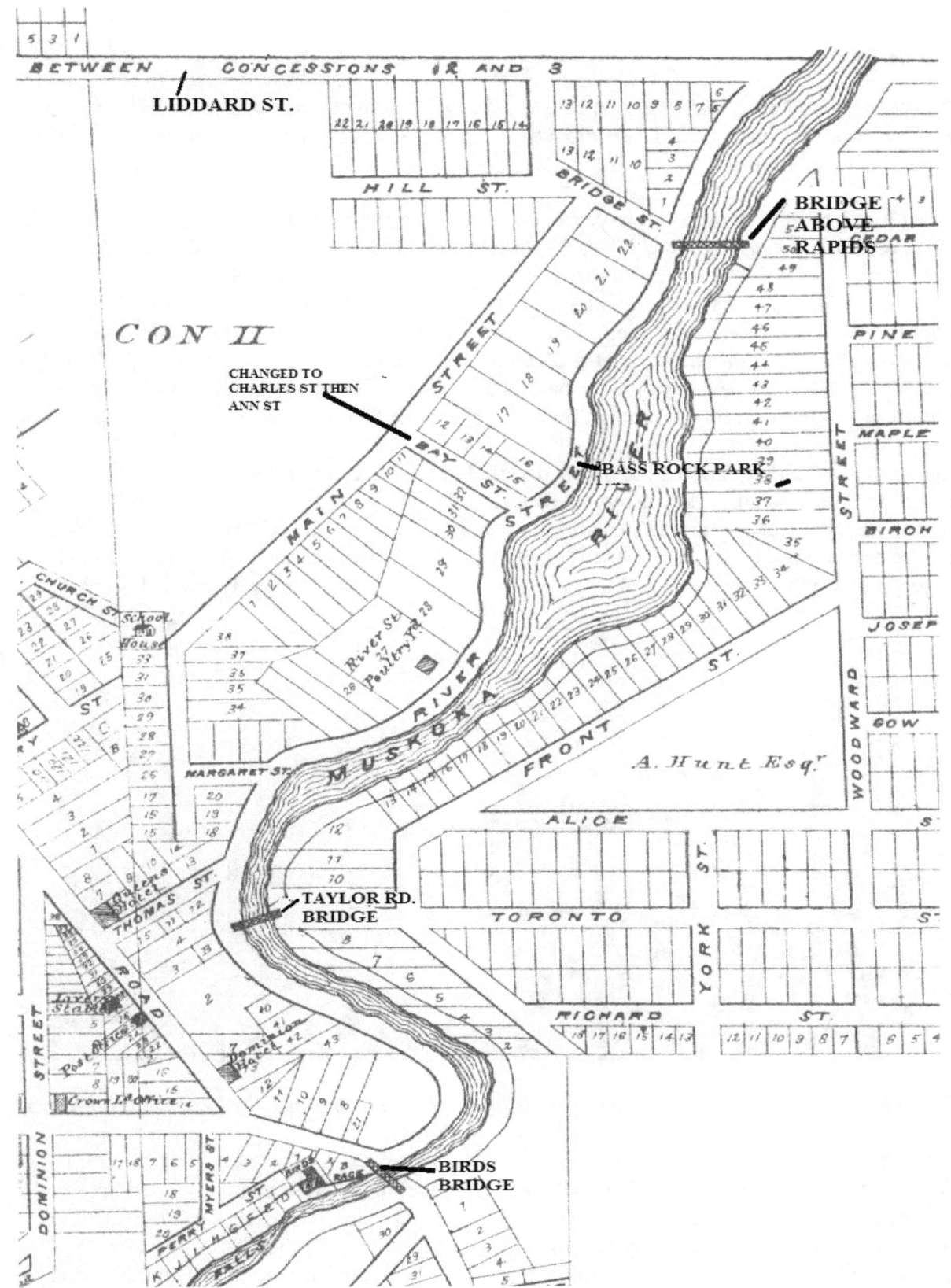

1879 map showing that Birds Bridge, Taylor Road Bridge and a long-gone Bridge upstream from Bass Rock Park were all in use at that time.

It continues,

"The "new road" on Hunts Hill was reached from downtown Bracebridge by a low bridge crossing between Thomas and Toronto Streets, a bridge which seems to have been constructed only a few years before."

In fact it had been built quite a few years before because the map of the Village contained in the ***Guide & Atlas of Muskoka and Parry Sound Districts 1879,*** in addition to showing the bridge above the rapids at Bass Rock, also shows a bridge connecting Thomas Street and Toronto Street, (both now called Taylor Road). In a letter written by Joseph Cooper at the age of 94 possibly supplied by his daughter Annie, he writes, ***"As I was a carpenter I had to build bridges one where we cut the pine tree and one where the Station now stands."*** That would be the ***"frail bridge"*** referred to by Thomas and it would probably have been built some time after Bird's Bridge which he built in 1861 as part of the completion of the Muskoka Colonization Road.

Apparently it could not handle the traffic diverted to it as a result of the demolition of the Wilson's Falls Bridge by Macaulay Township, so Bracebridge decided to replace it. With the assistance of the Provincial Government, and in spite of objections expressed by one of the Town Councillors that the proposed new structure was far too grandiose and unnecessary in the first place, they proceeded with the construction of a new steel bridge which was officially opened in 1906.

The 1906 new bridge, showing the "frail" bridge below that had not yet been removed from service.

While Township and Village officials searched for suitable (or more suitable) locations for bridges, there were some early travellers, probably settlers looking to access their Free Grant Land property in areas beyond Bracebridge or loggers heading for their camps, that weren't about to wait for the result of their efforts. In an 1888 news article reference is made to a road that was created by those looking to gain access to the north-east portion of Muskoka, especially the Baysville (or Trading Lake) area. It reads as follows, ***"(the connection between the parts of Bracebridge west and east of the river had been by way of King Street and a road*** *between lots 3 and 4 of Macaulay, to Richard Street).* Obviously, those who chose to live in the *"Hunts Hill"* (as it is known in 2013) part of town also played a role in creating this road because it provided a convenient way for them to get to the downtown business section prior to the construction of (and even after) the *frail bridge* that many didn't trust.

This road was at the top of *"Free Methodist Hill"* and ran easterly from Muskoka Road along King Street passing in front of the first church building in the community; built by a Presbyterian congregation who had previously held their services in Alexander Bailey's trading post near the mouth of the river. The church building was shared with the Methodists and located roughly on or adjacent to the parking lot of the Chapel Gallery, a building that was built to emulate that first church structure. The road continued on from there through the property known as Birds Grove and provided access to the Taylor Road/Richard Street (Hunt's Hill) area. Although it is unclear when this long-forgotten road ceased to be used, in recent years a pedestrian pathway was developed there following a similar route after this pioneer public access was confirmed by discovery of a resolution passed by the County of Victoria, of which Bracebridge was a part at the time, where it was authorized that a load of gravel be placed on *"…the road leading from Muskoka Road to Baysville past the Presbyterian Church…"* This conclusive evidence of there being a publicly funded road in this location enabled the Bracebridge Council to insist that a public walking path be maintained through this beautiful part of town.

This road was also very accurately described by James Boyer in 1905 as reprinted in the 1986 newspaper serial *Muskoka and Bracebridge,*

"The Presbyterians built the first church, a small frame structure on the hill, above Mr. Birds house. It was a short distance from the Muskoka Road, from which branched off a road, running alongside the church, which was then the only road to the 2nd, 3rd, 4th and 5th concessions of Macaulay on that side of the river."

The article goes on in the Explanatory Notes to say:

"A continuation of this road went on to what later was called Toronto Street, and this 'was then the only road to the 2nd, 3rd, 4th and 5th of Macaulay on that side of the river'."

It continues,

"In other words, there was no bridge as there was later between Thomas and Toronto Streets across the river, the only bridge (except at Wilson's Falls) being the one at the top of the Falls."

That article of James Boyer seems to focus on events in 1870 and 1871 and indicates that the Joseph Cooper's *"frail bridge"* (today's Taylor Road Bridge) to Hunts Hill was constructed after that date and the Wilson's Fall Bridge before it. Lacking however, is reference to the bridge at the Bass Rock rapids, in spite of the fact that both G.H.O. Thomas and Redmond Thomas suggest that it *preceded* the Wilsons Falls Bridge and the fact that a decision had been made by the newly formed Village of Bracebridge in 1875 that it be kept free of snow. Could it have been built between 1870 and 1875? Not likely, James Boyer as Municipal Clerk of the Village in 1875 would not have missed it. It is more likely that, in spite of the fact that it was considered important enough to keep it free from snow, the instability of the bridge rendered it not worthy of mention considering the easier route and more reliable crossing at Wilson's Falls.

Another early bridge over the Muskoka River North Branch in the centre of Bracebridge deserves to be recognized because of its oddity. It was called *"The Scows"*, consisting of the large scows of the tanneries lashed together end to end and anchored firmly at each shore.

Redmond Thomas in **Reminiscences** said it was in the same location as the present day Wellington Street Bridge, but in a 1922 newspaper article it is stated to have been between the old wharf which was located on the north side of the river just upstream from the mouth of Bracebridge Bay, and the foundry site which was adjacent to the launching ramp at Shaw Street on the south.

It was placed there only in the winter well after the end of the navigation season through the courtesy and co-operation of the tanneries. In either location it was a very convenient connection, especially for the staff of the tanneries, and possibly a shortcut for the heavily laden horse drawn sleighs enabling them to avoid some of the steep hills; piled high as they would have been with hemlock bark so essential to the hide tanning process,. It was also an asset to residents of the area allowing them to cross the river without having to walk all the way into town where they would cross the river on Bird's Bridge.

When the Provincial Government proceeded with the construction of the Ferguson Highway in the 1930s, Bracebridge got a new bridge. It was an enormous undertaking to carve a roadbed out of the steep south bank of the Muskoka River in Bracebridge Bay and build a new structure over the Bracebridge Falls. In fact, the Silver Bridge is two structures, one of which can only be seen when viewed from the bottom of the falls. That new access into downtown was a wonderful addition and provided a greatly improved route to handle the increasingly heavy traffic on what would eventually become Provincial Highway Number 11.

A secondary benefit resulted from the huge silver bridge that towered over the falls; it gave Bracebridge a very picturesque identity that may endure forever. Even during a recent complete rebuild which rendered the high superstructure section of the bridge totally unnecessary, it was decided to leave it in place because of its scenic value and the distinct identity it gave Bracebridge Bay Park.

Year in year out the Bracebridge Falls with that bridge in the background appears on logos, letterheads, advertisements and newsreels and immediately identifies Bracebridge. It is probably the most photographed feature in Muskoka. In the late 1930s, with a world war looming due to the aggression of Hitler's Germany, the Chairman of the Water Light and Power Commission Wellington Reid was lamenting at the family dinner table that he wished he could do something to lighten the gloom that had descended on the community knowing that it would not be long before the country would be engulfed in a bitter conflict. In response, his daughter Ruth said *"why don't you put coloured lights on our new bridge?"* Her father thought that was a wonderful idea and made it happen and the people of Bracebridge were delighted.

Those lights have been on ever since except for one brief period in the 1980s when the Town Council attempted to convert the rather expensive bulb system to a fibre optic type of lighting, which of course was just a white strip that took the place of the wires with the attached bulbs. Within days following the installation of the fibre optic lighting the complaints started pouring in. Comments in the local newspaper, letters to the editor in the Toronto Star, presentations to the Council members and the Town Office staff all pleaded for the return of the coloured bulb lighting system.

As an acknowledgment of the wishes expressed by the community the Council decided to return to the bulb system and in celebration thereof organized an event on a Friday night in late November dubbed the *"Relighting the Lights"*. It was advertised in the newspaper but everyone expected it to be a rather quiet affair. Allan Armstrong, foreman of the Public Works Department and his staff made sure everything was ready and we patiently waited for the advertised start time, wondering if anyone was going to show up. To our amazement, the sidewalks of Manitoba Street suddenly started to fill up and before long a crowd of close to 1000 people gathered in the cold evening weather chatting excitedly about this great event. When the switch was thrown and the bridge again shone with brilliant coloured lights the crowd cheered wildly and the Bracebridge Kinsmen Club provided a brief fireworks display. It was a heart-warming event to see a community so thrilled that this simple little part of Bracebridge heritage was restored. What made it even more rewarding was that Ruth (Reid) Taylor, the young lady who put forth this idea many years before, was on hand for the event and had tears in her eyes when she saw that her idea had not been forgotten.

Although it originally had little to do with Christmas, that seasonal celebration has continued ever since, expanded to include lighting on other public buildings and functions for children, and renamed *"Lighting of the Lights"*.

An additional bit of lighting was added during the war years in the form of a huge lighted "V" for victory in the middle of the upper span of the bridge.

The ingenuity and determination of our early pioneers is clear in this chapter. They were going to find a way across, or around the river, in the location they wanted no matter what; the same way they found places and built their sawmills wherever there was a reasonably reliable flow of water. Out of necessity they had to be creative in order to scratch out a living in this Muskoka wilderness and these hardy entrepreneurs took advantage of everything available, determined that they were going to be successful in this new land in spite of the many obstacles.

16. HER MAJESTY'S OLD RELIABLE SHAVING SALOON…

Redmond Thomas wrote a wonderful article in **Reminiscences** about **Her Majesty's Old Reliable Shaving Saloon** that opened in Bracebridge around 1879. It was there that his father G.H.O. Thomas took him for his first haircut as a boy because the owner, Gustavus Adolphus Binyon, had a reputation for getting along well with kids. He was also a coloured man, a rare sight in early Muskoka, and therefore a subject of curiosity for children.

The business had a number of different locations during its tenure in Bracebridge, which actually was of substantial length compared to many early businesses. It also had a name change when Queen Victoria died and King Edward 7th assumed the throne of England, becoming ***HIS** Majesty's Old Reliable Shaving Saloon*. Interestingly, while recorders of our history refer to one or the other of those names, Binyon himself had earlier advertised his services in the ***Guide & Atlas of Parry Sound Muskoka Districts 1879*** as ***THE** Old Reliable Shaving Saloon.* Perhaps he was so impressed by the large number of British emigrants moving to Bracebridge that he made a strategic name change reflecting royalty to get their business.

Mr. Binyon was very active in the community. He was appointed a member of a committee to plan the opening event for the new Town Hall in 1881, was sworn in as a constable to act in cases of emergency progressing to Chief Constable in 1886, played cricket and participated in creating a new cricket field for the community. Another interesting item about Mr. Binyon is that on the 1880 assessment role he is shown as being 30 years old, but just 5 years later on the 1885 roll he is shown as 39.

Maybe he wasn't sure how old he was; records were not kept as carefully then as they are now.

17. WILLIAM HOLDITCH'S TWO HORSEPOWER BOAT…

To say that William Holditch had a significant influence on Bracebridge would be a huge understatement. He came to North Falls in 1862 (according to an 1868 report he owned 200 acres of property that included much of the settled area of North Falls) and became a partner with Gillman Willson in the Norwood Mills sawmill operation at Wilsons Falls. Another report states that in 1863 he started the first post office at Falkenburg and that he later surveyed lots in North Falls and sold them from his boot and shoe store on Dominion Street. He was obviously a shrewd businessman and a tough negotiator. He knew his property well and was firm on its value, exhibited by being difficult with the Town and E.P. Cockburn regarding a proposal to establish a new wharf in Bracebridge Bay. His property included where the Bracebridge Public School is located; another occasion where he stubbornly negotiated to get what he thought his property was worth.

As mentioned earlier, his relationship with the Willson family went beyond business. The first marriage ceremony ever performed in North Falls was when he and Elizabeth Willson, Gillmans daughter, were married in 1866. In recognition of his great contribution to his community, Holditch Street was so named in his honour.

There is a lot that could be said about William Holditch's achievements and participation in community affairs. His most lasting achievement, one that we have had before us every day since and probably will live forever, took place on Confederation Day, July 1st, 1867. In recognition of that wonderful event the residents of the whole area converged on the property between Manitoba Street (Muskoka Road then) and the river commonly used as the fall fair grounds at the time, and had a community picnic. It is was during the speeches welcoming Confederation that William Holditch suggested that certain streets be named in recognition of Confederation and proposed Main Street, Ontario Street, Manitoba Street, Quebec Street and Dominion Street. Robert J Boyer in *A Good Town Grew Here* wrote that each name was placed in a box, covered and delivered to each street. It was later that night that the covers were removed and the residents found out which name was in the box and that became the name of that street. Mr. Boyer's comments were supported by a letter he had received from Mrs. Forbes McLaren of Pipestone Manitoba, a daughter of Mr. & Mrs. Gordon Ewing, who as a very young girl was at that picnic and had witnessed this process.

However, this chapter is not about him. It is about his daring attempt to build a boat.

It wasn't long after the early explorers and surveyors had travelled the lakes and rivers of Muskoka in the performance of their duties using canoes provided by the Natives that Holditch recognized the need for larger crafts to serve the growing population. In fact, he was ahead of the founder of the Muskoka Lakes Navigation Company A.P. Cockburn in attempting to create a craft that could accommodate a larger capacity of passengers and freight.

Prior to the 1866 launch of the first steamer the ***Wenonah*** by Cockburn there had been sailboats and rowboats attempting to fill the need. They were slow and awkward in Holditch's opinion so he built a large flat-bottomed boat that was propelled by a paddle wheel on each side activated by horses on a treadmill turning a rotating post that transferred power to the wheels.

It was creative and innovative, but unfortunately it didn't work. It only made one trip, according to ***Muskoka and Haliburton 1615 to 1875,*** that being from North Falls to McCabe's Landing, later named Gravenhurst. Even then it only went one way; it was unable to return to its home base because the propelling system had failed and besides, it took 12 hours to make the trip. No doubt the experiment gave Cockburn encouragement to get on with *his* plan.

Who knows, Mr. Holditch may have created the rating system applied to engines ever since when he referred to his power source as having 2 horse power.

18. HOUSE OF COMMERCE...

What must have been direct competition for Teviotdale's District Exchange and its various owners was James P. Humphries **House of Commerce**. One thing they obviously shared was a penchant for choosing exotic names that probably exaggerated the reality of their retail operation.

Like Teviotdale, Humphries was very active in the community as a member of council, school board and affairs of his church following his arrival in the 1870s. He was instrumental in the construction of the Methodist Church building on Dominion Street, later to become the United Church in the same location.

The House of Commerce no doubt carried similar merchandise such as groceries and dry goods as the District Exchange, but it lasted a lot longer in business and seemed to be more creative in its advertising and promotion. Humphries had purchased the store from Alfred Hunt, better known in history for establishing the first bank in Muskoka, **Hunt's Bank,** and they operated side by side in the same building; in 2013 appropriately named Marrin Building in recognition of being the location of P.J. Marrin and Sons grocery and wholesale business.

A feature of the store that attracted a lot of attention was a small narrow-gauge railway that travelled the length of the store and was used to carry supplies to and from the street to a warehouse at the back. He creatively promoted his business in an 1878 advertisement in a local newspaper of the day where he included the following poem:

> *"While round your Tea Table, Fire or Hearth,*
> *Talking over your wants and money's worth,*
> *We give our advice-pithy and terse-*
> *Get your supplies at the House of Commerce."*

Well, maybe his creative ability failed him a little when it came to poetry. James P. Humphries died in 1909 at the age of 62.

19. DOWLER MATCH FACTORY...

George Dowler came to Canada in 1876 from Birmingham, England where he owned a very successful manufacturing business employing over 500 people. Along with many brass products, he also manufactured matches. After a disastrous fire he limited his product to ammunition, his market being Napoleon who was in the midst of the Franco-Prussian war. Unfortunately though, Napoleon didn't pay his bills so Dowler packed up his belongings and moved to Canada.

George Boyer wrote in **Early Days in Muskoka** that Dowler purchased the extensive property of Col. Maude, an English officer, who had attempted to create a farm at Prospect Lake. Imagine the culture shock, moving from what must have been relative comfort in England to trying to plough the rocky ground of Muskoka. Dowler couldn't make farming work there either and eventually moved into Bracebridge where in 1886 he applied for and was granted a five year exemption from town taxes and established a match factory on the river side of Dill Street just a little east of its intersection with Victoria Street.

George Dowler's ingenuity is evident in the system he created for drawing water from the Muskoka River. He rigged up a series of poles connected together at the ends and attached at the top to a circulating wheel that, when turned, caused the poles to jerk back and forth activating a pump at the river which then pushed water up the steep incline to the buildings on the street.

He operated there for a number of years, his son Joseph Dowler continuing the business following George's death. An interesting aside, Joseph Dowler was a member of the first baseball team ever assembled in Bracebridge. The team probably played their games on the vacant property that would later become Jubilee Park and in 2013 the home of Nippissing University.

New government regulations on some of the components used in manufacturing matches brought an end to that production and Joseph went into the grain-chopping business. Maybe that was just as well because it seems using the matches could be dangerous. Once struck, they flared up so badly that they had to be held at arm's length until the sulphur burned off before they could be used.

Needless to say, instructions on their use no doubt suggested that a good deal of caution was required if one wanted to light their pipe or cigar with one of Dowler's matches; maybe even life threatening if one happened to be near combustible materials.

20. BRACEBRIDGE BRILLIANT LIGHT COMPANY...

The identity of the founders of the *Bracebridge Brilliant Light Company* is unclear but it is a matter of record that Alfred Hunt (founder of Hunt's Bank) was the Secretary Treasurer and John H. Jackson was an officer. Others named, although not identified as to the degree of involvement, were Fenn, Buckerfield, Tom Johnson, T. J. Anderson, and William Kirk.

Redmond Thomas wrote that there were two light manufacturers in Bracebridge, one being the subject in a building on Dominion Street, the other the *Bracebridge Acetylene Company* owned by a Mr. Marskell who he states operated from a building on the property where the Bracebridge Memorial Community Centre is situated on James Street.

It is also unclear when these companies came into being but it had to be well before 1904 because it was in that year the Board of Directors voted to pay a 10% dividend to their shareholders.

The process of creating light consisted of a large cylindrical drum that permitted water to trickle over calcium carbide producing a gas that could then be lit. It all sounds pretty archaic but one of those firms boldly put on an exhibit at the Toronto Exhibition Grounds to show off their product.

Their existence was short lived, no doubt because of the rapid expansion of electrical power provided by the Town's newly acquired electrical generation plant and the ready acceptance by the community of the trouble free lighting process. In 1906 the patents registered in the name of the *Bracebridge Brilliant Light Company* were put on sale and were purchased by James Marskell in 1910 who continued to produce acetylene lighting at the Dominion Street location.

When that production ended is not known. No doubt it was a victim of new technology; commonplace in any era. In those days producing light with such machinery must have been perceived as an incredible phenomena and one users could understand because they could *see* it. On the other hand, many of those experiencing electrical power for the first time were very wary of this strange new force that they *couldn't* see yet it could make a piece of glass light up like magic. Like the introduction of any new revolutionary product, no matter what or when, rumours were rampant about what illnesses this *'lectricity'* would cause and what terrible afflictions those exposed to it would know in the future.

Fear of the unknown haunted them back then as it does us now and brings to mind the old axiom, the more things change the more they stay the same.

21. BRACEBRIDGE MARBLE AND GRANITE WORKS...

Like the Bird Woollen Mill, the *Bracebridge Marble and Granite Works* served the public for a long time, almost 50 years to be exact. It was often referred to as the *"tombstone factory"* and operated from a building on Queens Hill on Manitoba Street opposite the Queens Hotel.

It started in 1880 but there is some confusion in historical records about who started it. Robert J. Boyer, in *A Good Town Grew Here* and *Bracebridge Around 1930*, says that Henry Boyer started the business after learning the trade in New York, where they lived after emigrating from England and before moving to Bracebridge in 1867. However, in *Muskoka Memories,* while he mentions

Henry, he states that it was *Harry* who in 1871 heard of a marble shop in Orillia and applied for a job there. He worked there for a few years and eventually returned to Bracebridge where in 1880 he started the marble works, assisted later by his sons Harry Jr. and Sam.

***Many, if not most, of the older gravestones in Muskoka
cemeteries were made right here in downtown Bracebridge***

Redmond Thomas in ***Reminiscences*** states that it was Henry Boyer who started Bracebridge Marble Works and that he served on the Town Council and School Board. He also praises Boyer's artistry that still adorns many of the older tombstones in cemeteries throughout Muskoka. In 1930 Sam Boyer moved the business to Haileybury.

Regardless of whether it was Harry or Henry (it could have been both or that they were one and the same) who started the ***Bracebridge Marble and Granite Works***, it was a good operation that served the community well for a long time. Like The ***District Exchange*** and the ***House of Commerce***, in modern day terms it could be considered as an *anchor store* that attracted many shoppers to the community.

22. DUFFERIN HALL…

Dufferin Hall was not significant for its contribution to the business community and the economy like the retail stores; it was more for its interesting name and its final owner.

It was located on the south side of Ontario Street near its intersection with Dominion Street and was built sometime before 1874, although its ownership is not mentioned. Sometimes it was referred to as Village Hall and served the community as a public meeting place; many groups used it regularly for their meetings.

It became ***Dufferin Hall*** after a very distinguished couple made a brief visit to the pioneer town on July 17, 1874. That couple was the Governor General of Canada Lord Dufferin and Lady Dufferin. This visit of the representative of Queen Victoria is well described by Robert J. Boyer in *A Good Town Grew Here* and in newspaper reports contained in *Muskoka and Haliburton 1615 to 1875*. To say the least, the community provided a grand welcome and while the Mayor and Council were front and centre at a reception for the vice-regal couple, the only recorded note in the Council minutes regarding the visit is to pay a bill of $19.00 incurred for the construction of the stage where the reception was held.

In recognition of that visit, ***Dufferin Hall*** was so named. Meetings of the Municipal Council were held there until the new town hall was completed in 1882. Public groups continued to meet there until 1884, including the newly formed Salvation Army, who around that time acquired the property and established their first *barracks* later to be referred to as the ***"Citadel"***.

It is recorded that the hall was still around in 1891, but at some point it was demolished and a new Salvation Army Citadel erected in its place.

23. NEW YORK HORSE SHOEING EMPORIUM…

Ranking among the most exotic in the list of strange pioneer business names is this one. Its operation was mostly what its name suggests but it was in fact an old fashioned blacksmith shop typical of those we heard about in our childhood. The owner referred to himself as a blacksmith.

There is no explanation of its connection with New York, either city or state, other than perhaps the owner was trying to attract the business of emigrants from the United States. If that was the case it would be a curious thing to do because the vast majority of immigrants to Muskoka were British, who as a nation were paranoid about being attacked by the United States as explained in Chapter 1.

The owner, Richard Swain, was not a United States citizen. For a number of years he was member of the Municipal Council including that of 1889, making him a founding member of council for the new designated *Town* of Bracebridge. Previous to that and since 1875 Bracebridge had been designated as a Village.

The ***New York Horse Shoeing Emporium***, spelled ***Horseshoeing*** in some records, was located on Thomas Street just below the ***"old"*** Post Office at the corner of Manitoba Street and Taylor Road, probably at or near the location where for many years Seth Hillman and Arthur Crockford operated the Downtown Garage.

Richard Swain was active in the community, as most business people were back then. As a member of Council he was involved in the *Flora Barnes* lawsuit against the municipality (the subject of another chapter), was an active member of the Agricultural Society and the Independent Order of Oddfellows. Unfortunately, shortly after Swain was elected to the first Town Council, he died, never having the opportunity to experience the benefits of that new municipal designation.

24. THE GOLDEN BEAVER STORE…

The name itself conjures up a variety of images in one's mind but there is no record whatsoever regarding the reason for such a moniker aside from what is described below. While the anchor of any pioneer community was the *"general"* store, occasionally a retail operation would assume a more focused product line. Such was *The Golden Beaver* because it sold dry goods, presumably meaning clothing and like materials.

The store was started by Thomas Crompton according to the notes of G.H.O. Thomas in a building owned by Mr. Myers, but in an unexplained transition, John W. Ney who was a clerk in the store got ownership in 1884. Ney had arrived in Bracebridge in 1879 and Robert J. Boyer quoted him in *A Good Town Grew Here* as saying *"..that after over 20 years of a successful business career in Bracebridge.."* due to ill health he was forced to give up his dry goods business. That was in 1904.

The store was then sold to an adjacent storeowner, The Hunter Bros., who combined the inventory with that of another store they had purchased and had the audacity, in spite of Ney's claim of success, to advertise that they were going to *"…give Bracebridge people something they have been needing for a long time, an up-to-date store."* The nerve! Ironically, there is little reference to any success of the Hunter Bros. thereafter, and it is noted that they sold their business a couple of years later.

The endearing feature of *The Golden Beaver* though is that they had just that, a golden beaver statute that served as the store sign mounted on a post at the front of the store.

The Golden Beaver Store, proudly displaying its mascot (a beaver of course) on a pole in front.

25. THE OLD ESTABLISHED WAGGON SHOP...

G.H.O. Thomas, in *Bracebridge in 1884* wrote that an 1878 list of businesses indicated there were 124 commercial operations in the pioneer community. That's a lot, considering that the first settler, John Beal, came to the dense wilderness just 19 years earlier. The rapid growth of the area is evidence that Bracebridge quickly became the business centre for Muskoka.

That list of businesses includes three *"waggon"* shops, and spelled as such, although later historical reports spell it as *"wagon"*, and lists the various owners as Thomas Magee, Storey, Warner and in the case of *The Old Established Waggon Shop*, John Glover.

The curious thing about this name is the reference to *"old established"*. With the business community having only existed for a few short years, it seems unlikely that any business could claim such status.

Perhaps Mr. Glover was exaggerating his title to get a leg up on the competition. He might have come to Bracebridge with a great deal of experience in the trade; one thing for sure is that he knew how to advertise his product:

> *"Waggons, Buggies, Sleighs, and cutters*
> *Manufactured at short notice. Repairs neatly executed*
> *Rear Huber's Book & Variety Store"*

It would seem he had every angle of the horse drawn conveyance business well covered.

26. THE BRACEBRIDGE LIQUOR COMPANY...

George W. Sibbett was way ahead of his time, but not in a good way in the eyes of the temperance movement. He was experienced in the liquor business, partly through his work at the British Lion Hotel and partly with the assistance of his father William who was the manager there. With that support he decided to open his own liquor store, appropriately named the *"Bracebridge Liquor Company"* in a building beside that of the Independent Order of Oddfellows on the west side of Manitoba Street.

It must have been a favourite hate for the prohibitionists but it was popular with society, evidenced by the fact that it stayed in business for 25 years, according to Sibbett, when it suddenly had to close because a 1911 referendum in favour of *"local option"* made liquor sales in Bracebridge illegal. Sibbett may have been good at selling liquor but not so good at keeping track of time. It is reported that they started in 1894 and had to close in 1911, a total of *16* years. Maybe the difference was that they had been selling liquor either long before they officially started or long after they were told to stop.

Regardless, it was a very successful business in early Bracebridge. Many were of the opinion that Sibbett made liquor from basic ingredients, which made it more of a novelty, but others claim that was not the case. That opinion was based on the fact that his employees were seen carrying pails of water from Teviotdales spring, as explained in a previous chapter, and that it was used in the brewing process.

However, when this writer suggested that Sibbett made liquor from scratch in a public presentation, an elderly gentleman stood up and said, ***"No, no, no. Sibbett did not make liquor there, what he did was make liquor WEAKER*** meaning of course, that he imported liquor and mixed it with the spring water to produce a bigger volume to sell.

We will never know if that was so.

One of the few remaining "jugs" used by the G.W. Sibbett Liquor dealer in downtown Bracebridge in Pre-prohibition days.

27. CHANCERY LANE...

Reading between the lines in Bracebridge history, it would seem that the construction of the beautiful, large, modern, town hall building on Dominion Street in the 1880's caused some consternation among the people in the downtown business area. There were some who considered that it was **"out-of-town"** and that the economy of the main street was going to suffer; not that different from complaints expressed when the **"new"** town hall built in 1957 to replace the original destroyed by fire was sold and the Municipal Offices relocated to Taylor Court in the 1990s.

In an attempt to mitigate the concern, the 1880s council purchased a strip of land 12 feet wide that led from Dominion Street, along the side of the town hall, and down the steep hill to connect with the west side of Manitoba Street.

Initially it was called the **"alley way"**, or **"alleyway"** depending on which book you are reading.

When the new courthouse was built in 1900 the furor came alive again, resulting in improvements being made to the lane and somewhere along the way named **Chancery Lane,** after the famous London, England street which was so closely associated with the legal profession. It was fitting that it should be called that because of the close proximity of the municipal building, the courthouse, land registry office and the numerous legal offices located in the immediate area, especially on Chancery Lane. In fact, at one time it was said there had been a law office presence on Chancery Lane continuously for over 70 years.

Chancery Lane has experienced many things since it was created including disastrous fires, especially one in 1912 that destroyed both sides of the lane and another in 1981 that wiped out the north side. It was also very near the upper end of Chancery Lane where scaffolds were constructed to carry out the death penalty bestowed upon two convicted murderers. The steep incline of the lane was great for kids to slid down during a winter snowfall but not so great for adults, especially senior citizens. On particularly slippery days pedestrians would lose their footing and go on a wild ride down the lane, slide right across the sidewalk and land on Manitoba Street.

During a rebuilding program in 1981 that was all resolved. As part of the construction, heating cables were installed in the newly laid concrete of the lane and the slipping and sliding stopped, to the disappointment of the kids.

28. DOBBIN'S TOWN PUMP...

John Dobbin was an entrepreneur extraordinaire in Bracebridge history. Strange and erratic as his methods were, he still created a lot of interest and a lot of business in the early years of the Bracebridge economy.

In 1874 he was appointed the commissioner to take a census of the population of the community in support of a resolution asking to have Bracebridge designated as a separate municipality from the Township of Macaulay. He must have conducted a very thorough survey because it enabled

Victoria County to decide quickly and Bracebridge became a separated, stand-alone municipality in 1875.

However, this section is not about him. It's about his ***Dobbin's Town Pump***.

Considering the rapid growth of the community in that era, it is not surprising that many residents did not have ready access to a potable water supply. The Muskoka River was a long walk away for most and the quality of the water questionable at best. Dobbin saw this need and in 1878, at his own expense, had a well dug on Manitoba Street, directly across from the Taylor Road intersection (then called Thomas Street after Thomas Myers), and had an ornate wooden pump placed on top of it for the use of the public.

It was free and immediately put to good use. Many businesses, families, pedestrians and travellers appreciated the fresh water supply for years. Some local businessmen helped in the maintenance of the well but many citizens were of the opinion the municipality should have been more responsible for its care. In response to the criticism, Town Council gave Dobbin a formal vote of thanks for providing such a badly needed facility, (a feeble token of appreciation to say the least), but in due time the council did help out and the Muskoka Herald reported that ***"..the well has been cleared out, a new pump placed on it and there is an abundance of water"***.

Dobbin was in the mercantile business, whatever that meant in those days, and operated from a ramshackle building on Dominion Street that he called ***"Dobbins Gardens"***. Because he was appointed by the Provincial Government as an Immigration Agent to help immigrants get jobs and give advice on real estate and business matters, he anointed himself publicly ***"The Settlers Friend"***.

His well however, in time fell out of favour. The town developed a municipal water supply system and the well became a mere ornament in the busy downtown area. After a few years it started to show a serious state of impurity and the water from it was tested by an accredited agency in 1891 who filed a report stating, ***"…on no account should it be used for drinking purposes"***. Is it possible the well contributed to the diphtheria epidemic of 1887/88? It will never be known but no doubt the epidemic was the incentive that brought about the introduction of proper testing for public water supplies.

The community was obviously not in a hurry to depart with such a significant piece of heritage though because the pump still appeared in photographs of the downtown area well into the 1900s.

It was finally filled in and put to rest, possibly around the same time as the Women's Christian Temperance Union donated the watering trough that was placed almost directly across the street from the pump.

John Dobbins contribution to the community, picture dated around 1900

29. CRYSTAL PALACE…

The naming of a structure *Crystal Palace* in pioneer Bracebridge is indicative of the creative thinking of the entrepreneurs that seemed to abound in the community in its formative years. Again, like the early hotels, it carried a connection to Royalty and England where many of the early pioneers were born and raised. The name alluded to a famous building in London, England, which, as noted by Redmond Thomas in his column *Comments* in the Bracebridge Gazette of Sept. 13, 1945, was the location of the Great Exhibition of 1851. Thomas made the connection but not-so-subtly suggested that there was little similarity between the two buildings.

No kidding. The *Crystal Palace* here was a wooden, two story structure located near the east side of Jubilee Park and created through a partnership between the fall fair committee and the Town. It served as a display area for the various products and produce of the local farmers and various other functions of the community.

On the other hand, the 990,000 square foot, cast iron and glass Crystal Palace built in Hyde Park, London England to house the 1851 exhibition accommodated 14,000 exhibits and was a massive structure surrounded with extensive gardens and walkways. Some nerve, many thought, to infer that the wooden rambling fair building in Jubilee Park had any resemblance to that in Hyde Park.

The Crystal Palace in Jubilee Park in Bracebridge was as important to the society of Bracebridge as the Crystal Palace in Hyde Park was to London England

It is unclear when it was built. It was in the 1880s though because one of the great pictures of it states that it was **"circa 1880"**. It is described as having 7 square arches which precisely fits with the picture. Other records indicate that the new fall fair building erected on the fair grounds in 1888 was the **Crystal Palace**.

In its day it was certainly a wonderful structure for Muskoka and it was heavily used for many years. In spite of the fact that fires destroyed many of the fair buildings, this one was simply removed in 1962.

Although the record is sketchy, the fair board apparently had asked the town to replace the 1880s fair building with a new 2 story one, although it is not stated which building they wanted to replace. It's possible that the building they got could have been the **Crystal Palace**. We may never know.

There were a number of buildings erected in Jubilee Park by the fair board over the years, one being a horse stable called the **"red barn"** built in 1895 that burned in 1942. Others met the same fate while some collapsed after heavy snowstorms.

None of them, however, would ever compete with the glorious structure that was the namesake of that in Hyde Park in London England.

30. BRACEBRIDGE CHEESE FACTORY…

A fine example of anticipation of future success getting ahead of reality can be seen in the development of the *Bracebridge Cheese Factory.*

Picture the time and place. There was a multitude of new settlers in Muskoka each with a section of property under the Free Grant Land and Homestead Act and all convinced that this was going to be the farm of their dreams. It was something they could never have had in their homeland, and they were sure their future here was guaranteed to be successful. All this land! How could they miss?

They laboured their hearts out to clear the required section of their land, acquired some livestock and planned their dairy production. A part of that plan would have included getting their products to market and, while the council of the Village of Bracebridge provided a place for a farmers market on Market Street, later to be called Kimberley Avenue, some decided that would not be enough. Their dairy production would be very extensive, they were sure. The future looked so positive.

As a result of a number of meetings it was agreed to develop a cheese factory that would provide a ready and reliable market for their dairy products, which led to the formation of a company. A cheese factory was chosen over a creamery, for reasons that are unclear, although there is little doubt that the result would have been the same. It had to be in Bracebridge, the centre of the area, but those involved in its creation and management represented a large part of Muskoka. The names of the promoters and Board of Directors of the new company are readily recognized as key businessmen of the area, a mix of farmers and entrepreneurs, and the place they chose for the factory building was at the north end and on the west side of Wellington Street.

The key ingredient was to have a manager who knew how to make cheese and could direct the affairs of the newly formed company. They chose Alex Anderson for that position because he was already in that business with production facilities in Watt Township and Rosseau. His operation in Watt Township was at the intersection of the Windermere Road and District Road 4, known for years after as *"Cheese Factory Corner".*

He agreed to build and operate the cheese factory in Bracebridge on one condition -that the farmers of the area guarantee a supply of milk from 200 cows for 5 years. Those involved were quick to agree; the future seemed to be bright, and in 1898 the *Bracebridge Cheese Factory* started production.

It didn't take long though before problems appeared. Either the cows couldn't supply enough milk or the farmers couldn't supply enough cows. It was reported in 1904 that it was *"...coming along well"*, but just a year later it was advertised for sale, so obviously it *wasn't* coming along well. It was purchased by James Rusk, (at a price that represented a big loss for the investors), who eventually demolished the building.

Many years later, following a re-alignment of the Monck Road/Wellington Street intersection, the Bracebridge Council contemplated renaming the northerly part of Wellington Street because it no longer aligned with the southern section. During the discussion, *Cheese Factory Hill* was mentioned as a possible name and a news reporter made reference to that in their report on the meeting in the newspaper the following week.

Well! It became clear very quickly that the residents of that section of the street had no interest in history and adamantly conveyed their opinion to their council representatives that under no circumstances would they allow their street to be discredited with such a disgusting name as *Cheese Factory Hill*. As a result the suggestion of renaming was withdrawn and the name remained the same; and an important part of our heritage disregarded, until now.

31. THE PALACE RINK...

Not many in 2012 would recall Bracebridge having an arena other than the Bracebridge Memorial Community Centre that stands proudly on James Street. It was officially opened in the spring of 1949 and was the first artificial ice surface in Muskoka. There have been many glorious celebrations in that building; winning hockey teams, figure skating carnivals, home shows, beer festivals, banquets, receptions, and the like.

Prior to the present arena though, there have been a number of earlier skating rinks in the community of Bracebridge dating as far back as the early 1880s that could all lay claim to hosting similar successful events. Redmond Thomas and his father G. H. O. Thomas were clearly hockey and figure skating fans and were diligent in writing about those sports, including the facilities that housed them, in their excellent historical booklets on Bracebridge. The first skating facility described was an open-air rink located on property just south of Memorial Park in the vicinity of the present location of the Norwood theatre/National Bank/Canada Post buildings. It was lighted for night skating by coal-oil lanterns.

It was on this same property where the original Bracebridge bandstand was located prior to it being moved in 1900 as part of the development of Memorial Park. That bandstand provided many hours of enjoyment for the people of Bracebridge but was in such ramshackle condition that it had to be demolished shortly after it was relocated and the present Memorial Park bandstand was built in its place. In the summer months the rink property was used for a variety of events, but the most memorable were circuses. In **"Reminiscences"**, Redmond Thomas wrote about one of those circuses and riding a steam powered merry-go-round, watching minstrel shows by the light of coal oil flares and listening to barkers rave on and on about their secret oil; **"best thing in the world for humans, horses and harness"**. It was sometimes generously referred to as the **"Broadway of Bracebridge"**.

The first *covered* skating rink came in the 1890s when John E. Dunn built a wooden structure adjacent to the west bank of the Muskoka River North Branch, not far from where in 2013 the Northern Buildal lumber storage building is located. It was a start but as hockey rapidly gained in popularity it became evident that the posts down the centre of the ice that held the building up were a bit of a problem.

As a result, Dunn built another covered skating rink a little further upstream adjacent to the east bank of the river at the east end of the bridge leading from the Bracebridge downtown area to Hunts Hill, often referred to back then as the road to Lake of Bays. He named it *Jubilee Rink*. It was a dramatic improvement because it had no posts and there was a section for hockey games as well as a separate small area for public skating. It was here that Redmond Thomas learned to skate and wrote about that experience, along with later skating rinks, in his many interesting newspaper articles.

John Dunn's skating rink can be seen on the far side of the 1906 bridge leading to Hunt's Hill from the downtown area. "Ace" Bailey, an NHL star with the Toronto Maple Leafs learned his hockey skills in this building. A fire destroyed the building in 1931.

Once again though, the popular past-time of skating outgrew the facility and Dunn decided to expand and remodel the building, providing a better playing surface for hockey games and a stage area set aside just for the Bracebridge Citizens Band which they used for their concerts. Appropriately, Dunn decided the greatly improved facility deserved a more dramatic name so he renamed it ***Palace Rink.***

Dunn's skating rinks produced a number of excellent hockey players. This is where Irvine ***"Ace"*** Bailey learned his hockey skills before advancing to the National Hockey League with the Toronto Maple Leafs. Although they didn't become an NHL star like ***"Ace"*** there were others who played in professional leagues; all graduates of the hockey system in Bracebridge who developed their skills in the skating rinks of John E. Dunn.

There was Clarence Louis Jamieson, nick-named ***"Dutch"*** when he played here and ***"Moose"*** when he played in Cleveland and later in Minneapolis and Kansas City. He was encouraged to go to the professional leagues by Ed Binyon, a Bracebridge native that became a lawyer and had his legal practice in Cleveland. Jamieson's claim to fame was that he could easily hit the arc lights that illuminated the ***Palace Rink*** with a wrist shot, no doubt to the chagrin of the owner.

There were others who first laced on skates in Dunn's Rink. Herbert Trimble, Roy Cooper and Earl (Squirrely) Walker joined Jamieson in Cleveland. Both Redmond Thomas and Robert J Boyer in their notes quoted news articles from a Cleveland newspaper that said these players ***"...covered themselves with glory"*** in winning the league championship in 1913.

To the dismay of the people of the community, the ***Palace Rink*** burned in 1931. It was thought the fire might have been started by railroad transients that sheltered in the building overnight. The building was completely destroyed along with its contents including the hockey equipment of Charles Hampson, a friend and team mate of Irvine ***"Ace"*** Bailey, who like Bailey had an invitation to try out with the Toronto Maple Leafs. Those who saw Hampson in action said he could easily have made the Leaf team as Bailey did, but he chose instead to stay home.

Bracebridge was not without a skating rink for very long. In 1932 George Yearley opened his new skating rink (complete with a section for curling) on James Street. By 1937 though, Yearley found that ice skating rinks weren't very profitable, not his anyhow, and newspapers of the day claimed that it was in danger of being torn down and the salvaged materials sold. To their credit, the Town Council stepped in and made a deal with Yearley to keep it going, although the specifics of the arrangement were never disclosed.

All went well for a number of years and then in 1943 tragedy struck again. It is thought that the huge wood stove that was used to heat part of the structure got out of control and the entire building, like John Dunn's **Palace Rink,** burned to the ground. Once again Bracebridge was without a skating rink and remained so until after World War 2 when the Bracebridge Memorial Community Centre was built on the same property as the Yearley rink and officially opened in 1949.

***The first official face-off in the new Bracebridge Memorial Community Centre,
February 1st, 1949. Left to right, Stu Reid, referee Frank Suter, Bus Brazier.***

Once again figure skating and hockey flourished in Bracebridge. Aside from the success achieved by those who used the new arena, one of the most significant events that occurred there took place on January 25th, 1952 when for the first time *two teams consisting of retired NHL hockey players competed*. It was organized by the Bala Lions Club and the Bala Legion, but held in the larger venue in Bracebridge because of the popularity of the event. The players were thought to have been organized into teams by broadcaster and long-term Muskoka summer resident Gordon Sinclair, recognized by the fact that he was appointed as honorary manager of both teams. If that is in fact the way the teams were organized, that would make Gordon Sinclair the founder of NHL old-timers hockey that has flourished ever since.

In addition, the game was videotaped by the NBC television network of New York City (possibly arranged by Gordon Sinclair as well) and was broadcast on television there; Canada at that early date in broadcasting was not technically equipped to carry out that process. That made this the ***first hockey game played in Canada to appear on network television***; right here in the Bracebridge Memorial Community Centre!

It does not end there. This significant event is described in detail in a paper presented to the Society For International Hockey Research by Dr. Eugene Willis entitled ***January 25th, 1952 – The Town of Bracebridge Scores a Hat Trick*** and includes a claim that a third hockey *"first"* occurred in that game. Two of the players, in what started out to be a fun scuffle to provide a little additional entertainment for the fans, not uncommon in such exhibition events, became very serious to the point where the referee had to intervene and separate the combatants. The two players were Bucko McDonald, a Liberal Member of Parliament and Lionel Conacher, a Progressive Conservative Member of Parliament. The claim made was that this was ***the first time in history that two players who were sitting members of parliament got in a fight in a hockey game!***

32. MEMORIAL PARK…

The beautiful *Memorial Park* that adorns Manitoba Street in downtown Bracebridge is rich in the history of Bracebridge. It was created by the Council of the Town in 1900 and received its name because it was created as a memorial to two young Bracebridge men who were killed in action in the Boer War in South Africa in 1899.

The two young men were Fred Wasdell and James Findlay. They had enlisted in the Canadian Armed Forces and word of their deaths was received just as the people of Bracebridge were holding a celebration party in the Town Hall in recognition of victories achieved in that battle for freedom. A plaque on the foundation of the north wall of the bandstand, personally donated by G.H.O. Thomas when he was Mayor of Bracebridge in 1927, bears their names to commemorate their sacrifice, appropriately inscribed *"HEROS OF THE BOER WAR"*.

This plaque, situated on the north side of the foundation of the Memorial Park Bandstand, was placed there in memory of these two young men from Bracebridge who died in that conflict.

The bandshell in the park has a history all its own. The first bandstand, donated by W. S. Shaw of the Anglo-Canadian Leather Company, was the delight of music lovers and speechmakers of the community. It was located near the intersection of Manitoba and Dominion Streets and relocated to *Memorial Park* when it was established in 1900. The original bandstand was still in use when Giovanni (John) Morra was hired as Bandmaster of the Bracebridge Citizens Band in 1929. By that time the structure had seen its better days and Morra reported that it leaned badly and vibrated with the tapping of the 49 musician's feet. He was particularly concerned with the beating of the big bass drum.

The original "shaky" bandstand donated by W.S. Shaw relocated to Memorial Park

As a result, a proposal was made to replace it with a new structure as a memorial to those who lost their lives in World War 1. This proposal met with some opposition however, possibly because some felt that it would interfere with the original memorial intent of the park, while others thought that those who died in the Great War deserved their own recognition and a more appropriate memorial would be a hospital.

It was a hot political subject for a while but a satisfactory solution evolved, thanks to the efforts of those who returned from service following World War 1 (and who shortly thereafter founded what we know in 2013 as the Royal Canadian Legion), in the creation of the Bracebridge Memorial Hospital in 1928. The new bandstand plan was not abandoned though and in 1929, supported by fundraising and community minded citizens, a new one was constructed. The roof however, was delayed until 1933 when George W. Ecclestone jumped in and donated the necessary funds to cover the cost and except for minor repairs, the bandstand stands in 2013, 84 years later, basically as originally constructed.

The Memorial Park bandstand built in 1929. The roof was added in 1933.

No longer did the legendary Bandmaster John Morra have to worry about the bandstand collapsing to the beat of the big bass drum.

An additional tribute to Fred Wasdell and James Findlay was to rename the street on the west side of the park Kimberley Avenue after Kimberley, South Africa where one of the significant battles of the Boer War took place. It was known previously as Market Street because it was on that side of the park property where pioneer farmers would park their wagons loaded with their farm produce and offer it for sale to the people of Bracebridge. *Memorial Park* property had also been the location of the Harvie Stage Company depot for Muskoka. The *"stages"* carried mail, passengers and freight between the pioneer communities of Muskoka and southern markets as roads were developed. There are many interesting stories told by the passengers who used this early mode of transportation, especially the bone-jarring stage rides. When they weren't getting bounced about on rocks they would have to get off the stage and help shove it out of the mud holes and muskegs which dominated the famous Muskoka Road. For many years the postal service continued to be referred to by residents of the area as *"The Stage"*.

G.H.O. Thomas and his students raised the money and placed this fountain in Memorial Park in 1900. His 1898 house (in 2013 Nick's Family Restaurant) stands proudly in the background, giving the impression that he is still watching over this treasured part of our history.

It was dubbed the *"Boer War Memorial Fountain"* and was in the park for many years until it eventually fell into disrepair resulting in it being disassembled and left in pieces in Kelvin Grove Park. It was not until 1966 that Brenda Cox, Mr. Thomas's granddaughter, asked Town Council to do something with it and she was given permission to relocate it to her Bracebridge residence. Through her generosity, many years later during the celebration of the 125th anniversary of Bracebridge in 2000, Brenda and husband Art, along with Don Currie, Superintendent of the Bracebridge Water Department and his staff, worked together to refurbish and install it in operating condition back in its original location where it had been placed 100 years earlier.

Another part of the park development was a request of the Government of Canada that, in keeping with the memorial aspect of the project, they provide two cannons that had been used in the Boer War. They were received in 1905 and placed here, one at each end of the Park, in 1907. When the guns were received it was estimated that they were between 200 and 290 years old and that they bore the ordinance mark and crest of King George the 4th, which, to the disappointment of the Town, meant they were certainly not used in the Boer War but were similar to those in Halifax's Citadel Hill. They are estimated to weigh 5160 pounds each.

Also included in the 125th anniversary celebration of Bracebridge in 2000 was to change the name of the street along the south side of the **Memorial Park** from Park Lane to Rene Caisse Lane. This was done in recognition of the dedicated work of Bracebridge native Rene M. Caisse in easing the suffering of humanity through the development of her Essiac treatment which she provided for those afflicted with cancer. A separate chapter of this publication will be devoted to her work.

Is there another property *anywhere* that could be compared to this one when it comes to representing the people, heritage and history of a community?

Little wonder it is called **Memorial Park,** yet sadly, thousands drive by it every day and have little understanding of all it represents.

33. FLORA BARNES…

Few, if any, will recognize the name **FLORA BARNES** and know the part it played in the history of Bracebridge.

It was a 64 foot steamer owned by Capt. Thomas Barnes built in Port Carling as a tug, but the story as it relates to Bracebridge began when it was moored at the Bracebridge wharf in 1883 and left there for the winter. The town at that particular time was apparently having a difficult time financially and council implemented a policy to take firm action against those who were in arrears of taxes, particularly non-residents. Since the assessor had decided to place an assessment against the moored *Flora Barnes* a tax bill was issued and had remained unpaid.

This was exactly the kind of arrears that was the focus of the new policy -an unpaid tax bill and a non-resident property owner, Mr. Barnes being a resident of Wentworth County. Town officials acted promptly and seized the boat. Locks were put on the doors and the boat was advertised for sale for payment of the arrears.

That was when things went wrong. In the middle of the night the locked-up boat mysteriously caught fire and burned to the waterline. Speculation raged about how the fire would have started but the cause was never determined.

It didn't take long for Barnes to take action and the town received a lawsuit from his lawyers for damages in the amount of $3,500.00. The town responded by hiring lawyers and defended their actions in the ensuing court case that took place in Barrie in 1884. To the towns dismay though, after a lengthy hearing that included many witnesses, the decision of the court was in favour of Barnes and the town was ordered to pay him damages in the amount of $3,671.00. The town immediately appealed the decision but after a discussion with its lawyers the appeal was withdrawn.

In one account of this occurrence it is stated that the town then put a referendum to the people of Bracebridge to approve the settlement, which had now grown to $4,000.00. This must have seemed to many as a waste of time because it wasn't as if the town had any choice in the matter. It could have been that a positive referendum was necessary in order to issue a debenture to cover the court ordered payment rather than pay it out of current funds, which they probably didn't have. In 1884 $4,000.00 was an enormous amount of money.

In any event, the vote must have been positive because a debenture was issued and for 20 years, every tax bill issued in Bracebridge included a one line item that read *"Flora Barnes $7.79"*. The citizens were furious to say the least. Needless to say, few newborn baby girls, if any, were named Flora for years after.

It is interesting to note, that of the five member 1883 council (who had created this embarrassing situation), only one returned to Council in 1884. That was Sam Armstrong, and true to his conviction that the council had acted correctly in seizing the boat in 1883, was the only member of the 1884 council to vote against withdrawing the appeal against the Barrie court decision.

34. STONE COTTAGE, CASTLE DUNC AND LOCK-UPS...

They are not one of the more exotic and interesting parts of our history but jails were a necessity in this frontier town. Bracebridge had a lot of natural assets that were invaluable in bringing settlers and new businesses to the area, but the one asset that provided the greatest boost to the economy right from the start was the huge pine and hardwoods that covered the land. As far back as 1853 logging companies were setting up operations in Muskoka resulting in hundreds of workers moving back and forth between sawmills and logging camps; for the most part along the two branches of the Muskoka River.

There were sawmills in Bracebridge, a larger number in McCabe's Landing (Gravenhurst) locally referred to as *"Sawdust City"*, on the Moon and Musquash Rivers and as far west as Georgian Bay. Hundreds of thousands of logs wound up at those mills, many getting there via Lakes Muskoka, Rosseau and Joseph, but a large percentage of them were run down the two branches of the Muskoka River; therefore, right through the centre of the active settlement of North Falls.

Transient workers were a big influence on the Bracebridge economy. The many *"watering holes"* as listed in a previous chapter could not have survived relying only on the modest number of permanent residents in the community (many of whom were dedicated temperance supporters and would never have darkened the door of any place that sold liquor) so the taverns were usually associated with hotels and transient workers were a big part of their business.

Liquor, transients with time to waste and a hotel room was a good recipe for trouble. It was not long before the local authorities came to the conclusion that law and order, and a lock-up, were needed.

The first *lock-up* would seem to be a log one with a dirt floor located on provincial property; Bracebridge in 1868 having been recognized as the District seat. It was provided with a courthouse, registry office and a Crown Land Agent housed in a building at the corner of Dominion and Ontario Streets. The *lock-up* was mentioned by Redmond Thomas in *Reminiscences,* as part of a humorous event that he no doubt had heard from his father G.H.O. Thomas.

It was in this building where two men were placed overnight after a run-in with authorities following a drunken spree and were awaiting disposal of the charges against them. The year of this occurrence is not mentioned but it had to be prior to 1879. As they languished in their cell, impatience (and their thirst) got the better of them because from the window of the jail they could see the British Lion Hotel across the street. With time on their hands they set about digging into the dirt floor, under the wall and through to the outside. Just like that they were free! But they didn't attempt to run as one might expect. Instead they brushed themselves off, walked across the street to the tavern in the hotel, and proceeded to continue their drinking spree.

All the time though, they kept a careful eye on the jail and when they saw Warden White's helper Bab Simmons approaching with meals for his prisoners, they hurried back and crawled back into the jail. Simmons, however, beat them inside and when he found the window and door properly locked but no-one there he left to find the authorities. Not wanting to miss a free meal the prisoners chased after him shouting, *"wait, wait,"* and while the rest of the story fades away at that point, one can assume that they got their lunch and were released. Their voluntary return saved the authorities the work of having to assemble a posse.

Before we move on describing the next phase of incarceration structures, it should be noted that the log jail that is discussed above is still alive and well in 2013. It is located on the south side of Santa's Village Road at the northeast corner of Annie Williams Memorial Recreation Park, immediately adjacent to the sidewalk. The logs have been covered with board and baton siding but through the cracks in the boards the original log construction can be seen. The owner of that residential property is aware of the history of the building and has advised that the steel bars for the window are still within the building. A prized possession, for sure, and it is hoped that this 150 year old plus building will eventually become part of a public area where all can admire and ponder its place in the history of Bracebridge.

Has Bracebridge's first jail built in the 1860s been preserved for over 150 years? That would appear to be the case. The picture on the left shows a building on government property in 1871 that closely resembles the configuration of that on the right located adjacent to Annie Williams Memorial Recreation Park with board and baton siding covering the log walls in 2013. Apparently the bars for the window still remain in the building

The log jail was replaced in 1879 by a modern brick structure located in the same area but closer to Dominion Street. There is no record of how or when the log structure got relocated to Santa's Village Road, but this writer can recall historian and Magistrate Redmond Thomas asking about the fate of that first lock-up building. Apparently he knew it had not been demolished but was not aware of its new location. The new brick structure contained 5 cells and was built by Neil Livingstone. It was clearly a more substantial structure and many make reference to it being the start of a proper and officially designated District Jail.

It is recorded that an 1884 grand jury, charged with the duty of inspecting public buildings reported that the jail was *"old and looked it."* This harsh observation hardly makes sense since it is stated that it was just built in 1879. It may have been that a lot of time had elapsed between their inspection and the public release of the report and the members of the jury had inspected the log lock-up with its dirt floor, the new one not yet ready for use. This thought is supported by the report of another grand jury in 1888, just four years later that found the jail *"scrupulously clean."* That jury also recommended that an enclosure be added to the facility for the exercise of prisoners and that provision be made to accommodate *"insane persons"*.

A residence for the warden, or *"jailer"* was attached to the building and in 1909 Richard Mills was replaced by Duncan McDonald in that position. It didn't take long before the jail affectionately became known as *"Castle Dunc".*

An aerial picture of Bracebridge shows the wooden fence that surrounded the Provincial/Town jail beside the Courthouse on Dominion Street.

In response to the recommendations of the 1888 grand jury, a high wooden enclosure was built behind the jail to provide an exercise area for prisoners. A garden to produce vegetables for food for those incarcerated was included in the exercise yard and the prisoners were made take care of it as part of their exercise, along with cutting grass, removing snow and other janitorial duties. Another requirement of the prisoners was to put a coat of whitewash (a paint consisting of lime, salt and chalk mixed with water) on the boards of the enclosure, an exercise that led to a very ill-conceived but humorous attempt at an escape.

In the era of the attempted escape the prisoners were required to wear the prison garb of the day that consisted of the right half of a jacket yellow and the left half black, the right leg of the pants black (below the yellow top) and the left leg of the pants yellow, (under the black part of the jacket). It must have been quite a sight but a good selection of colours to make sure that a prisoner would stand out in a crowd if they tried to escape. One fine day when two prisoners were carrying out their whitewashing duties, they had an inspiration. They knew it would not be difficult to get out of the simple wooden enclosure but their clothing was a problem. Their solution was to paint their entire prison garb with whitewash. By doing so they were confident that they would be taken for tourists, white being the colour of choice for tourists clothing in Muskoka at that time.

To their dismay however, it didn't work and they were returned to the lock-up. The reason for failure of their plan is not mentioned, but one can imagine that their soaking wet clothes dripping with whitewash paint and messed up crawling under the board fence enclosure would have been a dead giveaway. Certainly they would not have looked like prim, neatly dressed tourists, especially to Jailer Duncan McDonald.

The brick jail served its purpose for many years until the province designated the Parry Sound Jail as the District facility in the 1940s. In 1946 it was considered a fire hazard and was remodelled to serve as an Ontario Provincial Police office. It had been the scene of hangings of two convicted murderers and other strange and curious events. Jailer Duncan McDonald, a proud Presbyterian, often bragged about the fact there had never in the history of the jail been a person of Presbyterian faith incarcerated therein. This bit of bravado eventually became too much for Magistrate Spencer, better known as *"Gattlin' Gun"*, so as a joke on his jailer friend, he had his staff rewrite the record of all those who had been in the jail since the beginning to show that *every* prisoner was a Presbyterian. The revised document was then presented to McDonald and the joke was complete. There is no report on whether that ended Jailer Dunc's bragging rights.

Duncan McDonald had an exemplary and distinguished career as jailer from 1909 to 1933.

The log lock-up and the brick jail that replaced it served both provincial and town needs for a number of years. The remodelled brick jail building was eventually removed to provide space for a number of expansions of the Provincial Courthouse and a new registry Office.

The operation of the jail seems to have become blurred between jurisdictions at one point and in due time the town set up its own lock-up in a corner of the Muskoka Herald building basement at the corner of Robert J. Boyer Lane and Dominion Street. In 1904 they bought a small piece of land behind the Town Hall from Sam Armstrong and hired John Baker to build a new jail containing 3 cells with heavily barred windows. The massive, solid stone walls were eighteen inches thick. There was no way a prisoner was going to dig their way out of that building. It quickly became known as *"The Stone Cottage"*.

With changes in the administration of justice and the addition of holding cells in the Police Department of the new Town Office opened in 1958, the Town Jail became unnecessary and was used for storing street cleaning equipment- and the occasional transient. In 1967, H. E. S. (Bert) Sugg approached the town and asked to purchase it and, since it adjoined the parking lot of his legal office, the Municipal Council felt it was fitting that it should be part of his property. To his credit, when the solid stone building was demolished Sugg left the bottom row of stone intact so that our history would be clear regarding the location of that *"lock-up"* built 108 years ago.

The original holding cells in the basement of the courthouse (referred to by staff as *"the dungeon"*) also became storage facilities, having been replaced by cells adjacent to new courtrooms constructed as part of a courthouse expansion. Throughout the years there were attempted breakouts at the various jail facilities; all successfully thwarted through the dedicated work of the authorities and often before the prisoners even saw the light of day.

***H.E.S (Bert) Sugg, solicitor stands in front of his newly purchased
"Stone Cottage", the last free standing Bracebridge jail***

Jails were an uncomfortable necessity in early Bracebridge. A solace, if there was one, was that in 1928 it was publicly announced that for the first time in years there was not one prisoner in any of the jail cells in Bracebridge over the Christmas holidays.

Gattlin' Gun Spencer might even have said to ***Jailer Dunc McDonald***, *"not even a Presbyterian!"*

35. AUBREY WHITE…

As described in Chapter 5, one of the early pioneer settlers in the Upper Canada community of North Falls in 1860 was a man by the name of Alexander Bailey. A man who obviously possessed a determined entrepreneurial and adventuresome spirit, he decided to settle in North Falls because he recognized the great economic opportunity available in the numerous waterfalls and huge stands of trees across the landscape. He developed a number of enterprises including a hotel, saw mill, grist mill and, of special note for the purpose of this chapter, a general store that stocked basic necessities for the settlers of the day.

With his numerous operations he obviously needed staff and the person he chose to be his assistant in his general store was a lad by the name of *Aubrey White*. He had no idea that he was starting the young man on an incredibly successful career in business and public service.

Aubrey White was born in Ireland on March 19, 1845 and at the young age of 17 immigrated to Canada. He must have shared Bailey's adventuresome spirit to take on the challenge of a new country at such a young age; he must have known that he would be facing an uncertain future containing many difficult and unknown obstacles. He arrived in North Falls in 1862. Why he chose this area is not known; perhaps he, like Bailey, sensed the great opportunities the north offered in its various attributes- dense forests, rivers, waterfalls and wildlife that was the inspiration for many of the pioneers who came to settle in Muskoka.

White was not destined to stay very long in the position of *"assistant"* in Bailey's general store. His character and ability was obvious and he was spotted by A. P. Cockburn who was in the process of creating a fleet of large steamships for his new venture, the Muskoka Navigation Company, which for many years would provide transportation services for passengers, freight and pleasure cruises on Lakes Muskoka, Rosseau and Joseph. Aubrey White was one of Cockburn's first employees in 1866 and rose quickly to the position of Captain, piloting the huge vessels on their voyages in the uncharted waters of these large Muskoka waterways. He would have been just 21 years old.

From there he joined the A. P. Dodge Company of New York, USA when they commenced operations in Muskoka harvesting the huge stands of white pine for distribution to world markets. It was in 1878 however, that he assumed a position that would lead him into an interesting and influential lifelong career. He succeeded George Lount as Crown Land Agent for Muskoka. It was a perfect fit for White. He knew the wilderness of Muskoka, the people and the problems new settlers would face as they struggled to carve a homestead out of dense bush on their Free Grant Land Act properties. He received applications for land acquisition, directed each settler to the location of their property and approved final patents for deeds once the settlers proved they had fulfilled the conditions set out in the purchase agreement under the Act. During these years, long before the introduction of the federal income tax system, it was a municipal responsibility to levy a tax on their residents based on their income. In the 1879 assessment role he was shown to have the enormous salary of $200.00 per year.

Aside from his work, he was very socially active during his years in Bracebridge. He served as an officer for the Mechanics Institute (later to become the public library system), Superintendent of Algonquin Park, Warden of St. Thomas Church, contributed to the production of the important promotional and historical book ***Guide Book & Atlas of Muskoka and Parry Sound Districts 1879***, a member of the Agricultural Society, and in 1879 became a member of the Masonic Lodge where, several years later, he was elected to the lofty position of Grand Master for all of Ontario. Robert J Boyer in his book *A Good Town Grew Here* quotes W. E. Hamilton as noting that Aubrey White was ***"gifted with a phenomenal memory and could tell the names of all the sitting members of all the parliaments, great and small, of Canada, their antecedents and their constituencies, together with the dates of the various by-elections since Confederation."***

He married Emily Agnes Bridgland and after her death in 1880 married her sister Mary Bridgland, daughters of a prominent Bracebridge family. Aubrey Street in Bracebridge is named in his honour.

Aubrey White was Crown Land Agent for Muskoka until 1882. His work in that position must have impressed his superiors because he was asked to transfer to a more prominent position in Queens Park. It is unclear what his duties were immediately following the move but clearly they were of significant importance because within five years he was appointed Assistant Commissioner of Crown Lands and Deputy Minister of Lands, Forests and Mines; a position he held until his death in 1915.

White is distinguished by a number of achievements during his term as Deputy in that Ministry. His succinct definition of the jurisdiction of authority over road allowances along navigable waters, in a letter dated October 15th 1896 to Monck Township in Muskoka, is a good example of his clear view on such matters when he said ***"..although the freehold of all roads is in Her Majesty, yet the jurisdiction is in the Municipal Council and it is conceived that the Municipality has the same powers as to preventing trespasses upon the particular road reservations…".*** Another example of his authority and respect is shown when he dealt with the serious conflict between the Navigation Company and the logging industry regarding the use of the Muskoka River.

Since the beginning the Muskoka Rivers had served as a transportation route, especially important in pioneer days for getting people upstream to work in the logging camps and for floating the resulting cut logs down to the mills. To say the river was taken for granted would be an understatement. The logging companies were of the determined opinion that they had absolute domination over the use of the river. Not so, said Mr. Cockburn; he knew *'the times they are a changin'* long before the popular song made that prophecy, no doubt because he saw how the logging companies were rapidly decimating the great Muskoka forests.

The river from the Bracebridge Falls to Muskoka Lake was increasingly used by his large boats and with logs clogging the route, colliding with and even smashing holes in the hulls of his expensive crafts, the river was in fact prevented from being a navigable water way. In 1913 the local Member of Provincial Parliament, former Mayor and Bracebridge resident Sam Armstrong, met with H. J. Foy Attorney General of Ontario to discuss the matter of logs blocking navigation in the river and Deputy Minister White was dispatched to resolve the problem.

Into this lengthy dispute waded ***Aubrey White***. He knew the river, he knew the lakes, he knew the log run, he knew the people and he knew the boats; he had done it all. He met with representatives of the logging industry, the Bracebridge Council and Board of Trade and, in spite of industry representatives declaring it impossible, ruled that all logs in the river had to be tied together and towed downstream from Bracebridge to the mills safely. To accommodate those involved, the logging companies were given until the end of July that year to remove their logs in this manner and leave that part of the river clear thereafter.

Aubrey White's greatest achievement though came from another direction. His experience in Bracebridge had taught him the importance of the massive stands of forest that blanketed Ontario and the enormous economic opportunities they provided. But they were of no value if a wildfire swept through them and left in its wake blackened stubs in a decimated landscape. Forest fires were an enemy in the rapidly developing Province. Aubrey White set about developing a fire-fighting plan for Crown forests for all of Ontario wherein he recommended appointing fire rangers and building fire towers. In 1885 the Honourable T.B. Pardee approved his plan and 37 fire rangers were placed on duty. White's advantage in setting up the system was that he was a skilled navigator, no doubt learned scaling the wilderness of Muskoka and driving big steamboats on Muskoka Lake, so he was at ease venturing into unsurveyed and unknown territory in association with this work.

Aubrey White was Deputy Minister until his death on July 14th 1915. He never severed his ties with Muskoka and it was at his cottage on Chief Island on Lake Muskoka, after enjoying a day of rowing, swimming, and fishing that he passed away. He is buried in the St. Thomas Cemetery in Bracebridge.

On the fiftieth anniversary of his death the Ontario Ministry erected a cairn in his honour at High Falls Park in Bracebridge. Over 100 people from the Provincial Government and across Muskoka attended the unveiling ceremony on July 14th 1965. Deputy Minister of Lands and Forests, Frank A. MacDougall, spoke at the ceremony, noting that since Confederation Ontario has had 17 Prime Ministers and 42 Ministers of Lands and Forests but only 6 Deputy Ministers; citing that Aubrey White served the longest in that office and was one of the most distinguished. He mentioned in particular his abilities as an aviator that enabled him to travel extensively over the Province to carry out his important work. White's interest and participation in early aviation again confirms the dedicated spirit of adventure of this great leader.

Incredibly, after more than one hundred years, the Ontario Provincial Ministry of Natural Resources still consider *Aubrey White* as the founder of their forest fire fighting system.

The memorial cairn for Aubrey White erected in 1965 at High Falls in Bracebridge

36. RENE M. CAISSE AND ESSIAC...

The story of **Rene M. Caisse** and her treatment of cancer sufferers is an impressive one. It is the subject of many books, thousands of newspaper articles and testimonials telling of her success in easing the suffering of humanity. She was born in Bracebridge in 1888 and after acquiring a Registered Nurse qualification, spent a number of years in Northern Ontario where part of her work included contact with First Nation communities. It was during this experience in the north that she became apprised of a treatment that removed tumours. Having acquired the knowledge of the ingredients and preparation of the concoction, she treated a member of her own family that resulted in a successful recovery from cancer. For the lack of a better name, she called it Essiac, her name spelled backwards.

That started a whole new career for **Rene M. Caisse**. After further development of the process, she opened a clinic in her apartment in Toronto that she eventually had to leave because there were so many people coming to receive treatment, and set up business in Peterborough. She was there for a number of years and then decided she wanted to return to her hometown. With the assistance of Dr. A.F. Bastedo, the Bracebridge Town Council agreed to let her use part of the bottom floor of the British Lion Hotel, which they had seized for taxes in 1934. She operated her clinic there from 1935 to 1941 with significant results. There are pictures of the street lined with the cars bringing sufferers to her clinic and endless stories of miraculous results. The writer's grandmother, Eliza Veitch, was one who raved about how *"Nurse Caisse"* had saved her from the ravages of cancer.

All through her clinic years she was constantly harassed by medical authorities; she was not a doctor and therefore untrained and unfit, in their opinion, to treat anybody for anything. In spite of a petition containing thousands of signatures and an incredible amount of anecdotal evidence, a private members bill in the Provincial Legislature that would have allowed her to treat cancer sufferers failed to pass by a handful of votes, and the harassment continued. She had an offer of one million dollars to take her operations to the USA, another to work with Dr. Banting because he felt her concoction also helped diabetics, and others; all of which she refused saying she could not leave her patients in Bracebridge.

She would not reveal the ingredients of her concoction, something she would have had to do if she had accepted one of the offers. Authorities insisted that her treatment had to go through testing to establish if it really was beneficial to the patients she treated. She absolutely refused to do that, saying the results of her work was proof enough. Was she right? There are thousands who say she was. There are also many who say she should have agreed to the testing; participating in it personally to make sure it was done correctly. Her main concern was that a huge drug company would get exclusive rights to the treatment and it would never be heard of again, a legitimate concern in the minds of many.

However, time takes its toll. On March 29, 1995, long after Rene's death in 1978, her lifelong supporter and co-worker Mary McPherson of Bracebridge, close to 90 years old herself, in the presence of the writer, Chairman of the Bracebridge Historical Association Bill Glennie, Town Treasurer Andy Nelan and solicitor Nick Roche, in her own handwriting wrote out the exact Essiac recipe and instructions on how to prepare the concoction. Mary agreed to do that providing the accurate information was protected and enshrined in the Town archives.

It was witnessed, notarized and placed on file in the Town of Bracebridge historical records. It was not easy for her because she had promised Rene she would never reveal it.

Rene M.Caisse, the "Cancer Nurse" was adored by hundreds, perhaps thousands, who claimed she cured them from the ravages of cancer.

37. THE TANNERIES...

A massive contribution to the economy of Bracebridge, in fact all of Muskoka, was the development of the leather tanning industry. Massive indeed, because they not only employed hundreds of people in their manufacturing operation but were a steady source of income for many rural residents who laboured in the Muskoka wilderness cutting hemlock trees in order to harvest the bark; so essential in tannery operations.

That is why they came here. In that era tanneries turned cowhides into leather through a process that involved using tannic acid which was derived from hemlock bark. Who knew, in those first days of harvesting the huge pines and hardwoods of Muskoka, that right under the noses of the logging companies there was a whole new, and valuable, industry.

The writer's grandfather as a young man was one of those who dropped the huge hemlock trees, stripped off the bark, loaded it onto a sleigh or wagon and pulled it into Bracebridge for delivery to the tannery. Stripping a hemlock tree of its bark, while it sounds awkward and difficult, was easy as long as the tree was green and the bark was removed in strips 12 to 18 inches wide. Once a strip was started it could be removed from the entire length of the log in minutes.

It was unfortunate though that at the start the hemlock logs were just left to decay on the forest floor; after all there was an endless supply of nice clean pine for lumber. Besides, those in the lumber business learned quickly to avoid working with hemlock if possible because it presented a bit of a problem -slivers. To handle hemlock lumber workers had to wear gloves otherwise at the end of the day they would be removing painful slivers of wood from their hands. That feature of hemlock has never changed but what did change was that hemlock was finally recognized for its true value. In addition to the value of its bark and aside from its slivers, it proved to be a very strong and resilient lumber product. The record will show that the timber of choice when building the Toronto subway system was hemlock and many of the historic buildings, still standing strong and true in Muskoka towns, have hemlock foundations and roofing. The key was to keep it away from dampness.

The first tannery to arrive in Bracebridge, always referred to as the *"old"* tannery, was Beardmore and Company Limited. It had extensive operations in Acton, Ontario. A document on the company history entitled ***A HISTORY OF BEADMORE AND COMPANY LIMITED AND ANGLO CANADIAN LEATHER COMPANY*** by Abbott Conway states that, *"the Beardmores decided to locate their operations in Muskoka, where hemlock formed part of the 'climax forest'. The supply was considered by some to be 'inexhaustible'"*. In *A Good Town Grew Here* Robert J. Boyer notes that the Beardmores chose Bracebridge over Penetanguishene and Gravenhurst, possibly because of the availability of hydraulic power from the falls and perhaps that it seemed to be a more progressive area, having achieved the status as a *Village* municipality just two years before.

As was the custom then, the company asked for financial assistance from the Village so a referendum was put to the electorate resulting in a $2,000.00 bonus plus a 10 year exemption from municipal taxes being approved. As a result a large tannery was built in 1877 on property in Monck Township purchased from John Adair on the north side of Muskoka River. It was later the site of Canada Wood Specialties, later still by the Forgione lumber mill, and in 2013 the site of a condominium project *The Waterways*. The fact that the tannery was built in Monck Township didn't matter because the Village immediately expropriated the land from the township and expanded the Village boundaries. There is no comment on how that affected relations between Monck and Bracebridge but it was the right thing to do, the Village having put up the incentives and did all the work in encouraging the Beardmores to settle here.

As an interesting aside, in that same year of 1877, possibly buoyed by the success of the Beardmore referendum, another application for assistance was received from Jonas Bowman and David Barber who proposed to build a tannery on land occupied in 2013 by Northern Buildal and the now unused water storage reservoir beside Bird's Bridge. G.H.O. Thomas, in **Bracebridge in 1884** reported that they were given a 10 year exemption from taxes, information that was repeated in **A Good Town Continues**, but there the story seems to end. Certainly no tannery was built on the proposed site, but Redmond Thomas in **Reminiscences** mentions a *Barber Tannery* that was located on the northeast corner of Hiram Street and MacDonald Street, for many years the location of the Newark boat-fender factory. In fact, at one time there were 4 tanneries in operation in Bracebridge, including the Beardmore Tannery, the Anglo-Canadian Tannery, Barbers and another located on the northeast corner of Monck Road and Wellington Street owned and operated by E. Garrett.

It was a wonderful day in this part of Muskoka when word got out that this wonderful company had chosen Bracebridge as their home. Writers of history variously refer to the *Beardmore Tannery*, the *Muskoka Tannery* and *Muskoka Leather Company* all in the same breath but there is no doubt they were one and the same. No matter, the town and its residents were ecstatic, and no wonder. There would be jobs for everyone. As part of the deal the company had to hire at least 12 men, which proved to be easy because within a short period of time they had 30 employees and eventually became one of the largest tanneries in Canada. It was so active in fact, that in order to improve access to the tannery for the many sleighs and wagons hauling tanbark there, the steep hill on the easterly section of Ontario Street where it intersected with Victoria Street was closed to traffic and Rosemount Avenue (which quickly became known as Tan Bark Hill) was built connecting Quebec Street with Victoria Street and the westerly section of Ontario Street. Both Rosemount Avenue and the westerly section of Ontario Street became part of Quebec Street in more recent years.

It was a very successful operation and in 1882 just 5 years after start-up, perhaps to take advantage of an offer too good to refuse, the tannery was sold to Charles W. Tillson. One report states that it was when Tillson took over that it became known as the Muskoka Leather Company or Muskoka Tannery. However, the writer can remember seeing a large picture in the Town Office files of a tannery operation with the caption *Tillson Tannery*. Nevertheless, it didn't stay that way for very long because Mr. Tillson died in 1890 and the Beardmores were once again in the tannery business in Bracebridge.

There were a number of interesting situations that occurred during the Beardmore experience in Bracebridge. In 1910 the company made a pitch to the town to have a railway siding extended to their property. A survey was drawn up for it to travel from Manitoba Street along Wharf Road and Dill Street across Wellington Street to their tannery.

Following a discussion with reeves of the adjoining townships another plan came into being, that the siding already serving the J. D. Shier Lumber mill be extended across the river on a swing bridge which would have been located near the location of the Wellington Street bridge of 2013. Both plans were abandoned for financial reasons, fortunately, considering that just 12 years later in 1922, the Beardmores pulled up stakes and moved their operations back to Acton.

Things had changed in the tanning business. New chemicals had been developed that served the same purpose as hemlock bark and the need to be close to that resource became less important. In any event the *"inexhaustible supply of hemlock"* in Muskoka forests *had* become exhausted to the extent that there was difficulty in meeting the needs of the two huge tanneries that had made Bracebridge the tannery capital of Canada

Some residents were not unhappy about the plant closing down. A number complained to town council that the water in the river *"…down past the Beardmore Tannery is hardly fit for a dog"* during a 1903 debate about public swimming in the river. It was at that time when new rules were drawn up regulating the hours, incredible as it might seem, to control when swimming was allowed and including a prohibition against swimming in the nude. There is no comment about increased sales of bathing suits as a result of that council action. Some no doubt would have missed the bridge provided each winter by the tannery when they attached their scows end to end across the Muskoka River that allowed the residents to access the other side instead of having to make the long walk into town where they would cross Birds Bridge.

While there were 4 tanneries in Bracebridge at one point, there were two major ones, the Beardmore Tannery (the *"old"* tannery) and the Anglo-Canadian Tannery (the *"new"* tannery). Although they were competitors, they partnered for many years, sharing logging camps, helping the community in many ways and joining forces when there was need. A good example of that, at least amongst the employees, was in 1916 when an attempt was made to bring 10 Austrian prisoners of war into Bracebridge to work at Muskoka Leather Company. In a demonstration of intense patriotic fervour the employees of both tanneries refused to work beside these enemies of Canada and an *"indignation"* meeting was held at the town hall with the Town Council. Many residents of the area agreed with the employees and, mysteriously, in the late night hours following the meeting, a house that had been prepared to house the prisoners burned to the ground.

A.W. Beardmore had sent a letter that was read at the meeting suggesting that if the company plan to employ these prisoners was opposed then he would close the plant, making one wonder if the negative reaction to it played a part in the Beardmores leaving Bracebridge just 6 years later. The prisoners arrived by train and were delivered to the tannery office where they were met by an angry mob. In spite of Mr. Beardmore's threatening letter, the tannery manager, Peter A. Smith, decided to have the prisoners taken to their Acton operation and, as a result, Police Chief McConnell escorted them to the train station. The angry mob, clearly displaying their determined stand, followed them and remained standing in the rain for hours until the prisoners were on the train; no doubt cheering as they watched the steam engine chug out of town.

It was in 1890 that a local newspaper reported that David W. Alexander negotiated with the town to create what became known as the *new* tannery. The town agreed, again based on a referendum to the people, to give them a $2,000.00 bonus, and an even greater economic life came to Bracebridge in the form of the **Anglo-Canadian Leather Company**. In **Early Days in Muskoka** it states that the same approach was made to the council of Huntsville in 1891.

To the people of Bracebridge, who already had the Beardmore Tannery operating very successfully since 1877, the news of another huge tannery operation on the horizon was especially exciting. The land they chose was on the south side of the Muskoka River near the J. D. Shier Lumber Mill in Macaulay Township; at that time not part of the newly, and proudly, formed *TOWN* municipality of Bracebridge, but no matter. An October 1890 newspaper reported that "***The residents of this section applied to be taken into the town. A private bill of the Legislative Assembly would be*** *required for the annexation and the Council set aside funds for this purpose, also offering $150.00 to the Township of Macaulay if the Council there would assist in having the act passed. This section was to become Ward IV of the town."*

As in the case of the Beardmore Tannery setting up in a corner of Monck Township, the Town of Bracebridge brought the area into its jurisdiction. It included the property that became the home of the Anglo-Canadian Leather Company as well as several homes and the commercial operations of the J. D. Shier lumber mill and Singleton Brown's shingle mill.

As noted in the newspaper report, the annexed area was designated for electoral purposes Ward 4 of the municipality, giving birth to a heritage occasionally heard to this day when reference is made to this part of town as the *"4th Ward"*, or *"across the tracks"*. If some of the residents in that area got the impression that they were considered second class, Johnny-come-lately citizens of the town, they needn't have been concerned because from that *side of the tracks* came many entrepreneurs and astute business people who worked hard to make sure Bracebridge continued to be a thriving business community.

As one might expect, writers of the day referred to the new tannery by a variety of names. ***Early Days in Muskoka*** states that *"…a tannery was established in Huntsville in 1891 by the Shaw Cassels and Company owned and operated by the Anglo-Canadian Leather Company."* In "*A HISTORY OF BEARDMORE AND COMPANY LIMITED AND ANGLO CANADIAN LEATHER COMPANY LIMITED"* written by Abbott Conway, the proper spelling of the word Cassels is Cassils. However, that document also states that *"..,as supplies of hemlock bark began to decline, the Shaws began closing the smaller tanneries, until by 1905, when the Anglo Canadian Leather Co. Limited was formed, tanning had been consolidated into two large tanneries at Bracebridge and Huntsville."* Then again, in *A Good Town Grew Here* it is stated that in 1905 the *"Anglo Canadian Leather Company was the new name for the Huntsville and Bracebridge Tannery Co".*

So who cares. The result is still the same. The brothers C. O. Shaw and W. S. Shaw were movers and shakers in this industry. They were first class entrepreneurs and had a vision for the future few could ever possibly possess. In ***Power From Water*** it is stated that W.S. (William Sutherland) Shaw from Boyne Michigan managed both Bracebridge and Huntsville operations but Huntsville later came under the management of C.O. Shaw. What a find the Shaw brothers were for Muskoka! C.O. Shaw was the creator of the Anglo Canadian Band, (according to news reports of the day it was originally called the Anglo-Canadian *Italian* Band), and builder of the fabulous and renowned Bigwin Inn resort on Lake of Bays.

With his brother running the Huntsville operation, W. S. Shaw assumed management of the Bracebridge tannery. He also had a determined entrepreneurial flair and vision of the future and it didn't take long before he put it to use.

The town council had already been active in trying to develop a generating station to produce electricity primarily to power street lights; they had even entered into an agreement with a company to do so after a referendum to authorize such a move was approved by the ratepayers in 1889. They were way ahead of their time. But nothing happened and legal action was taken against the company for non-performance. They got nowhere with that however, and as they were searching for an alternative, to their delight W.S. Shaw stepped forward in 1891 and advised that his tannery plan included a generating station. Shaw was a man who got things done. His generating station was completed in 1892 and electrically powered streetlights appeared on town streets that same year, the town having partnered with Shaw to make that happen.

The town was still determined to create their own generating station though so more meetings and referendums were held resulting in approval to proceed. They acquired the land at the foot of Bracebridge Falls from Alfred Hunt, in spite of opposition expressed by Samuel Armstrong, Henry J. Bird and Singleton Brown - all respected businessmen. As a result, a secondary plan was put forward to purchase the generating station of Shaw and in October 1894 Bracebridge became the *first municipality in Canada* to own and operate a water-powered electricity generating system.

The Anglo Canadian Leather Company, by whatever name, was an enormous boost to the Bracebridge economy, especially considering it was in addition to that provided by the Beardmore Tannery. Those were great years in Bracebridge. No doubt they damaged the water quality of our rivers, but in fairness, they did not know the effect their discharges would have on aquatic life. The same could be said of the logging companies that came to Muskoka in the mid-1850s and decimated the landscape thinking the forests here would last forever, not realizing that in a mere 40 or 50 years there would be little standing timber left to support the industry. It took more than 100 years for the forests to resemble the original that stood here and while forestry still exists as a viable industry in Muskoka it is now done in a sustainable fashion ensuring that it will last as a viable business, albeit without the volume that existed in those early days.

Like his brother, W. S. Shaw was a music lover. He was a member of the highly respected Bracebridge Citizens Band and donated a bandstand where they could perform their concerts. As noted in Chapter 33 describing Memorial Park, it was located in a small community park near the intersection of Dominion and Manitoba Streets when the property now occupied by Memorial Park was still the location of the Harvie Stage Line and a farmers market. The small bandstand was moved there when Memorial Park was created in 1900 but due to its deteriorating condition was replaced in the late 1920s.

As good as the tannery business was in Muskoka it was not without its problems. There was often difficulty getting tanbark out of the bush some winters due to mild weather conditions; heavy frost was necessary to firm up the draw roads. In 1906 the two tanneries had 20,000 cords of tanbark in the bush that could not be accessed; the lakes did not freeze over until late January. Once out of the bush, the huge loads of bark then had to be delivered to Bracebridge over rough roads and steep hills or held until the navigation season when they could be delivered by scows. Even that had its problems because the Muskoka River often was clogged with logs being floated downstream to the mills.

Availability of workers was another problem, to the extent that imported workers were recruited from Italy (why Italy is not explained) and when one labour dispute caused 40 to leave for home others were brought in from Poland. There were strikes in 1908 and 1916 for higher wages, lock-outs, constant appeals for freezes on municipal assessments and accidents, some fatal. Bert Bailey died in 1915, James Prentiss in 1923 and injuries were commonplace.

The Beardmore Tannery operation was closed in 1922. The Anglo Canadian Tannery was shut down for an indefinite period, but by 1927 it again was at capacity, employing 100 men processing 500 hides per day. The company buoyantly predicted that they would be employing 225 eventually and capable of handling 2500 hides per day. In 1930 however, calamity struck. The market for leather was mostly in the United States and in a vicious protectionist move, legislation was enacted there raising the tariff on Canadian leather from 27% to 50%. As a result the Bracebridge operation was closed, or at least reduced to almost nothing, and the Huntsville operation struggled on through the great depression. The Board of Directors were prepared to declare bankruptcy but financially astute C.W. Conway and chemist F.R. Mosbaugh were given control of the company and kept it going - but the writing was on the wall.

The last use of hemlock bark was in 1942, and since hides continued to be processed until 1960, presumably the South American chemical product *quebracho* replaced it. Canada Packers bought both properties in 1953, kept processing hides for 7 years in Huntsville and used the Bracebridge buildings that had been unused for over 20 years to raise poultry. A tragic fire in 1959 killed 4000 chickens and 3000 turkeys and the buildings were demolished in 1977

In "***A HISTORY OF BEARDMORE AND COMPANY LIMITED AND ANGLO CANADIAN LEATHER COMPANY LIMITED***", it is stated *"...when tanneries of both Beardmore and Anglo were operating in Bracebridge, this town in the "backwoods" of Muskoka was probably the largest centre of sole leather tanning in the British Empire."*. While the ready availability of hemlock bark was a prime reason for the tanneries to come to Muskoka, another reason expressed years later by Canada Packers was that it was because of the *"soft water"* of the Muskoka River. The Beardmore and Anglo Canadian companies were merged in 1964, both by that time apparently through with making leather.

The Anglo-Canadian Leather Company was a huge contributor to the Bracebridge economy.

As a matter of interest, during the period when the Huntsville tannery was still operating under C.O. Shaw and the Bracebridge operation shut down, if Shaw had any kind of dispute with the town officials in Huntsville, he would activate his rail siding and run a boxcar full of hides into the Bracebridge property. Terrified that he was considering abandoning Huntsville and, God forbid, reactivating the Bracebridge operation, the town would suddenly have a change of heart, most willingly capitulate and grant his every wish.

38. THE RIVER...

Throughout this book there is a thread that ties everything in Bracebridge, and most of Muskoka, together. It is the ***Muskoka River***. It has served many masters; early explorers, surveyors, first settlers, entrepreneurs looking for hydraulic power, tanneries looking for ***"soft water"***, loggers as an access route, firefighters for fire protection, tourists for recreation, and before all that the natives travelled it for ages long before the white man ever saw this land. It has been a good servant but it has also been cruel master. Many who did not show it the respect it deserved paid the price. A newspaper article in the year 1900 listed close to 100 men who had died in the rivers of Muskoka during log drives.

It is the most taken for granted asset that could ever be imagined, for the most part by those closest to it. Essentially it is the same now as it was when all those mentioned above saw it and, while those educated in the evolution of the land tell of how it at one time was a much larger river as part of the huge Lake Algonquin that covered most of Muskoka, we will never see it any other way than it is right now.

The level of the river will continue to rise and fall, alarmists will blame something for the fluctuations, probably global warming, and rant wildly that we must do something to make it stop; forgetting that the evolution of this earth of ours will continue to change our river as it always has.

There is magic about moving water. The rippling sound, the crash of waves, the spray of mist that sweeps over us, the otters that play on the slippery rocks; all bring a peace of mind to those exposed to this wonder of nature. It is true that as time passes the rocks that create the waterfalls will, in the fullness of time, slowly erode so that our waterfalls will flatten and those pleasures will diminish. But don't be alarmed! That will take millions of years and those experiencing the river then will accept it *the way they see it*, as we do now. One of the greatest documents ever written on the Muskoka River is ***THIS RIVER THE MUSKOKA,*** a fabulous work by ***Gary Long***. Thorough, accurate and inspiring, it is the yardstick by which all other descriptions of the river should be measured.

Bracebridge claims to have 22 waterfalls of significance when the two branches of the Muskoka River and the Black River are considered. In fact, there are a lot more than that if all the smaller streams like Sharps Creek and Beaver Creek are included. Those falls are not considered significant because few if any had a sufficient and consistent flow of water to attract the builders of sawmills.

No wonder lumbermen flocked to the area considering the hydraulic power so available within easy walking distance of the growing community. Readily accessible on the North Branch are four- Bracebridge Falls, Wilsons Falls, High Falls, and Duck Chute. The South Branch has three-South (or Muskoka) Falls, Hanna Chute and Trethewey Falls. There could be eight in total if Halsteads Rapids near Bass Rock Park on the North Branch was included, but it is just that - a fast water rapids, although it was considered sufficient for the sawmill of Halstead and McNicol Company in 1870.

They all have a history, but the four largest falls nearest Bracebridge got the most attention, not only because they were so picturesque but they also presented the greatest opportunity for commercial development. As a result they were the ones most written about by the explorers, surveyors and historians of the era. The following paragraphs describing them were prepared as scripts to assist tour guides involved with various festivals in recent years and, while much of the information has been included elsewhere in this book, for the most part they are repeated here in their entirety. They are interesting enough to deserve to be repeated.

BRACEBRIDGE FALLS, with its 52 feet (16 metre) drop, is the first falls upstream from Muskoka Lake on the north branch of the Muskoka River. Its importance in the development of Muskoka and Bracebridge in particular cannot be overstated. While McCabes Landing (Gravenhurst) was the first settlement on Muskoka Lake to be accessed by the Muskoka Road and the Northern Railway, it was Bracebridge, known as North Falls until 1864, that was the focus of growth. It was here that hydraulic power was available in abundance and, situated in the centre of Muskoka, entrepreneurs recognized that this was the place to be. The deep-water access to Muskoka Lake for large boat travel was a huge asset. It is because of these falls Bracebridge exists in this location.

To illustrate the rapid growth, picture that the first white settler came in 1859 and by 1871, just 12 years later, there was an established settlement here with churches, a grist mill, a woollen mill, lumber mills, a newspaper, hotels, taverns and a number of stores. As described earlier, a combination of members of the Cooper family built the Muskoka Colonization Road to Bracebridge in 1861 and located the first bridge at the top of the falls.

There have been 4 public wharfs in the bay, according to Redmond Thomas in **Reminiscences**, as explained to him by his friend Richard Harper. One was on the north side of the river near the mouth of the bay (on which I have seen no other written evidence), another at the beach at the bottom and to the left of the falls, (primarily there to serve the grist mill of Alexander Bailey and which kept getting pulled apart by the current), the third about halfway around on the right (north side), and the fourth in its present location. The most active was the third wharf and the pictures we see of it show a number of big lake boats moored here, an indication of the extensive commerce going on in the community.

In the late 1800s the south side of the Bracebridge Bay below the falls was occupied by the Singleton Brown Shingle Mill, producing 20 million cedar shakes per year. Singleton Brown's grandson Norman J. MacMillan, born in Bracebridge in 1909, in 1974 retired as President and Chairman of Canadian National Railways and was appointed the same year as a Companion of the Order of Canada. After Singleton Brown's sudden death part of his property became undermined by floodwaters and the buildings were demolished. It later became a gathering place for those involved in a new fad -motorcars, not unlike modern day snowmachine clubs, and was generally referred to as the *motor park*. Following that it was a campground for many years until converted to this beautiful part of Bracebridge Bay Park. In the deed to this property the town committed to it being called Kelvin Grove Park, named after a park in Glasgow and Lord Kelvin of Scotland, obviously a request of Scottish native Mungo Park McKay from whom the property was purchased.

Adjoining the boat launching ramp located in the park for many years was the Minett-Shields Co. Ltd boat manufacturer where the incredibly talented Bert Minett designed and built 250 classic lake craft; treasured as works of art by their owners on one hand and as winners of Canadian and international racing competitions by others.

The north shore, after the latest wharf was built in 1905 and the third one demolished, became lined with private boathouses and marinas on the road allowance. Around 1970 Bracebridge Council began buying the decrepit boathouses and with Provincial help created Bracebridge Bay Park, complete with walkways that linked all parts of the property, viewing areas, historical message signs, viewing areas, playgrounds, a beach and a picnic area. It quickly became a significant and welcome addition to the community.

Above the main dam along the south shore a walkway leads to Entrance Drive (formerly Muskoka Road) and Bird's Bridge. This was originally Mill St. which gave access to the Grist Mill at the foot of the falls. Once across Entrance Drive. perched on the hill amidst huge pines is Woodchester, the 1880s octagonal home of Henry J Bird, founder of the Bird Woollen Mill.

On the north side of the river adjoining Bird's Bridge is the Bird Mill Pumphouse. As more thoroughly discussed in the chapter on tanneries, this was built by W.S. Shaw in 1892 and was the introduction of the magic of electricity to Bracebridge. The Town Council quickly recognized the importance of this and purchased the plant from Shaw in 1894, primarily for streetlights, and that purchase established Bracebridge as the first municipality in Canada to own an electrical generating station. It didn't take long before the service caught on and a much larger power plant was built at the bottom of the falls in 1902. The Bird Mill generating station was then converted to a water pumping station, continuing in that capacity until a new water transmission line was completed to Muskoka Lake many years later.

The Northern Railway, after a lengthy local promotion, commitment of funds and a number of corporate restructurings, cut through a 300 foot long, 60 foot deep rocky hill and built their massive bridge over the Bracebridge Falls in the 1880s, the first train crossing it in 1885. The part of the plan for the development of Bracebridge Bay Park that included the construction of a walkway on each side of the river under the towering bridge created a very interesting situation. When first approached about it the Canadian Nation Railway, in no uncertain terms, demanded that if there was going to be a walkway under their trestle it had to be covered with a steel roof to protect pedestrians from *"things"* falling off their train overhead. When the town protested about these large additional expenditures and why there were *"things"* falling off their trains in the first place, the adamant reply was that federal legislation gave them authority to demand this protection because they had their right-of-way established before the municipality had theirs.

They shouldn't have thrown down that challenge because we replied that they did not have that authority because the municipality had roads there long before the railway came to Bracebridge. On the north side of the river there was a road allowance that ran from Bird Woollen Mill property to the wharf to facilitate their deliveries to the lake steamers and on the south side the village had established Mill Street when Alexander Bailey built his gristmill in the 1860s. The original road allowance plans were submitted to CNR and after a number of months they finally replied that we had convinced them that Mill Street was there before their right-of-way. However, they said since the road allowance on the north side ended at the property line of Birds and did not adjoin another road allowance, then it could not be considered a public thoroughfare and therefore their rights took precedence.

In fact, they were right. Bird's property included a sliver of land on which the road to the wharf abutted, and only the point of a 90 degree angle corner of the allowance touched on Muskoka Road, which did not provide any width that would allow for a vehicle of any kind to cross. The fact that one could stand just inside the triangle and hop over the point onto Muskoka Road cut no ice with them so we lost that part of the argument.

But then a funny thing occurred. Because we had priority on the south side the CNR concluded that no protection for pedestrians was needed and a cover over the walkway unnecessary, but on the other side where they did have priority, protection of the pedestrians was definitely necessary and before they gave permission for crossing their right-of-way, a steel roof had to be constructed. As a result, several thousand dollars later, a steel roof gave protection to the public.

The town could never get an answer to the question why *"things"* could fall off the train on the north side of the river but not on the south.

The building on the north side of the river beside the Silver Bridge, where the Chamber of Commerce visitor centre is located, was built in 1918 as a warehouse for the Birds Woollen Mill. Its first use however was when the Bird family invited the entire community to a celebration of the end of World War 1 following the surrender of Germany to the Allied forces. One can only imagine the joy and relief that would have been expressed during that celebration, tempered no doubt by the families of those young men who perished in that conflict.

As a final link in the development of Bracebridge Bay Park, the town purchased this property, along with the adjoining property at the corner of Entrance Drive and Manitoba Street, formerly the location of Rombos Pizza and Russ Salmon's Texaco Service Station before that, and developed it in 1994 as a centre for the Chamber of Commerce, rental space and public washrooms. It was officially opened that year by His Worship Mayor Roland Hurst and Councillor Bud Robinson of Lincoln England where the Bracebridge of Washington Irving's book ***Bracebridge Hall*** still exists.

WILSONS FALLS is located on the north branch of the Muskoka River about halfway between Bracebridge Falls and High Falls. It drops level of the Muskoka River North Branch 41 feet (12.5 metres). This picturesque stretch of the river from Wilson's Falls upstream to High Falls was identified by early adventurers as the ***"Muskoka Canyon"*** and is still indicated as such on some maps.

In their pursuit of electricity, the Town of Bracebridge built the generating station here in 1910 in the same location as a sawmill known as Norwood Mills established by Gillman Willson in the early 1860s, as described in an earlier chapter. For some unknown reason his surname lost one of its *"l"*s when it was applied to the Falls. He was the first resident missionary minister (Methodist Episcopal) to come to Bracebridge but somewhere along the line Willson decided he was more of a lumberman than a lecturer. His daughter Elizabeth was the bride in the first wedding to take place here in 1866; she married William Holditch after whom Holditch St. was named by the municipality

The sawmill, under different ownership and converted to a shingle mill, was destroyed by fire in 1892.

Although referred to in the previous chapter on bridges, some features of this waterfall are worthy of being repeated. Just above the falls and generally following a road allowance that crosses the river, easily identified by following the power lines in the same location, there was a bridge that provided access from Bracebridge to settlements to the north. In times of low water the footings that were used for support of the bridge are still visible.

The Township of Macaulay had constructed it in the early 1870s before Bracebridge achieved its own incorporated status as a village. It was well used by early settlers and companies in the logging business but it eventually fell into disrepair, was condemned and removed by the Township of Macaulay in 1902. They refused to replace it because they said it served the people of Bracebridge more than those of their Township. It was curious decision to make because traffic over the bridge went both ways and residents of the township needed to get back and forth to Bracebridge to work and get supplies. It is more likely there was some resentment still remaining in the minds of the township fathers because Bracebridge had the nerve to separate from the Township in 1875.

Understandably a lot of hard feelings resulted and Bracebridge appealed to the Provincial Government who then replaced the rickety first *"Hunt's Hill"* (Taylor Rd) bridge shortly after.

It was also in this location where for many years there was a post on each side of the river with pulleys attached and a cable that extended between them. A chair was attached to the cable and by pulling on the cable the chair could be moved back and forth across the river. Hydro workers who lived at these falls used this precarious contraption as a shortcut to the High Falls generating station where they would perform daily maintenance. While it did save them a lengthy walk into Bracebridge to cross on a safe bridge, it is unexplained why they didn't just use a boat. Perhaps they did, but it was more fun to ride the cable.

HIGH FALLS is part of the north branch of the Muskoka River just upstream from Wilson's Falls and adjacent to a roadside park maintained by the Province of Ontario. It consists of a number of cataracts that lower the river level by 48 feet (14.6 metres).

This waterfall was greatly admired by early explorers and some referred to it as the *"Niagara of the North"*. In Robert Bell's *"Diary of a Survey"*, written when he explored here in 1848, he refers to the river as the *"Muskako"* River as many others did at that time and notes that he *"…saw 3 magnificent falls"* referring to the number of cataracts which made up High Falls at that time. In 1935, the area of the river including High Falls north almost to Port Sydney was one of the candidates being considered for designation as a National Park by the Federal Government.

The generating station located on the most northerly of those cataracts was constructed there in 1948 by the Water Light and Power Commission of the Town of Bracebridge.

As with any body of fast flowing water its mystifying beauty can be very dangerous. A number of people have drowned at these falls and there have been many close calls, including a truck that went over the side of a bridge that at one time crossed the river at the top of the falls, and a bulldozer that slid into the river. They both occurred during the relocation and widening of Highway 11. In another incident a couple on their honeymoon were viewing the falls when the newly wed husband wondered out onto the rocks and slipped over the edge, luckily landing on a rocky ledge halfway down and escaping with only a broken ankle.

On the south side of the falls is a cairn erected to honour Aubrey White, formerly of Bracebridge and the subject of a separate chapter in this book, in recognition of his innovative development of the forest fire protection system for Ontario and service as a Deputy Minister from 1887 to 1915. Emigrating from Ireland at an early age and starting as a store clerk for Alexander Bailey, he progressed to a number of positions including Steamboat Captain, log run organizer, Crown Land Agent and Supt. of Algonquin Park before the Provincial Government recognized his talents and transferred him to the head office of the Ministry of Lands, Forests and Mines in the Provincial Capital in Toronto.

The cairn was erected by the Ontario Ministry of Natural Resources where White is still recognized as the founder of that ministries forest fire prevention system, over 100 years later!

MUSKOKA FALLS was also given a number of attractive names by early explorers and surveyors. When Henry Briscoe, during his exploration of the Muskoka River in 1826, came to this thundering cataract he called it **"the Wild Falls"**, in French **"Sault du Sauvage"**. When Robert Bell came to it in 1848 he called it **"the Great Falls"**, and J Stoughton referred to it as **"Grand Falls"** in 1861. For a more recognizable identity, it became better known as "**South Falls**" because it was on the South Branch of the Muskoka River; the same reason Bracebridge Falls was referred to as North Falls on the North Branch. Somewhere along the line South Falls also became known as Muskoka Falls and although it is not written anywhere, I suspect it became known as that because it was so symbolic of the Muskoka District's abundance of rivers and wild waterfalls.

Muskoka Falls drops the level of the South Branch of the Muskoka River 141 feet (43 metres), and has been described as *"..the highest, wildest and most powerful waterfall in all of the Muskoka watershed…"* and *"…an awesome spectacle unmatched in mid-Ontario wilderness."* What is known now as Hanna Chute contributes 9.8 metres (32 feet) to that total drop but the early explorers and surveyors saw the whole falls before dams, powerhouses and bridges got in the way. It would have been an incredible sight.

Robert Bell liked these falls so much that he recommended that it be considered for a townsite and eventually the Town Plan of Muskokaville was created. Over the years though, the community has become better known by the same name as the falls that the subdivision surrounds.

Choosing the area for a town site wasn't a bad idea because it, like Bracebridge Falls, had unimpeded access by water to the big lakes. The only, but important, difference was that the depth of the south branch was insufficient for the large boats. As a result, the settlement didn't develop commercially like Bracebridge. It did give rise though to having the first post office in Muskoka and the first bridge over the river.

It took a concerted effort to design and build it but a log slide from top to bottom was built in 1878 on the left side of these falls by the Province Ontario, not The Muskoka Slide, Dam and Boom Co as was the case for the log slides on most of the other falls on the river. An interesting aside, one of the men involved in the dangerous work of building this lengthy structure was so proud of his work that he boasted he would ride the first log that went down the slide at the ribbon cutting for its opening ceremony. Ride it he did, but it was not a happy ending. He was found a few days later in the river downstream. He misunderstood; his good work was meant for logs, not human beings, no matter how dedicated.

The Town of Gravenhurst acquired water rights and built a generating station at the bottom of the falls in 1907. It proved to be more than the town could handle and it was purchased shortly after by Ontario Hydro who greatly increased the capacity and added the generating station at Hannah Chute in 1926. It was considered important enough to be protected by guards during World War 2.

Spectacular Muskoka Falls, or South Falls as first named, showing the log slide

In summary, the three waterfalls on the North Branch (Bracebridge, Wilson's and High) have a combined drop of 141 feet (43 m) and Muskoka Falls/Hanna Chute drops the South Branch by about the same. Gary Long in ***This River The Muskoka*** explains how combined they drain a watershed of close to 2000 square miles, just slightly smaller in size than the Province of Prince Edward Island; and it all flows through downtown Bracebridge.

39. DR. JAMES FRANCIS WILLIAMS MD…

Dr. James Francis Williams was born in Dalston, Oro Township in Simcoe County in 1858. He studied at McGill University, graduated in 1886 and continued his education in hospitals in England before returning to Canada where, in 1889 he married Gertrude Annie Bird of Barrie, Ontario, a sister of Sir Lyman Duff, Chief Justice of Canada. They moved to Bracebridge in 1895 and made it their home; he was one of three doctors practicing in Bracebridge at that time and was joined in his practice by Dr. Peter McGibbon in 1905. Dr. Williams died in 1926 and his wife in 1929. On the day of his funeral flags in Bracebridge flew at half-mast and the funeral blinds were drawn in the windows of downtown businesses. Sadly, their only child, a son, died at a very young age.

Dr. Williams had served in the North West Rebellion and would serve again in World War 1 attending to the wounded. His medical practice in Bracebridge was renowned and for years he was faithfully committed to his patients, traveling by horse and buggy to every corner of central Muskoka. Historical reports exist about him racing furiously to the bedside of a sick person, or sitting beside a dying pioneer surrounded by his family in their log shanty in the dense and difficult Muskoka wilderness. One such incident is recorded in Bert Shea's ***History of the Shea's and the Paths of Adventure-***

"Early in the afternoon, the old collie seated in the yard before the door, uttered a short, sharp bark and we looked out of the window. We saw coming over the hill the foam lathered horses, heads held high, travelling under a tight rein, as fleet as the wind and hitched to a buggy bearing Dr. Williams to mother's bedside. In less time than it takes to tell, the fiery bloods landed the buggy and Dr. Williams on the dooryard and came to a sudden stop. With not a word spoken, Dr. Williams stepped out of the buggy, valise in hand. One of the boys took the lines and drove the noble beasts, who had brought the doctor the sixteen miles from Bracebridge in record time, to the stable. A half-pail of water each and after a good cooling down they were given a good feed of Black Tartarian Oats."

Shea went on to describe the dedicated work of Dr. Williams with those in the community who were afflicted with the dreaded diphtheria, claiming he *"...had gained for himself a great name in the treatment of the disease, at Dee Bank."*

Dr. James Francis Williams, a dedicated, selfless friend to early pioneers

Dr. Williams was deeply involved in his community, serving as Magistrate, as a member of the Patriotic Fund which provided support for families of Canadian Soldiers, President of a newly formed Children's Aid Society in 1910 and as a member of the Methodist (later United) Church. He also was as an environmentalist long before most had ever heard of that word. He planted over 50,000 red pines in Oakley Township on a property owned later by Jack McVittie and his son Don who have continued Dr. William's heritage by maintaining the acreage as a managed forest. Dr. Williams loved the outdoors, the land and living things. Who else but a completely unselfish man in his mid-sixties would plant thousands of seedling trees that would take 80 to 100 years to mature, and whose maturity he would never see.

Another wonderful gift that becomes more valuable as time passes is Annie Williams Memorial Recreation Park, left in a trust by Dr. Williams for the benefit of the people of Bracebridge. Always one to think to the future, he also provided ongoing financial support for its maintenance. He originally bought this property that surrounds the United Church Cemetery for the purpose of an extension to that burial ground which he then proposed to give to the Church providing it be named Williams Memorial Cemetery. Apparently the congregation declined the proposal because of the naming provision. In a way though, Dr. Williams did get his way because in the centre of the Park is a small cemetery containing the graves of himself, his wife and his child.

He also established a scholarship in medicine at McGill University, a fund providing ongoing financial support to his church and a trust fund for needy sufferers of cancer and tuberculosis.

Their beautiful home and property in Bracebridge, which they called **"Carn Brae"**, was located at the south end of Manitoba Street, adjacent to the parkette in front of Bird Mill Mews where in 2013 the Chamber of Commerce Visitor Centre is located. When Wharf Road was being constructed in 1906, dynamite stored in a shack along the construction area exploded and did extensive damage to that whole area of Town, particularly the Williams residence. A popular feature of the William's home was a Pianola, a machine which, when placed against the keyboard of a piano, would play it as directed from a roll inside the machine. Les Hart, founder of the popular Hart's Flowers business in Bracebridge, a Bernardo Home Boy, was placed in the William's home when he came to Canada. This was another indication of the kindness of the Williams family because they also welcomed another Bernardo Home Boy by the name of Johnny Moon into their house, as described in a separate chapter.

Their house was demolished when the Ferguson Highway (later designated Highway 11) was carved into the steep south bank of Bracebridge Bay and the Silver Bridge erected in the early 1930's to provide for an ever increasing flow of traffic.

Dr. Williams was a keen motorist in the early years of automotive travel and, while it is claimed in one book that he was the first citizen in Bracebridge to own an automobile, other historical documents claim that it was the Mahaffy Brothers in 1911 or Arthur A. Mahaffy MPP that had the first automobile. The list of owners of motorcars in 1913 did not include the name of Dr. Williams. He was very much an entrepreneur, accumulating valuable property and partnering with the White Brothers in a silver mine in Cobalt which produced fine examples of silver ore.

His medical office at one time was over MacMillan's (Norman J. MacMillan's parents) Grocery Store at the foot of Chancery Lane. In 1904 he built a small store beside the Independent Order of Oddfellows building and when the Town changed the road levels in front he laid a claim against the municipality arguing that the grade alteration was harmful to his property which, in due course, was resolved and he received a settlement of $906.00.

Dr. Williams and Mrs. Williams were highly respected people of Bracebridge. They were generous, thoughtful and dedicated to all. Following Dr. Williams death, Mrs. Williams lived for some time in the front room of the second floor of the Inn at the Falls where she was often seen in the window in her rocking chair.

Elijah Veitch of Ufford often told of the time when Dr. Williams visited Mr. Morley as he lay dying in his little log shack well back in the bush in Ufford where he had tried to build a homestead on Free Grant Land Act property. His wife and their young family were gathered in the room crying, saddened by their father's suffering. They recognized that the hard work of their father trying to create a home for them in an unforgiving and impossible land for farming was now taking its toll.

Mr. Morley was lamenting to Dr. Williams that he was a failure and had not been able to achieve his dream, and now lay dying a poor man. Dr. Williams asked him to look around the room where his family was gathered and said to him ***"No, Mr. Morley, you are a rich man. You may not have*** *a lot of money but you have these children who all love you and will remember you. I, on the other hand, have a lot of money but my only child died when he was only a year old and I have no one to regret my passing the way your children will yours. No, Mr. Morley, you are the rich man and I am the poor one."*

Dr. Williams good deeds and acts of kindness are described in great length in Robert Boyer's book ***A Good Town Grew Here*** and Redmond Thomas' ***Reminiscences.***

40. PAWSON HARNESS SHOP…

Artefacts from our pioneer heritage are commonplace and plentiful, especially farming implements and, in particular, equipment for horses. A visit to the annual Muskoka Pioneer Power Show in Bracebridge makes that very obvious. Until the introduction of the railroad and aside from walking, a good horse was priceless for land transportation when this country was being developed. Old wagon wheels, plows and hay rakes are featured in museums almost everywhere and often displayed as front yard decorations. Personalized items like bridles and harnesses are of particular interest, especially when they can be identified as having been manufactured locally. There were a number of businesses in the horse trade here but little evidence of their existence remains. The one exception is Richard (Dick) Pawson, a harness manufacturer whose business was generally referred to as the *Pawson Harness Shop.*

He had moved to Bracebridge from Hamilton with his parents but on May 18, 1883 tragedy struck. In his father's absence, their house on Ontario St. caught fire. Mrs. Pawson, after getting her daughter out of the house safely, re-entered the house to rescue a son and sadly both perished in the fire. The family reportedly lost all their money with which they hoped to start a business in Bracebridge. Although it is not clearly stated inference is made that Richard and another son Jack were away from the house at the time.

His shop was located on the north side of Thomas St, (Taylor Rd) in the building that later housed the Bracebridge Bowling Alley, more recently the Muskoka Heritage offices, beside the former Muskoka Trading store, now Lakes of Muskoka Cottage Brewery. One report states that its location was in the former Crystal Theatre building on the north side of Thomas St. where the bowling alley was later located and in another reference *"behind the Queens Hotel roughly across from Downtown Garage".*

It is said of Richard Pawson that he kept alive the honourable profession of making and repairing leather harness for horses. He had apprenticed for many years with W.W. Kinsey as a harness maker before opening his own store. He was also musically inclined, playing trumpet in the Bracebridge Citizens Band. It is recorded that *Jack* Pawson played in the Bugle Band which accompanied the 23rd Regiment Canadian Volunteers to Niagara-on-the-Lake in 1913

Richard Pawson died in 1929 but he left a lasting legacy in his handmade bridles and harnesses upon which he had proudly stamped his name. They are precious to those who own a piece of this priceless Bracebridge work, one of those proud owners being Muskoka's best respected horse logger Gerald Cook.

41. THE "OLD" POST OFFICE…

THE "OLD" POST OFFICE was not so old in 1915 when it was officially opened as a state-of-the-art federal building, making Bracebridge the envy of every other municipality in the region. It did not come easily; it took monumental coaxing, prodding and pushing by the town to get it here.

Since receiving its first designation as such in 1864 the Bracebridge Post Offices were in a number of private premises in Bracebridge. The first record of lobbying for a new Post Office and Federal Building appears in 1902 and continues sporadically in the written histories of the municipality. It seems that every little settlement in Muskoka that had a corner store was given a post office designation and, because it would have been the store owner that had applied for it, without fail it would be located in his or her store.

In 1911 a promise of a Federal Building was received and when nothing had materialized by 1912 a delegation was assembled to go to Ottawa to plead their case. Just as they were about to depart however it was made known that $18,000.00 had been allocated to build a *"Dominion Government Building"* in Bracebridge.

A number of locations were suggested for the new building and the site that was chosen was that of the Whitten Hardware Store which, along with a number of adjoining stores, had been destroyed by fire in December 1908.

Robert J. Boyer, in *A GOOD TOWN GREW HERE* describes the progress of the building in great detail. Construction started in 1913 with an increased budget of $30,000.00 to build a 45 foot building and a 75 foot tower. The contract was given to Simcoe Construction of Toronto. Apparently there was a need to have piles driven into the ground in order to provide solid footings for the building, in spite of the fact that a rocky ridge dominated the opposite side of Manitoba Street; more evidence of the remarkable geologically features of Muskoka.

The work proceeded throughout 1914 but the Town became concerned when they heard there was not going to be a clock in the tower; something they had every right to expect in this glorious new structure. They were relieved when they were informed that J. H. Elliott of Bracebridge would install a clock with dials 4 ½ feet across. The Post Office moved from its existing location just south of Chancery Lane to the new building in 1915. It was the first Federal Building of its kind in Muskoka, duplicated in Gravenhurst and Huntsville in 1926 following the 1st World War.

The clock itself deserves special mention. In spite of the massive clock face on each side of the tower, the mechanism that runs it is relatively small, not much larger than a laundry basket. But out of it there is a spider web of rods and pulleys running to the clock faces that turn the hour and minute hands, and cables that connect to two huge lead weights. The lead weights provide the energy that runs the entire operation. Once a week, a huge crank is used to pull the weights to the top of the tower by their cable and gravity slowly pulls them back down to the bottom, thereby running the clock mechanism for the week. The slightest addition of weight stuck to or removed from the lead weights is used to make the clock run a little faster or slower as the need arises.

Bob Burton, long time former owner of *THE "OLD" POST OFFICE,* maintained the clock with loving care and allowed visitors to climb the clock tower where he would proudly describe this marvel of early engineering.

42. AN INTERESTING CORNER - DOMINION AND MANITOBA...

This intersection can lay claim to being one of the most historic sites in all of Bracebridge.

The block of land on the west side of the intersection, roughly including the property on which the Old Station Restaurant, the Bracebridge Public Library, Bracebridge Seniors Centre, Rogers Insurance and their respective parking lots are located, in the earliest days was a town park. It was in this park where the original bandstand donated by W.S. Shaw in 1898 was located, moved in 1900 to the new Memorial Park just up the street. As described earlier in **Chapter 33. *MEMORIAL PARK*...**that bandstand provided many hours of enjoyment for the people of Bracebridge, but eventually became so rickety that it had to be demolished and the present Memorial Park bandstand built in its place. It has been said that the Bandmaster of the day asked the bass drummer to use his instrument gently because the whole bandstand trembled when it was used normally.

As related in **Chapter 32. *THE PALACE RINK*...** and worthy of repeating here, the property was used for many community functions; the most memorable being circuses. In *"Reminiscences"*, Redmond Thomas wrote about riding a steam powered merry-go-round there, watching minstrel shows by the light of coal oil flares and listening to spielers rave on and on about their secret oil; ***"best thing in the world for humans, horses and harness".*** It was sometimes generously referred to as the *"Broadway of Bracebridge".*

We think the Queens Hill is steep now, but when Bracebridge was a pioneer settlement, it was far steeper. Picture John Beal in 1859 parking his canoe at the bottom of the falls and traversing steep hills and valleys as he searched for a piece of flat land where he could build his shanty. During excavation required for municipal services at the bottom of the hill in recent years stumps of cut trees were found over 10 feet below the surface. In fact, it was so steep originally that some avoided walking north on Manitoba Street.

Adjacent to the intersection was the location of the Rogers Pump Works manufacturing plant that produced the long-handled manual pumps used for pulling water from the dug wells of the community. In fact, a number of these pumps were still in use on Woodchester Avenue prior to the installation of the municipal water supply being installed there. In 1928 J. Hudson Burton bought the property of a Mr. Nelson, added 14 feet to it, which he purchased from the town (part of the Public Library property), for the purpose of starting a service station business to serve the rapidly growing automobile trade. The building was built by Ed Hunt and, when completed, the business was operated by Burton's son Douglas. The service station, known as the Uptown Service Station, came under the ownership of Earl Rosewarne at one point and then Ernie and Fenton Patterson, where at one time they sold Studebaker automobiles. These business entrepreneurs were very successful and an integral part of Bracebridge economic affairs. After many years the business was taken over by Ted Smith, a long term and trusted employee of the Patterson brothers. An entire generation can remember wheeling their first car up to the antique gas pumps between the concrete pillars in front of the building where Ted Smith would be waiting to ask ***"Fill'er up?"***

However, life goes on. In 1980 the business closed and the building was renovated to the Garden Café restaurant. In 1985 it was sold to Mike Warr who re-opened it under the appropriate name of *The Old Station*.

Besides the parades, street shows and personalities this intersection has known, other less routine occurrences deserve mention. Around the same era as the circuses the W.W. Kinsey funeral home was located across Manitoba Street on the east side of the intersection. At the conclusion of a funeral service for Robert M. Browning, the coffin was being loaded into the back of a funeral carriage pulled by a team of horses. However, just as it slid into its proper place, the horses bolted with such violence that the coffin broke free from its fastenings and was ejected out the back of the hearse; fortunately the bearers reacted quickly and stopped it from crashing to the ground. Redmond Thomas in ***Reminiscences*** wrote that one of the pallbearers was heard to say ***"Oh no, Robert---you don't get out yet."***

In 1935, Fenton Patterson, who was covering the evening shift at the service station, was alerted by the sound of the cash register being opened. He rose from his desk and was confronted by two thieves. He was held at gunpoint until the thieves were satisfied they had all there was to be had, then watched them escape in a waiting vehicle.

This intersection, not unlike most other Manitoba Street properties, has witnessed many interesting events in the evolution of Bracebridge.

43. AUBREY STREET...

One would hardly expect to read about *AUBREY STREET*, a popular residential area in the northeast corner of urban Bracebridge, in a book that talks so much about the history of the area as far back as the 1860s, but the fact is that the history of this street *does* go back to that era. On the 6th of May 1884, Joseph Cooper filed Plan of Subdivision #21 with Charles W. Diggle, Dep. Reg. on which Aubrey Street, Cooper Street and Charles Street are designated. The plan was drawn by Robert T. Pope, Provincial Land Surveyor. Coopers statement on the 1884 plan reads,

"I hereby certify that this Plan correctly represents the manner in which I have caused part of Lots 2 & 3 Concession II Township of Macaulay to be subdivided into Building Lots and also the manner in which I have caused part of the Original Plan or survey of said lots to be resurveyed."

This statement infers that there was an earlier plan for the area, according to one report as early as 1872, however, for the purpose of this chapter the 1884 Plan of Subdivision will suffice to establish the fact that *AUBREY STREET* was created long before it developed into what we see today. The property was the subject of later surveys as well wherein lot lines were relocated reducing the lot frontages from 1 chain (66 feet) to 50' more or less, and renumbered Plan 23. Although there is little to confirm it, the name *"Aubrey"* probably evolved from Cooper's association with Aubrey White who came to Bracebridge in 1862 from Ireland. As described in **Chapter 36. *AUBREY WHITE...,*** he worked briefly with Alexander Bailey, became a Captain with the Muskoka Navigation Company, worked with a lumber company harvesting timber and in 1878 became the Crown Land Agent for Muskoka. Charles Street on the same plan was probably named after Charles W. Diggle the Deputy Registrar for Muskoka, possibly another friend of Coopers.

It wasn't until 1948 though that Bylaw #802 was passed by the Town authorizing *AUBREY STREET* to be *"...opened for Public Traffic, and assumed by the Town of Bracebridge as a Public Street."* It also states in the *"Whereas"* paragraphs that the reason for passing the bylaw was that *"...the Town of Bracebridge has entered into an Agreement with Central Mortgage and Housing Corporation for the erection of Twenty Five Houses in the Town of Bracebridge."*

That is when *AUBREY STREET* had its real beginning. In *A Good Town Continues* for the year 1948 it states, *"...a contract was made with Wartime Housing Ltd. to build 35 approximately $6,600.00 four and five room homes on the Boake property near the hospital. Rental preference was given to veterans or their families with an option to buy after two years occupancy."* In the same publication for 1963 there is a picture of the newly constructed South Muskoka Memorial Hospital showing some of the Aubrey Street houses in the background, bearing the caption that reads, in part, *"Visible along Aubrey Street at the top of the picture are several of the 1½-storey "war-time" houses built to ease the housing shortage created by returning veterans after World War II."*

This Federal incentive program to resolve the housing shortage, probably doubling as a make-work program as well, gave *AUBREY STREET* its start. Most of the first residents were returning veterans, newly married and eager to start a new life after experiencing the terrors of the war with Germany. They had already seen more suffering in their lives than they deserved.

While many details are lacking, the names of those who became part of this newly created meca for young people were shown on a chart compiled in 1975 and again in 1987 by two of the original residents of the street. The charts list the following as first residents of the *"war time"* houses on *AUBREY STREET:*

On the west side - Ken Downey, Townsend, Reid, Commandant, Mrs. Earl Clarridge, Taplin, Kettle, Harold and Peggy Hart, Vic Trustrom, Downey, Patterson, Bob Everett

On the east side – Norm and Dolly Miners, Ron and Jean Olan, Jim and B Raeburn, Gallanger, MacIver, Wilf and Shirley Shier, Harry and Doris Lidstone, Moore, Sedgwick, Lomas, Magee, Laquer, Rutledge

There are some conflicts between the two lists, one saying Olan the other Lou Specht, Magee -the other Ball, Commandment -the other Morrison or an OPP officer named Alex something, Taplin -the other Tange, and Clarridge -the other Petry. No matter, the lists probably have it reasonably close.

The many common interests among those who first occupied the *"war time"* houses drew people together. For the most part they were young married couples with new careers, new jobs, relieved to be home following their service in World War 2 and eager to get started on a new way of life. It was a perfect formula for the creation of life, that is to say, babies. It didn't take long before it acquired the affectionate name of *Diaper Row*. It has been estimated that at one point there were 70 children living on the short street in the 25 homes.

The enthusiasm and exuberance of these young families contributed to make this close knit community a wonderful place to live. Along with that came having fun and many zany, creative and incredible events that will live forever in the minds of those involved, and their descendants.

As an indication of the spontaneity of the residents, in 1955 they put their heads together and decided, since there was no town organization doing it, to have a *street* Canada Day Fireworks display. Since moving into their cozy little *"war-time"* houses in 1949 individual families on the street had been having their own little show so it was an easy transition to get together and go big.

Just like that it became a tradition, one that residents from all over Town came to enjoy. Every July 1st an immense crowd would gather around the small (and only) vacant property left on the street and under the supervision of Harry Lidstone, Norman Miners Sr. and Ted Boyer a glorious display was provided to the delight of everyone. The vacant lot was only 100 feet wide by about 110 feet deep, a dangerously small area for a fireworks display and in today's world would be absolutely forbidden, yet everyone crowded within spitting distance of the launching site. Ice cream and popsicles, courtesy of Duffy Fraser and Gerry Short, were provided for the kids and a collection taken to cover the costs of the fireworks.

A Good Town Continues reads that in 1972, ***"The Kinsmen Club hosted the fireworks display at Jubilee park with Don Coates and John Davis in charge and Bob Spence as president of the club."*** Although it is not mentioned there, that is when the *"Aubreyites"* as Harry Lidstone called the residents of the street, relinquished the Canada Day public fireworks display; after nearly 20 years of excitement.

Most of the ***Aubrey Street*** fun took place in the day-to-day interaction between those who lived there. For the most part it seemed as if a party could break out anytime and anywhere, although there was one occasion when two wives had a disagreement and wound up having a fist fight in the middle of the street. That was the only negative recollection anyone can recall between adults, although by times there would be a dust-up between the kids.

There were many fun loving characters that lived on Aubrey Street and the antics that took place there were known far and wide, to the point that people wanted to move there in order to be part of it. Humorous events were numerous and many deserve to be recognized here.

One long term and early resident had never seen a party he didn't like, and he saw lots. Always popular and the life of any party he had a little act that everyone marvelled (or grimaced) at. He would bring a roll of toilet paper and, with a drink in hand of course, put the end of the roll in his mouth. Then he would chew and swallow the tissue as the roll tumbled and rolled around on the floor beside him. Occasionally he would bring a little jar of small live minnows and every now and then pluck out one of them and swallow it. He died at a young age of natural causes but there were those who wondered if the minnows and toilet paper were a contributing factor.

If a neighbour didn't cut their grass regularly they would come home to find a threatening swath cut through the front lawn by their friend next door. In one case two neighbours were watering their lawns in front of their house when one accidentally (or on purpose) sprayed a little water on the other. Well, that was reason for a little retaliatory spray back and before long they were exchanging full-blown soakings. Finally one gave up and ran into the relative safety of his house, the neighbour however, not to let the other off the hook that easily, followed him inside and continued to administer the soaking in his living room.

Then there was the outhouse. A resident contracted with a carpenter to build an outhouse which he was going to put in place at his hunt camp located well back in the bush far from Bracebridge. That was fine, but it got delivered before the resident was ready to put it in his truck and take it to the camp, with the result that it sat in his front yard on ***Aubrey Street*** for several days. With all the kids on the street, here was an opportunity too good to miss so they started using it instead of heading home when they needed a bathroom break. The result was just what one might expect, and gone unnoticed by the owner until it was 'way too late. That was just the incentive needed for the owner to find the time to get it moved to its proper place.

Every rainstorm provided a great opportunity for fun for *Aubrey Street* kids. The way the street was built, fairly wide, no storm drains, sidewalks on both sides of the street and no ditches; just a slope off the side of the payment to a low area that rose again to the sidewalks, resulted in large ponds of water gathering along the sides of the street. Some kids would put on their bathing suits, although most didn't, and sit at the sidewalk edge of the puddles breathlessly waiting for cars to come by so they could get drenched when the cars ran through the water, no matter that it got increasingly muddy as the game progressed.

Dangerous activity, but those who drove the street were generally used to this happening and were pretty careful. In fact, as a car approached the kids would wave their arms, motioning for the car to come closer so it could hit the middle of the puddle thereby providing a bigger splash. Amazingly, many drivers did co-operate, in fact, sometimes parents of the kids sitting there would be driving the cars. The kids loved the freedom to have fun!

Marbles and road hockey were two other sources of recreation for Aubrey Street kids. Again, the games were played right in the sandy area beside the pavement and road hockey was right on the street. During one road hockey game, the kids all moved aside as one of the neighbours drove up the street on their way home. The kindly fellow waved a friendly greeting to the players as he drove past, one of whom was his own son, however, the kids had not removed the goal net, thinking that he would just drive around it like everyone else. Not so, in fact the neighbour was so busy waving he didn't even *see* the net and ran right over it. It took an hour for the neighbour and the kids to disengage the net from the grill and undercarriage of the car; of course the net was demolished.

In various stages, some residents had titles. At one time Harold (Ding) Bell was the ***"Left Handed Governor"***, Ted Boyer was ***"The Registrar of Dirty Deeds"***, Noel (Turk) Lees was the ***"Solicitor in Generalities"***, Harry Lidstone was ***"His Worship the Mare"***; but none of those titles stuck for long because they were forever impeaching each other, usually every Saturday night.

"Ding" Bell was a veteran of World War 2 and had many stories of combat that he often emotionally shared with the rest of us, including one where he and a number of other soldiers were taking cover in a gravel pit when allied bombers mistakenly took them for the enemy and began strafing them. He was like a godfather. A man that would argue endlessly over drinks in the evening and the next morning be there helping put up your storm windows. A dedicated hockey fan that followed the street kids with a passion and after every game would gather everyone around to analyse the performance. Opinionated for sure, he was always claiming that, working for Fowler Construction in free enterprise, he was paying the salaries of those of the rest of us who were working for government.

Strong and tough as they come, it was Ding that in a restaurant downtown wrestled a gun off a renegade who was threatening to shoot one of the Town police officers. If he saw someone on their front lawn on a Sunday morning he would wonder over and talk about his favourite subject of the day. His endearing quality was that he always wanted to talk close to one's face and in doing so his large chest would be constantly bumping and knocking you off balance and forcing you to back away. The rest of would often compare notes about how many times we walked backward around our front yard talking to Ding.

An often used favourite demand of Dings, if he knew of someone planning some house painting or yard work, was to casually wonder over to them and say, ***"It had better look right or we'll burn you out!"*** It was a laugh to the rest of us but he occasionally pulled that little act with newcomers to the street, which to say the least, was a little upsetting until the rest of us clued them in to the situation. However, one year when he had applied a sickly yellow basecoat to the bare, unpainted aluminium siding that was a standard for all wartime housing units, Tom Robinson and the writer decided to turn the tables. Just after dark we got a long pole, wrapped a rag around one end, soaked it with motor oil, set it on fire and slowly walked back and forth across Dings front yard. It didn't take long before he came storming out of the house roaring at us to get the hell off his property. Suddenly he didn't quite see any humour in the fact that we didn't like the colour of his basecoat.

On another occasion, Tom Robinson somehow came into possession of a goat. Whether he had acquired it for this purpose or not was never revealed, but after dark one evening he took the goat and tethered it in the middle of the Bell's front lawn, knowing that they were away on an overnight visit. Of course it stayed there all night and well into the next day. By then it had cleaned off most of the grass within reach and promptly replaced it with manure. As an explanation he insisted that he thought he was doing Ding a favour by providing him with some fertilizer for his garden, which did not seem to be a fair exchange in Ding's opinion. The rest of town enjoyed it though; the street was busy with people wanting to have a look at the goat and the decimated lawn, chuckling over another Aubrey Street prank.

Another of his stories involved a visit during the war to a house in Scotland on a New Year's Eve when the man of the house suggested that he and Ding visit a neighbour for a drink to celebrate the New Year. One house led to another and Ding woke up sitting in a kitchen chair back at his friends as the family was getting set to enjoy a nice breakfast. The clock on the wall said 9:30 and he expressed to his friend that he had enjoyed last night's New Year's Eve get together, when his friend's wife spoke up and said, ***"I'm glad you had a good time, but this is January the 2nd!"***

Ding had a brother that lived in the western United States that he and Irene visited occasionally. It was when they were on one of those visits that a number of neighbours decided to call him to see how he was enjoying the holiday. Their teenaged kids having remained at home, the neighbours decided, since they did not have the telephone number of his brother in the States, to go over to their house and get it. Of course they were let in and they proceeded to make the call. There were about six neighbours and everyone talked to Ding, dragging out every conversation on every subject they could think of, to the extent that it went on for about 45 minutes or more. Finally he said, ***"I had better let you guys go, it must be costing you a fortune for you to call me all the way down here."*** That was when Tom Robinson was talking to him who replied, ***"Not at all Ding, we're calling from your place!"*** The call ended quickly at that point following many expletives; Ding never mentioned how much that call cost him, nor did we ask.

If there were ever a gentleman in this world it would be Ted Boyer. A descendant of pioneer Muskoka families, his recall of their experiences was invaluable to those who love the history of Muskoka. His character matched his ability and his personality went even farther. It was impossible to stir him to impatience and his ability to settle everyone down in a dispute was classic. His very presence brought peace to any setting. He was a remarkable canoeist and his ability to carry a canoe on his shoulders over difficult portages was legendary.

Ted was a great supporter of Bracebridge and his work with the Lions Club proved it. Often called on as a surveyor to settle property line locations, his decisions gave him a reputation of fairness and accuracy. No matter that it disagreed with any one person's claim, it resulted in satisfactory conclusions, *because it was Ted*. That is how his neighbours on Aubrey Street felt about him as well. He was always nice to be with, and *always there,* for us.

Besides that, he was Harry Lidstone's *"seeing eye dog"!* They played golf a lot and Harry, whose eyesight was failing as time passed, relied on his partner Ted to watch where his ball went. That went on for a number of years, never mentioned by Ted, but always by Harry; Ted was Harry's life support for golf. During a scourge of forest tent caterpillars in the 1980s, this writer, who had a pump-up spray can, and Ted went on a campaign to assist their neighbours in protecting their trees from the infestation.

Every day, the two of us would wonder around the immediate neighbours and try to rid their trees of this pest. This impressed the creative Harry Lidstone, inspiring him to compose the following:

To Tonto:

Here comes the worms
(Chorus) Let us spray, let us spray.
Get out the dioxin
(Chorus) Let us spray, Let us spray.
Supervisor and seeing eye dog
(Chorus) Let us spray, Let us spray.
The worms they go away
(Chorus) Let us spray, Let us spray.
I would like to repeat
Don't invade Aubrey Street
Or all we can say---
Tonto will get you, Today.
(Chorus) Let us Spray, Let us Spray,
Let -----------Us----------Spray

Cheap
Inc.
Cards

It is almost impossible to talk about one resident of **AUBREY STREET** without involving many others. That is especially true with Ted Boyer and Harry Lidstone. Harry was the artistic and creative leader of the street, especially evident when, for a number of years, we built snow sculptures. What a great street event. *Aubrey Street* resembled a beehive the weekend prior to Winter Carnival with people crawling all over huge mounds of snow in their front yards trying to create a sculpture that made sense. When one ran out of ideas they would call on Harry who would take one look at the pile of snow and say what he thought it should be, and then proceed to explain how to go about it.

The writer's house, right across the street from Harry and Doris' front window, received a lot of scrutiny form this creative neighbour. Whatever was done to the front of the house had to receive approval from Harry. *"After all,"* he would say, *"we are the ones that have to look at it all the time, not you."* In fact, when a proposed plan for a facelift for the front of the house was suggested to Harry, he insisted that we leave it to him. Sure enough a couple of days later, he delivered a watercolour drawing and with no discussion, explanation or suggestion of compromise said, *"Here, do this."* And that is what was done, no matter that it had little to do with the original thoughts of the owner. It was a delight.

Harry Lidstone's version (demand, that is) of how the front of our house at 44 Aubrey Street must appear after our alterations. The bottom yellow and the cedar shakes brown; no discussion allowed!

In front of the Lidstones house there stood a huge Manitoba Maple tree - a species that grows very rapidly - and Harry and Doris were forever trimming and cutting it back, usually to little avail because within a year or two it would again cover their front yard. One of those cutbacks was so severe that all that remained was a stump about 8 or 9 feet high. Why leave a stump? No-one ever asked but we suspected that Harry with his keen artistic ability had a plan, although for years it a remained a stump until shoots grew up from the roots to restore it to its former glory years later and as it still remains in 2013. Nothing could kill that tree.

Whether or not he had a long term plan to carve it into something will never be known, but what he did do was to wind coloured lights around it as a Christmas decoration. Curiously, although Harry may have had this in mind all along, the lights stayed on the stump all year long and without fail, if Harry heard that one of the kids from the street had won some kind of trophy, when they arrived home, usually late at night, the lights on the stump would be glowing like a beacon.

It wasn't like they were brilliant lights; it was just the thought that Harry and Doris were telling the world that an *"Aubreyite"* had done good. The kids absolutely loved it. When the Bracebridge Midget hockey team won an all-Ontario championship and were riding around Town on the top of a fire engine, they insisted on driving along Aubrey Street so they could see Harry's tree and know that he was celebrating the victory with them. Like Ding Bell telling the rest of us that *"you can't have grass and kids too"* and that *"home plate and first base should never be near a window,"* it was those little things that occurred on ***AUBREY STREET*** that will remain forever in the minds of those who grew up there.

Growing up in Ufford where a family car was unheard of and 15 miles from Bracebridge, the writer hardly ever got to see the glories of the big town. With one exception; a neighbour liked going to hockey games and occasionally, feeling sorry for those without that opportunity, would stop and ask if I wanted to go to see a Bracebridge Bears hockey game. Well, for a kid that had tried to learn how to skate on yellow ice in front of our stable and in skates that were a cast off from some adult, going to a Bears game was like a dream come true. When my grandparents scratched around trying to find a few coins for my admittance fee, our neighbour would usually speak up say not to worry about that because they would pay my way into the game. I will never forget that.

Arriving at this huge building and seeing so many people were unforgettable experiences. Once inside, the crush of people became incredible, compared to what I was used to in Ufford. The seats were filled and the walking area around the arena was so congested with fans that I couldn't get near the railing to see the ice surface. Desperately, I put my hands in the form of a wedge and shoved my way between adults until I came to the front of the standing area. There it was! Brilliant white ice and the Bracebridge Bears skating from their dressing room. The crowd went wild and I could hardly believe my eyes.

I cannot recall the score of the game because that was not what was important. It was all about being there and seeing this wonderful new world. One thing I do remember was hearing those around me talk about one of the players, Turk Lees. The details of the game were lost to me for the most part, but many years later, in 1967 when my wife and I moved onto ***AUBREY STREET*** our neighbours across the street were Turk and Wilda Lees. It was Turk (Noel - he was born on December 25th) who started the winter snow sculpture activity and after a while we became involved in Minor Hockey where we spent several years coaching. To my surprise, I found that Turk was not that much older than I, meaning that when I was clutching the steel rail around the arena at 12 or 13 years of age watching the Bears, he was a *very* young member of the Bracebridge Bears Intermediate Hockey Team.

Turk and Wilda Lees were farmers at heart, proven in time by their building a new home on an acreage south of Bracebridge. On *Aubrey Street* though, the size of the lots and questionable soil conditions greatly limited gardening opportunities. Nevertheless, with the hope of getting into the lucrative apple growing industry, they planted two apple trees in their front lawn. With great expectation they nurtured the little trees carefully, pruning them in accordance with established practices, but after 2 or 3 years – nothing. No apples. Every spring was greeted with excitement; maybe this would be the year they thought, but none appeared.

The opportunity was too good to pass up, so neighbours Harry Lidstone and Ralph Young purchased a basket of nice red apples, and in the dark of night, proceeded to tie them onto the branches of the apple trees. It was a glorious and exciting sight the next morning, albeit short lived. It created a lot of laughs but Turk and Wilda could finally say they had apples on their apple trees, no matter how they got there.

Many simple situations on *Aubrey Street* turned into memorable events. On one occasion when the writer was visiting Turk Lees across the street enjoying a cold beverage in the driveway, a stray cat jumped onto the back deck of Turks car. It was shooed off immediately but it persisted and kept jumping back onto what it considered a nice warm place to rest. So, aware that one of the neighbours, Don Thur up the street, had a particular dislike for cats, we decided we would carry it to his place and leave it with him, so to speak. Turk picked it up and was stroking it nicely as we strolled up the street. The cat however, detected that something was wrong and as we approached the Thur house it became increasingly agitated to the point that it was clawing Turks arms and hands with its razor sharp claws.

By the time we arrived at our destination Turk had the cat clutched in a bear hug, desperately trying to avoid being scarred for life, so we quickly opened the door and threw the cat inside. Then we stood back and waited for the fireworks. It didn't take long. There were shouts and screams; Don was running around trying to find his gun and shells, his wife Carol was yelling for help, and the terrified cat, desperate to get out of the house, burst through the screen on the door and made its escape. It had to be the funniest spectacle of the year, even though Turk and I received a blast of comments clearly indicating that the Thur family didn't appreciate the humour of our prank nearly as much as we did. It was just another Sunday afternoon on *AUBREY STREET.*

Aubrey Street at its best! Ralph Young, Tom Robinson, Ken Veitch and Turk Lees below the falls on the Muskoka River bagging smelts for a late night snack. Photo by a mutual friend Aldyn Clark

Every spring for a number of years the Muskoka River would be clogged with smelts, a 5 or 6 inch long fish that when dipped in a flour and egg batter and deep fried or fried in butter were delicious to eat. One of the best places to catch them was along the shore of Bracebridge Bay Park. A call that the smelts were running would be a cue for the *AUBREY STREET* guys to dig out their nets and buckets and, always late at night, head for the river. The smelts would be so thick along the shore around midnight they looked like a dense grey cloud moving in the water. We would all get a supply that we would enjoy over the next few days, but on the night shown here we decided to have a mini-banquet, prompting Ralph Young to suggest that we meet at his place where he felt his endearing wife Ida would prepare the feast that we all had in mind. However, when we arrived there, Ida was upstairs in bed, understandably because it was late at night, so we decided to do the cooking ourselves. Ralph's voice was always loud, but on this occasion it seemed unusually loud, saying, *"How many eggs do you think we need, six, eight? What should we use for a frying pan, any ideas?"* It didn't take long before we heard Ida's determined footsteps pounding down the stairs, demanding loudly, *"You guys get out of my kitchen, I'll cook the smelts!"*

When the writer's wife Sharon was ready to head to the hospital to deliver our third child, our daughter Debra, Mary Robinson came to our house at 44 Aubrey to watch over our two boys Ken Jr. and Dave while I went with Sharon. Debra was born around 3:00 am and when everything settled down and all were resting, around 4:30 AM I slipped home so Mary could return home to her family up the street. When I walked in the door the phone was ringing and it was Harry Lidstone across the street. Knowing I had taken Sharon to the hospital he had waited up so he could call and make sure everything was all right. A few days later when we brought Debra home, sitting on the front steps of our house patiently waiting to see the new baby, were Cathy Lees, Warren Rowe and Carolyn Bell. How could neighbours be more caring than that!

With the close friendships that had developed in the **AUBREY STREET** community since that magic year of 1949, it was inevitable that reunions would be organized. The first was held in 1975 in recognition of the 100th Anniversary of the incorporation of the municipality of Bracebridge. The second was in 1987, prompted by the success of the first. The street was closed by bylaw of the Town Council for the purpose of the reunion in both of those years. Ted Boyer and Harry Lidstone created maps showing every lot on the street and every family that had ever lived there, canvases were spread over front yards, games organized for the children, parades, picnic tables covered with snacks, etc. A feature of the day was a rope tied to hydro poles on opposite sides of the street from which hung diapers, each with a letter painted on them that spelled ***AUBREY STREET.***

There are lots of stories about hi-jinks on the street, many that would be improper to include here and are better left in the memories of the participants. There were road hockey games that often resulted in pieces of car grills lying in driveways, kids coming home puzzled because they saw two dogs ***"stuck"*** together, Ralph Young's laughter echoing from their front porch, Ida Young's faithful bicycle, Wally Rowe's bread truck starting up at 4:00 am as he started his day's work, Gord Lefebvre's determination to be independent in spite of having lost a leg in a land mine explosion in WW 2, and his friend from Newfoundland that slept all night in the wet grass in his backyard after drinking someone's home brew.

It just went on and on. Joseph Cooper and Aubrey White would have been proud. I think.

44. THE "TOWN" HALL WAS REALLY THE "VILLAGE" HALL…

Whatever the reason, even though Bracebridge was a *Village* municipality, designated as such in 1875 and long before it attained *Town* status in 1887, all reference to a building to accommodate staff to administer municipal business was referred to as the ***TOWN HALL***. In 1880 William Duffus submitted a design for a municipal building and it was accepted by the Municipal Council. Tenders were submitted for the construction, but the Village Council was so shocked at the high prices submitted by the bidders they amended the plans and called for new tenders. It doesn't sound like much now but the adjustment saved them $690.00 which made them happy and they entered into a contract with Charles Storey to build the ***Town Hall*** building at a cost of $3,275.00.

It was a glorious building for its day in spite of there being a number of problems that arose during its construction. Village Clerk James Boyer on a number of occasions had to settle disputes, finally taking action against Storey, and Council had to call tenders again to have the work completed. After paying Storey $2,000.00 Council contracted with Neil Livingstone to complete the work at a cost of $1,285.00.

There were many who were proud of this grand new ***TOWN HALL,*** especially when they knew the surrounding townships ran their affairs from the kitchen table of whoever was appointed the Clerk at the time, but there were also those who despaired at the extravagance of the Council. They need not have been so concerned; the building served the community for 76 years with dignity.

I guess some things never change. Closely resembling present day complaints about Town facilities being moved to the perimeter of the business area, it is quite likely there were those in the 1880s that would have preferred to have the ***TOWN HALL*** in the middle of the thriving downtown rather than on Dominion Street; it was just too far *out of town* on Dominion Street. However, it did give rise to another important part of our heritage that is still enjoyed today; the dignified Chancery Lane that was created right along the side of the *TOWN HALL* and connected Dominion Street with Manitoba Street as more fully described in **Chapter 27. CHANCERY LANE…**

Still on display in 2013 at the Bracebridge Municipal Office is this watercolour painting of the first Town Hall built in 1881. It was presented to the Town of Bracebridge by Robert J. Boyer as a gift on its Centennial in 1975. James Boyer, Robert Boyer's grandfather was the Village Clerk at the time and no doubt played an integral part in the supervision of its construction.

As with many of the *"firsts"* for Muskoka that happened in Bracebridge, the *TOWN HALL* that opened in 1881 was ahead of its time. It was a classy structure that prompted other agencies, when they were building their facilities, to copy its example. The School Board built the Bracebridge Public School at about the same time, the Provincial Government built the Courthouse also on Dominion Street in 1900 and the Government of Canada built their new Federal Building and Post Office in 1914. They were all attractive architectural achievements.

The sections that housed the municipal office, council chamber, police office and fire department were wonderfully functional compared with anything that had ever existed previously. It included holding cells and a nice accommodation for Rock and Tom, the two faithful horses that pulled the fire pumper but the endearing feature of the TOWN HALL was the upstairs auditorium. It was acoustically excellent, according to those who used it, with a large stage and front curtain that bore a painting of Windsor Castle; another indication of the connection between the residents of the area and Great Britain.

The seating facilities were humble by today's standards consisting of long moveable benches and the isles were identified (and adjusted as necessary) by drawing lines on the floor with chalk. Across the back of the hall and behind the main seating area was a slightly raised section of seats similar to a balcony. It was reserved for what was described as *"…enthusiastic and uninhibited drama critics."* Somewhat disrespectfully, those who sat in this area were called *"The Gods"* by those who occupied the regular seating area of the theatre, no doubt reflecting the resentment they felt for those who thought they were better than everyone else.

In *A Good Town Grew Here,* it is reported that by 1908 the auditorium was becoming a *"..dingy and unattractive place…"* and many were advocating a new auditorium for the town. Nevertheless, a number of premier events continued to be held there. It also describes its condition in 1924 stating, *"The upper room and stairs of the Town Hall were renovated by Mr. Will Adamson; we now had opera seating and could reserve for 228."* There is no explanation of how they arranged the seats in order to accommodate an audience that large. Later it reports that in 1957, *"The Town Hall auditorium got new seats for $4.00 each from the company demolishing Shea's Theatre in Toronto. Nelson A. Goltz was in charge of installation."*

It would be nearly impossible to list all the events and functions that took place in the *TOWN HALL* auditorium during its 76 years of existence. They are well described in great detail in the numerous books written on our history. A synopsis of them would include: political party rallies, ratepayers meeting, musicals, local groups meetings, receptions for dignitaries, church special events, drama societies plays, traveling shows, minstrel performances, comedians, early *"moving picture shows",* Bracebridge Citizen's Band performances, lectures, charity balls, performances by the Royal Scots Concert Co., and in 1904 a special reception was held for a recital by Pauline Johnson. It's unfortunate that present day videotaping wasn't available to record all of that; it would have been a delight to see.

Bracebridge Firefighters struggle to control the devastating fire that destroyed the historic 1881 Town Hall on December 13, 1957

To the dismay of all, on the bitter cold night of December 13, 1957, something unknown ignited a fire in the basement of this famous building. It started in late afternoon and, in spite of all attempts, eventually engulfed the entire building. Lyle Cathcart, a town councillor at the time, Dr. R.J. Dodds and others, removed the leather bound elegant council chamber chairs, table and antique clock just in time to avoid the fire and they still remain in use at the ***TOWN HALL*** of 2013.

Unfortunate that after getting those nice comfortable chairs from the Shea's Theatre in Toronto that replaced those miserable wooden benches, few got to use them because they were lost in the fire just a few months later.

45. VIOLA (HUGGARD) MACMILLAN...

During the early 1960's I held the position of Assistant Accountant at the Bloor and Yonge Branch of the Bank of Nova Scotia in Toronto; a large, busy office that boasted about having one of the largest client bases in all of Toronto.

One of my duties there involved buying and selling stocks and bonds for clients, an active job that carried a lot of responsibility and demanded great concentration; a mistake could cost thousands of dollars in damages. One day in midafternoon, the branch manager approached my desk with two well-dressed men in tow that he introduced as fraud squad investigators from the Ontario Provincial Police. There was nothing new about having police drop into the bank; they were constantly trying to chase down suspected scammers, forgers and the like. But these two, in their undercover role, were a cut above the normal uniformed officers we had seen in the past.

The two officers took a seat in front of my desk and, after the usual recording of my name, position, duties, etc., asked if I had done any trading for clients in the shares of a company called Windfall Oils and Mines. I replied that I processed dozens of orders each day and could not recall processing anything for that or any other company in particular, so I suggested we check through a few days entries. To their delight (and my surprise) there were dozens of purchases and sales of Windfall shares and the officers recorded the details of every one.

After we had finished, I asked them what this investigation was all about and they explained that they were considering laying charges against certain officers of the company for fraudulent business practices, in particular *Viola MacMillan*. Immediately I said, *"You mean Viola Huggard?"*; a blank look crossed their faces and they responded *"Who?"* I went on to explain that *Viola MacMillan's* maiden name was Huggard, she had grown up near the area of Ufford where I came from and that my father knew her and her family well. Suddenly the discussion took a funny turn, their eyes narrowed and one of them said *"Was your father ever involved in mining?"* Happily, I was able to assure them that my father was involved in a lot of things but mining wasn't one of them. I suspect I saved him from being subjected to a lengthy interview with the authorities although I am sure they would have enjoyed traveling to Muskoka as part of their investigation.

Viola (Huggard) MacMillan was born in 1903, one of the 15 children of Mr. & Mrs. Thos. Huggard, an impoverished family that operated a pioneer farm northwest of Bracebridge on the north side of the Dee River which forms part of the watershed feeding Lake Rosseau. It is reported that she was actually born *"Violet"* but chose to become known as *"Viola"* for reasons that are not stated.

Her mother died at a young age when Viola was just a teenager. One can imagine the tough times that ensued with 15 children to be fed and a farm to operate; made more difficult when a number of her older brothers enlisted in the Canadian Armed Forces in World War 1. Viola had to quit school and help her father as best she could and in her spare time, if there was any, worked as a maid at Windermere House and other resorts in Windermere. In the book, *Women Who Made a Difference,* in a chapter dedicated to her, it is stated that she would peer through the resort windows to observe the lavish lifestyle of the rich people of society. Although her income had to be very limited, she managed to gather up enough money to pay the tuition for a secretarial course that had been a childhood dream and a move that would eventually lead her to an incredible career.

Following the end of World War 1 she visited a brother who worked at a silver mine operation in Cobalt, Ontario who took her on a tour of one of the mineshafts. She had to dress as a young man because a woman in a mineshaft in those days was considered a bad omen. It was then and there that she decided she would work in the mining industry for the rest of her life. No doubt she fell in love with all that wealth hidden in the ground, just waiting to be discovered.

In 1923 she married George MacMillan, a man already deeply involved with the mining industry. Except for the time she spent working with Federal and Provincial governments in World War 2, she would work where she could in secretarial positions in the winter but with her husband head for northern Ontario every summer searching for gold. She became an expert at identifying potential mineral deposits, staked claims all across Canada and founded a number of mining companies to develop her discoveries. It very quickly became her life.

Her husband has been quoted as saying that her ability always amazed him and that he would just follow along behind her. He said that she was as comfortable and as much at home sleeping in an old tent in the wilderness as she was in the Royal York Hotel in Toronto.

As successful as she was in the industry, her greatest achievement came through her involvement with the Prospectors and Developers Association of Canada. It was during the difficult years of World War 2 that she and her husband got involved as leaders of that organization, Viola eventually becoming President. At that time the membership consisted of around 100, mostly local people in the mining region of Timmins, Ontario. Through her efforts it became a classy, professional and influential organization and by the time she retired as President in 1966 it had an international reputation and a membership in excess of 4000. She was so loved by the members that each year when she opened the annual meeting they all rose to their feet and sang **"Let Me Call You Sweetheart"**.

In contrast to her popularity and status in the industry, in the 1960s she was the subject of an investigation by authorities on complaints of improper reporting on core samples by her company Windfall Oils and Mines. It was during that investigation that I was re-introduced to the adventures of Viola Huggard.

Although those allegations were found to be baseless, she did run afoul of the law because of a series of convoluted trading of shares of that same company by other companies also controlled by her. Although she pleaded that she didn't know she was doing anything wrong, she was convicted of stock manipulation and sentenced to eight months in prison, of which she only spent a few weeks. She said it was an experience that she would highly recommend.

She was later granted a pardon by the federal government and went back into the mining business but in a greatly diminished way. She donated 1.5 million dollars to the Canadian Museum of Nature to assist in the purchase of one of the world's most famous mineral collections which was placed in an area in the museum designated the **"Viola MacMillan Mineral Gallery"** in her honour. Because of her enormous contribution to the success and growth of the industry in Canada she was appointed a Member of the Order of Canada and the Canadian Mining Hall of Fame in 1993.

Viola didn't need any trumped up help from some government funded support group to find her identity. She knew where she was going and how to get there from the very start.

Viola (Huggard) MacMillan was not a Bracebridge native. She was born and grew up nearby in the tiny settlement of Dee Bank in Watt Ward of the Township of Muskoka Lakes, not far from the Village of Windermere. She and the family were often in Bracebridge for the usual reasons those from surrounding townships gravitated to the business centre of their area. The Town of Bracebridge archives contains a record of her achievements but she has never been recognized by those in charge of the affairs of the Township of Muskoka Lakes, in spite of the fact that this native daughter became a national hero to thousands, been honoured with the prestigious Order of Canada and a member of the Canadian Mining Hall of Fame.

What would it take to recognize her incredible success by establishing a memorial on the homestead of her birth? A place where she spent those difficult, formative years of her life dreaming of that great future which she knew was hers.

It is another sad reminder how quickly great people and events of the past can be forgotten.

46. ARNOTTS NURSING HOME/GOGGINS PRIVATE HOSPITAL?...

How downtown Bracebridge's beautiful Memorial Park and its bandstand came in to being is well described in **Chapter 32. Memorial Park...** but for the purpose of this chapter on hospital services and the role the park played in acquiring them the following summary is provided. There was a movement to create something as a lasting memorial to those from Bracebridge and area who served their country in World War 1 and a replacement of the bandstand in the park was proposed. The veterans themselves stepped in at that point and suggested that any such memorial should be something more significant and strongly supported the establishment of a hospital, a badly needed facility in the growing community. No-one knew the value of a hospital like the veterans of that bitter blood bath with Germany.

The Bracebridge Municipal Council agreed and the Bracebridge Memorial Hospital, to be operated as a *"Red Cross Outpost Hospital"*, was born. A community hospital had been proposed previously by the Board of Trade and in 1914 Council held a referendum to authorize such an expenditure of public funds for this purpose but the proposal was defeated 136 to 130. *After* the Great War everyone knew how important a hospital was in the community and the project proceeded.

Prior to that, care for the sick had been provided by a number of care-givers in their personal residences; a number specializing in delivering babies. The one best known, endured the longest and was best equipped was that of Mary Ann (Rutherford) Arnott, which even included an operating room. It was located on the northeast corner of the intersection of MacDonald Street and Manitoba Street; in 2013 the location of the Kentucky Fried Chicken restaurant. Before that it was Les Rosewarne's Ford automobile dealership, operating from the same building as the private hospital. It was variably referred to as Arnotts Nursing Home and after the death of her husband and remarriage to William Goggin, as Goggins Private Hospital. It is mentioned in a number of books and articles on Bracebridge, one of the best descriptions being that written by Patricia Boyer in her booklet ***LOOKING AT OUR CENTURY***.

Mary Ann (Rutherford) Arnott/Goggin was stated to be a *"practical"* nurse and eventually had the assistance of trained staff to care for patients; further enhanced to a great extent by the addition of her daughter Fanny Arnott who became a Registered Nurse while working at Toronto Western Hospital and who returned to work with her mother serving the people of the Bracebridge area. Fanny shared the same determination and work ethic as her mother and to those who received their care they seemed like angels from heaven.

When the Bracebridge Memorial Hospital was opened in 1928, Fanny Arnott was appointed the first administrator according to some sources, as the first superintendent of nurses in others. Her mother died in 1933 and Fanny, who married William Hare in later life, died in1975. This mother and daughter team earned the right to be recognized and acknowledged as pioneers in providing care for the sick of Muskoka.

47. BRACEBRIDGE'S ABANDONED BABY…

To say this event was the talk of the town would be a colossal understatement. The speculation and yes, gossip, went on for decades. It all happened in 1948, when I was an eight year old riding my hand-me-down bike around Ufford, but when I came to work for the Town of Bracebridge in 1966 it was still a topic of conversation. Even then there remained strong opinions and suspicion about the circumstances; to quote a resident of Bracebridge of that era it was said, *"It was just a matter of the chickens coming home to roost"*, whatever that meant, and that was the end of the discussion.

It was in the middle of the night at a house on Woodchester Avenue where a lady claimed that she was woken by the cries of a baby and on investigation found a basket sitting on her front step and inside it, a baby boy. It was obvious that it was not a newborn, in fact it was estimated later that it was close to 3 months old and had been reasonably well cared for. So well in fact, that included in the basket were some supplies to provide for the immediate needs of the child.

There was no note or explanation provided and no evidence to indicate where the baby came from or why it ended up on the front step of a house in Bracebridge. Was the house picked at random? Was it a targeted house? Maybe someone knew that those who lived there would see that their baby received proper care. So many unknowns -no wonder speculation was rampant, fueled no doubt by what appeared to be a half-hearted effort by the authorities to take any enthusiastic action to solve the mystery.

The fact that the baby seemed well cared for and provisions supplied for its continuing maintenance clearly indicated that someone really cared about it; totally different than the tiny newborn baby strangled by a shoelace that was found in a garbage dump in Draper Township many years later in 1967. In that case there was an intense investigation by the authorities and rightfully so, but the search for the guilty party proved fruitless. However, in recent years the police received a message from a lady in western Canada, perhaps ridden with guilt for her actions, who confessed to that murder. The remains of the baby was exhumed and reburied in British Columbia. It was established that the pregnancy was the result of incest and whether or not charges were laid is unknown.

In a similar event, in 2010 an elderly lady went to the police and reported that when she was a young girl she witnessed a baby being buried in the yard of a house in Fraserburg. The police, with the woman, toured that community until she spotted the property where she felt the burial had occurred. The permission of the owner was secured and after a number of excavations the police did discover skeletal remains. There was no further action taken that was made public.

BRACEBRIDGE'S ABANDONED BABY was taken into the care of the Children's Aid Society and was eventually adopted by a family in the Niagara Peninsula who raised the child as their own. He grew up knowing he was adopted but as mid-life approached he couldn't help puzzling about his heritage. Through the appropriate channels, he found to his amazement (and that of his adopting parents), that as a baby he was found on the steps of that house on Woodchester Avenue in Bracebridge.

In spite of a dedicated effort that included the services of a private investigator, all attempts to establish his parentage failed to provide the slightest information of who it was that gently laid him on that front step, no doubt accompanied with the fervent prayer that the child's cries would alert the household that a very important gift was awaiting discovery.

48. GEORGE RICHARDSON (VC)...

Few will have ever heard of George Richardson. He was only in Muskoka for a short period of time (roughly 20 plus years during the 1880s and 1890s) but it is the story of his life and the fact that he *was* here and served his community that encouraged me to include him in this book. I had heard of him before but came to know his story a lot better through my friend Mark Boyes who had retired back to his home village of Vankoughnet after a distinguished career in dentistry and as a professor with the University of Toronto. I was honoured to have assisted Mark in a minor capacity in his determined effort to get the Ontario Government to erect a memorial plaque in the Vankoughnet Village Park commemorating Richardson's life. Mark's nephew Graydon Boyes assisted me in this chapter by refreshing my memory regarding some of the noted events.

Richardson was born in Ireland in 1831 and immigrated to Canada in the 1860s. He purchased a farm in Oakley Township near the community of Vankoughnet where he held numerous township offices including Reeve in 1895 to 1896 and participated in social events there. The most significant part of his life however, occurred before he arrived in Canada.

He served with the British Army as a private in the *34th Regiment of Foot* during the Indian mutiny of 1857 to 1859 where in one particular battle, in spite of being severely wounded, he succeeded in defeating a heavily armed rebel Indian soldier. Reportedly a number of senior officers were saved from harm because of his bravery. In recognition of his valor he was the Irish recipient of the Victoria Cross, the highest and most prestigious award for gallantry in the face of an enemy that can be awarded to British and Commonwealth forces. He was only 27 years old.

After arriving in Canada he joined the Canadian Army, rising to the rank of sergeant. For a number of years his regiment held reunions which took place on the Canadian National Exhibition grounds in Toronto. Part of each reunion included a parade around the square where his fellow soldiers would carry Richardson on their shoulders as a token of their great respect, showing that they had not forgotten his bravery.

In a strange turn of events, and unknown to either of them, there was another veteran of the Indian Mutiny conflict besides Richardson that had retired to the Vankoughnet area of Oakley Township. It was one Capt. Hornal (no first name is stated) who was mentioned by George Boyer in *Early Days in Muskoka* as an early resident of that township. Interestingly, George Richardson is also mentioned in the same paragraph as Hornal for the same reason. It is not stated whether or not Hornal was nearby when Richardson captured the rebel soldier but he was certainly aware of his heroics. On what must have been an historic event, they were both in attendance at a social function held in the Loyal Orange Lodge building in Vankoughnet when Hornal spotted Richardson across the room and shouted out, **"Richardson! Richardson! Richardson! Is it really you Richardson?"** It must have been quite a reunion.

George Richardson and his wife left Muskoka around 1900 and relocated to northern Ontario where misfortune struck a disastrous blow. In his absence their house caught fire and took the life of his wife. He eventually moved back to London Ontario where he died in 1923.

49. HOWARD VINCENT (DCM)…

Every year at the eleventh hour of the eleventh day of the eleventh month all of Canada pauses to reflect on those who served our country in the armed services in conflicts all over the world. Sadly, thousands of young men died; their names inscribed on stately monuments erected in their honour so that their efforts may never be forgotten by those of us who remain. It is a tragedy most of us will never be able to comprehend.

Those who died no doubt experienced unimaginable brutality, pain and suffering. No doubt also that they showed courage and character in battle; hard as that may have been in the wretched conditions of the battlefield. Their personal stories will never be told. There were others who had a similar experience in battle but for reasons they themselves would never understand, survived bitter death and their stories can be told. They have given us a valuable insight into the dark terror of conflict.

Their experiences are exemplified in the story of George Richardson as set out in the previous chapter and of **Howard Vincent (DCM)** in this chapter; the first Bracebridge resident to enlist for service in the Canadian Army at the start of World War 1.

Howard was one of the nine children of Thomas Ray and Suzan (Emerick) Vincent, and, while it is generally noted that he was a native of Bracebridge, Howard was actually born in the community of Fesserton, Simcoe County on August 21st, 1883. The family moved to Bracebridge around 1894 when he was eleven years old. They were a hardy bunch as most settlers to Muskoka had to be in that era and stories abound about their activities. Of the seven brothers, three served in the Canadian armed services in World War 1.

There have been volumes written about the horror of the battlefields of World War 1 and Howard Vincent's experience there is a good example of it. He enlisted at Bracebridge on August 20, 1914 and was a member of the 1st Battalion 1st Infantry Brigade Machine Gun Section of the Canadian Expeditionary Force. He was involved from the very start of the Canadian participation in that conflict. There were a number of different battles that comprised the assault on German troops at Ypres, Belgium and Vincent was there for the Battle of Passchendaele otherwise designated as the 3rd Battle of Ypres. In describing the conditions there he said the soldiers had to wade through mud to their knees, a situation they had to endure for days without rest, constantly being ordered to advance. What worsened the situation was that they could not lay down because if they did they would sink into mud; the only method of rest they could find was to sit with their feet on the firm ground under the mud and keep their weight on the calves of their legs.

Howard Vincent (DCM)

He survived many encounters with the enemy in the Battle of Passchendaele but it was the Battle of Givenchy that ended his active combat. His action there, for which he was awarded the *Distinguished Conduct Medal*, is recorded in **"THE OFFICIAL STORY OF THE CANADIAN EXPEDITIONARY FORCE"** as cited by Sir Max Aitken, (a war correspondent later to become noted publisher Lord Beaverbrook), where it describes the fighting there in June 1915 as follows:

"Lieut. F.W. Campbell, with two machine guns, had advanced in the rear of Captain Wilkinson's company. The entire crew of one gun was killed or wounded in the advance, but a portion of the other crew gained the enemy's front trench and then advanced along the trench in the direction of "Stony Mountain". The advance was most difficult and although subjected to constant, heavy rifle and machine-gun fire, the bombers led the way until further advance was impossible owing to a barricade across the trench…. The machine-gun crew that reached the trench was reduced to Lieut. Campbell and Private Howard Vincent (a lumberjack from Bracebridge, Ontario), the machine-gun and the tripod. In default of a base, Lieut. Campbell set up the machine-gun on the broad back of Private Vincent and fired continuously. Afterwards, during the retreat, German bombers entered the trench and Lieut. Campbell fell wounded. Private Vincent, then cut away the cartridge belt, and abandoning the tripod, dragged the gun away to safety because it was too hot to handle. Lieut. Campbell crawled out of the enemy trench and was carried into our trench in a dying condition by Sgt.-Major Owen. Those of them who knew Howard in post-war days remember that he proudly cherished the Distinguished Conduct Medal that he had so well deserved and that he also wore a heavy supporting cast from his armpit to his hips."

Well deserved indeed. A local newspaper article in 1916 gives another account of the action stating that the machine gun was kept going only by Vincent holding it on a plank on his back and while making his way back to the allied lines dragging his machine-gun, encountered two German soldiers whom he promptly took prisoner.

Another version of the action was contained in a 1984 Readers Digest article, **THE GAS OF YPRES, THE MUD OF PASSCHENDAELE**, a condensed version of *"MY GRANDFATHER'S WAR"* by William D. Mathieson. It is a dramatic, personal, firsthand view of the combat, reading in part,

"Gallant charges across no-mans-land form the popular notion of World War 1. At 9:15 a.m. on July 1st, 1916, for instance, the Royal Newfoundland Regiment went over the top to capture objectives a few hundred yards away. By 9:45 a.m., the Newfoundlanders were virtually annihilated. All the 26 officers and nearly 700 men were killed or wounded".

"I turn my head to the right. On his hands and knees I see Sergeant Vincent, a broad-backed lumberjack, a magnificent specimen of a man. On his back is the barrel of a machine gun. The tripod has been lost and Vincent is taking its place. Lieutenant Campbell is firing the gun. It is only a fleeting glance and once more my face is turned to the front as we go on, slashing, hacking and stabbing. I've stopped thinking of the Empire, the Allies, the glory of Canada, or my buddies. I'm thinking only of myself".

The misery of war couldn't be better described than that. It is a passage to remember when we meet each November in recognition of those who served our country in world conflicts.

A 1917 artist conception sketch by Frank Dadd of the scene where Howard Vincent supported the machine gun on his back while Sergeant F.W. Campbell kept the enemy at bay.

As a result of that encounter, Vincent was badly injured but because of the fury of the battle he was impervious to his wounds. Incredibly, after he captured the two German soldiers and found his way back to the Allied lines it was some time before superior officers recognized that he was wounded. In due time he was sent to a military hospital; eventually spending eleven months in a hospital in

England. On his return to Bracebridge in 1916, a reception was held for him and two other returning officers, Percy Cutler and Fred Wright; no doubt they had similar experiences to relate.

Each received a token $50.00 cheque, but the valor and bravery they exhibited in battle was beyond value.

Howard Vincent was the recipient of a number of medals for service in the Canadian Armed Service. Less its decorative ribbon, the above is his Distinguished Conduct Medal.

The Toronto Globe and Mail noted the death of a *"...well-known local resident..." Howard Vincent* on May 16th, 1939 as a result of a heart attack at the age of 58. He had served as a conductor for the Toronto Transportation Commission for many years.

Armed conflicts have produced many such stories of courage in the face of terror; it also produced many tales of sadness, suffering and death. Bill and Agnes Brazier of Bracebridge faced the horrors of war when seven of their sons enlisted in the armed service in World War 2. Charles, Robert, George, Victor, Percy, Edward and Buster (Bus) Brazier were all in combat overseas and, incredibly, all returned safely at the end of the war. While they were happy to see them home, the family never said much about it; they knew that many Bracebridge families had sons that served overseas and did not return. In 2012 a new children's playground in Annie Williams Memorial Park was named in honour of the Brazier family in recognition of their service to their country.

As horrid as the conditions were on the front lines of battle where death and suffering were constant companions, just as horrid were the conditions experienced by the thousands of people that were jammed into boxcars and starved in concentration camps. Few survived the brutality but those that did have been able to relate the stark reality of their experience in vivid detail.

Lest we forget!

50. ORGANIZATIONS WE HAVE KNOWN…

The municipal assessment roles of the 1800s provide interesting information on the earliest of Bracebridge residents. They include ownership of property, address, status in life, dog ownership, annual income, etc., but there is one thing of particular interest, that is the age of those listed as owning or otherwise occupying property. Almost every assessment role tells a story about the youthfulness of the population. Ages in the 20s and 30s dominate and ages of 60 plus are rare, no doubt reflecting the fact that it took young people with the stamina and strength of youth to develop the land.

They worked hard to create their new home, but they did not forget their homeland, as evidenced by the names of their hotels and businesses that so often reflect a British heritage. The same allegiance applied to the numerous community organizations that became part of the fabric of the small community and, while some quickly faded into obscurity, others continued to be part of Bracebridge society for many years. Those that disappeared may have amalgamated with associated organizations in other parts of Muskoka, reappeared under a new name or merged with others having similar objectives.

Our ancestors were enthusiastic about socializing and working together for a common cause, much more so it would seem, than in present society. The percentage of the population participating in local organizations was much higher than today; many belonging to two or more such community groups. As you read about the organizations that thrived in Bracebridge over the years, remember they were formed from a very tiny number of residents compared to that of 2013.

In his column **COMMENTS** in the Bracebridge Gazette of February 15, 1945 Redmond Thomas wrote, *"Why has membership in fraternal societies suffered such a decline in popular appeal?"* No doubt those returning from the armed services following the end of World War 2 helped the membership of many of the existing groups, and the war itself gave rise to a number of valuable organizations (mostly women) whose sole objective was to assemble aid packages containing items of necessity for those involved in that conflict. For the most part they faded away following the end of the war. It remains however, that we do not participate in local organizations like we used to, even more obvious in 2013 than that noticed by Thomas in 1945, almost 70 years ago.

An example of some of those long forgotten, or almost forgotten, community organizations of our ancestors, in no particular order, is as follows…

SONS OF ENGLAND…

The **SONS OF ENGLAND** was started in Toronto, Ontario in 1874 by English emigrant G. B. Brooks for the purpose of helping English emigrants in need by providing them employment and promoting support for each other in business and trade.

The founder was moved to form the organization because he was embarrassed by the number of his countrymen that, in public view, had to rely on the charity of the food distribution system of the St. Georges Society for their daily bread. Good evidence of the need was illustrated by the fact that five of the seven original founding members of the organization were unemployed.

The movement spread rapidly, no doubt because of the large number of emigrants from England arriving in Canada in their search of a better future, and was established in Bracebridge sometime before 1892 evidenced by the fact they had a representative at the inaugural meeting of the Sons of Scotland which occurred in September of that year. It was designated *"Lancaster Lodge"* and like the Sons of Scotland, held annual events as well as occasional functions throughout the year. It would seem the Sons of England did not carry the exuberance of the Scots who had trainloads of members attend their annual celebrations; it is said the English youth did not get the same kind of patriotic training like those of Scotland. Likewise, while the Sons of Scotland offered membership to anyone, the English were more selective, not welcoming Welsh or Roman Catholics into their midst; reportedly because the Welsh were held in low esteem by the English, the Catholics because it was felt they put priests before country and would probably rather belong to a Catholic organization anyway.

The Sons of England met in the Harold Hall, located at the southeast corner of the Ontario and Dominion Street intersection, and had Harry S. Bowyer as its President for 5 terms as well as one as District Deputy. Such dedication earned him the affectionate title *"Father of Sons of England"*. There is evidence of there also being a branch of the order in the community of Rosseau. They played a large role in celebrating along with the rest of Muskoka in the Diamond Jubilee of Queen Victoria in 1897, at which time Jubilee Park in Bracebridge received its name.

They may have lacked a little finesse in planning because in 1901, when electric power was in its infancy in the community, they held an evening public event at the Town Hall and relied on the new fan-dangled electric lights to provide the necessary illumination. After extensive decorating of the hall, to their dismay the lights were so weak that nothing could be seen, and one of the attendees had to retire and bring in a gasoline chandelier that lit the hall nicely.

There is nothing written about when the organization faded into obscurity or what caused its demise but it could be that a more diversified society in the rapid growth of Bracebridge, was a contributing factor.

SONS OF SCOTLAND…

The **SONS OF SCOTLAND** is a fraternal organization founded in 1876 by Scottish emigrants whose purpose was to bring everyone together to celebrate Scottish heritage and culture, provide social activities for its members and encourage them to become involved in their community. It also provided financial products for its members and was open to all for membership, regardless of race, religion and age. While there was an element of internal secrets, their goal was, and still is, to be *Canada's Scottish family*.

A *Camp* (or Lodge) of the *Sons of Scotland* was instituted in Bracebridge through the sponsorship of members of that order from Toronto. It was christened on Sept. 23rd, 1892 and named *Alloway Kirk Camp*. The founding members were: James Dollar (Chief), John Thomson (Chieftain), H. D. McInnis, Peter Hutchison, Alex Barron, John Baird, Dr. Bridgland, John McKinnon, William Fraser, Robert Leishman, William Webster and James Campbell (Piper). Bracebridge was not the first in Muskoka to have such a *Camp* however, because at the 1892 christening ceremony Alfred Kay and Joseph Weir, members of *Auldreekie Camp* of the Sons of Scotland in Utterson, presented a humorous Scottish recitation and speech.

This was a very busy and active organization. It held St. Andrews Day banquets where the Queens Hotel would be decorated with streamers, tartans and mottoes and an annual Scotsman's Day (referred to as *Scotchman's* Day by Redmond Thomas in **Reminiscences**) event at Jubilee Park that continued well into the 1900s. Toasts, songs, sword dances, tossing the caber and other sporting events were all part of the celebration, including a road race to Falkenburg and back. Special trains bearing several hundred members would come from the Toronto area to participate with the estimated 2000 others that attended the annual extravaganza.

A big part of the Scotsman's Day was music and it must have been classic with such bands of renown like the Royal Scottish Concert Co., the 48th Highlander Band and the 61st Highlanders Band performing. It often included boat cruises on the *Priscilla, Nymph* and *Cherokee*. The celebration received such attention that most of the businesses in Bracebridge closed up for the day so that the owners and their staff could enjoy the festivities.

It is unclear when the Bracebridge section of this fine organization faded away but it could be said the present day Highland Games and Scottish dance events emulate the original enthusiastic celebration of our Heritage. Nevertheless, in its heyday it was a huge part of the community for many years.

TORONTO-BRACEBRIDGE OLD BOYS AND OLD GIRLS ASSOC…

In the early years when logging was thriving and saw mills buzzed throughout Muskoka, those involved in that massive industry were convinced that the district's seemingly endless forests would last forever. However, reality set in very quickly and in just a few decades the landscape was decimated of trees and logging faded as the dominating industry. It would take 100 years of growth before the forests would bear any semblance of the way they were in the beginning,

As the logging industry faded away a new economic opportunity appeared -tourism. The world grew to appreciate the clear blue water of Muskoka's lakes and rivers and recognized the area as a place of beauty to visit and enjoy. The resident population was delighted to have the opportunity to improve their economy by providing the required amenities and, as a result, as the late 1800s approached, privately built, beautiful resorts started to appear along the shores of the larger lakes in Muskoka. They were gorgeous and luxurious and the exciting trip on the big lake steamboats to get to them made it all that much better.

The many attributes of Muskoka were promoted far and wide. The fresh air was recognized by medical authorities as beneficial to those suffering from lung disorders to the extent that facilities were built to care for those afflicted with tuberculosis, *Muskoka Lamb* became a delicacy, and the Muskoka Lakes Navigation Company introduced the exciting **"100 Mile Cruise"**. Tourism flourished with an energy and longevity that far exceeded that of the logging industry, and Bracebridge was front and centre of it all.

It is no wonder then that great relations were created between those visiting Muskoka and the permanent residents. Evidence of that good relationship is shown in the founding of the ***TORONTO-BRACEBRIDGE OLD BOYS AND OLD GIRLS ASSOCIATION.***

This group held annual assemblies, always in off-season one would imagine, and the local newspaper in 1930 reported on the one held in that year as follows…

"The yearly assemblies in Toronto of the Toronto-Bracebridge Old Boys and Old Girls Association had become fixed institutions of good fellowship, and the 1930 gathering at the Prince George Hotel was a happy occasion with 207 in attendance. President Dr. J. H. Speers welcomed everyone in a splendid address. It was gratifying that Joseph Cooper, 91, of Bolton, was able to be present. He spoke briefly and told of his arrival in Bracebridge 70 years before, in 1860, when he felled a tree at North Falls to enable him to cross the river to the north side where he built the first cabin on the north bank."

The article goes on to say that the following also addressed the gathering- Peter A. Smith, George W. Ecclestone MPP, W. S. Ferguson, Rev. Percy M. Peacock, Harry Linney, Leslie Perkins, Mayor George F. Gibson and others and that a number of Bracebridge young people who were attending university in Toronto were also present.

A good relationship indeed. Unfortunately it eventually faded away for reasons that have never been identified.

BLACK HAND…

One would hardly expect any reference to the violent **BLACK HAND**, whose proper name according to internet sources was extended to include *"Unification or Death",* to appear in the written historical records of Bracebridge, but it was so. It was a military organization formed in 1901 by members of the Serbian Army whose objective was to unify all the territories in the area annexed by Austria-Hungary where there were significant Serb populations. It has long been suspected as a participant in assassinations and even accused of being one of the catalysts in fuelling World War 1.

It became a subject of discussion in 1910 in a murder that occurred in Medora Township, now part of the Township of Muskoka Lakes. The case against an accused individual was heard in the Provincial Courthouse in Bracebridge and is described in *A Good Town Grew Here*, no doubt based on newspaper reports of the day, as follows,

"… Joseph Pisanis, a bushworker in Medora, was charged with murder in the shooting and killing of another worker, Raphael Dominsalo. The jury found him not guilty, and a charge was laid under direction of Mr. Justice Riddle, against Sam Salvadore for shooting with intent to kill. The jury found him guilty with intent to do grievous bodily harm, and His Lordship's sentence was ten years imprisonment for Salvatore. Another worker also charged was found not guilty. The Black Hand organization appeared to have been involved, in that some of the workers were being persuaded to hand over money and join."

Did the **BLACK HAND** really have an operative in Muskoka? That would seem to be the case. Certainly those involved were of appropriate origin but there is no further reference in any other document to its presence; not surprising though because the organization demanded a strong adherence to the pledge of secrecy required of each member, so necessary because of its covert and violent activities.

ORDER OF THE KNIGHTS OF THE MACABEES...

The 19th century version in Canada of the **KNIGHTS OF THE MACABEES** (spelled Maccabees in the encyclopedia) began in London Ontario in 1878 as a fraternal society. Its objective was to emulate the principals of *"steadfastness, persistence and wisdom of power"* of the original group which consisted of *"a priestly family of Jews"* that participated in a rebellion regarding the Temple of Jerusalem in ancient times. Its convoluted modern history from its resurrection in 1878 seems to indicate it gradually evolved into an insurance type of group protection for its members, eventually becoming part of an insurance company, then in more recent times re-establishing itself as an organization founded on the original objectives; this time also accepting women as members.

It was a widespread society, especially in Michigan and more recently, California. It is stated to have had a membership of over 200,000 in 1896.

Although there is little recorded about their activities and membership in Bracebridge, it is a matter of record that a *"tent"* of the order was established here on November 1st, 1893 with no indication of its longevity or fate.

INDEPENDENT ORDER OF FORESTERS...

Similar to many organizations that sprung up in Bracebridge in the 1800s, the **INDEPENENT ORDER OF FORESTERS** could trace its roots back hundreds of years, in this case as far back as 14th century in England. Like the others it was also founded on mutual aid and protection for its members who gained that membership through hand-to-hand combat, a practice that was abandoned in 1843. It was introduced in Canada in 1875 and developed into one of North Americas leading fraternal societies, eventually admitting women as members as well as men. It was a friendly society that focused on providing insurance benefits to their members at a time when the average working family could not get coverage of any kind. In Muskoka it flourished to a great extent because of the great number of men employed in the forest industry where bad working conditions and dangerous situations were plentiful.

The importance of the organization to working families was described in Bert Shea's book *History of the Sheas and Paths of Adventure* where it reads,

"Another organization that came to our community and was very popular in the whole township was the Independent Order of Foresters. A secret society with an insurance and sick benefit policy. The organization spread, especially through the northern Ontario district among the men working in the lumber woods and sawmills who were covered by a protection available from no other source."

Some sawmill owners when hiring would insist that a new employee buy insurance to provide for their families in case of an accident and the best (and usually the only) way to do that would have been through membership with the Foresters.

"Many were hesitant to subscribe but as time went by, accidents and even deaths occurred and benefits were paid to beneficiaries who without them would have been left in desperate straits."

In Bracebridge the Order was enthusiastically instituted in 1897, the members meeting regularly in the Herald Hall on Ontario Street. Among its members were G. H. O. Thomas and Lemuel Scott who, at his death and been a member for 40 years.

ANCIENT ORDER OF UNITED WORKMEN...

Like the *INDEPENDENT ORDER OF FORESTERS,* the **ANCIENT ORDER OF UNITED WORKMEN** started as mutual support, financial assistance and a collective voice for its fraternal brotherhood. The encyclopaedia states that it began its existence in Pennsylvania in 1868 with the aim of,

"adjusting all differences which may arise between employers and employees, and to labor for the development of a plan of action that may be beneficial to both parties, based on the eternal truth that the interests of labor and capital are equal and should receive equal protection"

It focused more on working class people, especially factory workers, and like the others included life insurance for its members. It had many of the characteristics of present day labour organizations.

When it commenced in Bracebridge is unclear but it was on or before 1879 because it is written that the Orange Lodge in that year let the **ANCIENT ORDER OF UNITED WORKMEN** use their lodge room for their meetings, and Fred Sander, who came to Bracebridge in 1871, was reported to have had a high office in the Order. Like many others it held annual summer events, including one in 1903 that involved taking a train to Toronto, steamship across Lake Ontario and electric railway to Niagara Falls; quite a trip for that era. Other members of the Order were James Whitten, D. T. Hogson, A. B. Coombs, E. Flaxman, John A. Caldwell, W. S. Ferguson, Judge W. C. Mahaffy and John Higgins.

Considering the number of business and political leaders that participated in the trip it would seem that for an organization focused on attracting labouring class people to their Order it wandered a little off course when they came to Bracebridge.

KALAMITY CLUB...

There is no link to an ancient order for this organization and it had absolutely no national or international connections. It was only here in Bracebridge and consisted of a group of young working men who banded together and shared a large flat in the **"Brick Block"**, Thomas McMurray's large business building located on the corner of Mary and Manitoba Streets, where now stands St. Thomas Anglican Church as described in **Chapter 10**.

The hotels were not interested in renting their rooms to young men of limited income, (the large number of transient workers flowing through Bracebridge allowed hotels to charge as much for one night's stay as the young men made in a day), and other accommodation being limited, they formed the reasonably well organized **KALAMITY CLUB** so that they could pool their resources and acquire a satisfactory place to live. G.H.O. Thomas, who came to Bracebridge in 1884 to teach school, was pleased when the club voted to allow him to become a member. They even had a Club pet; a bedraggled dog they found huddled at their door, so they adopted it as their own. They name they gave it? What else, they called it Kalamity.

Also as contained in **Chapter 10**, but worth repeating here because it relates so directly to the Club, was the condition of the building wherein their flat was located. McMurray was in a hurry to get his building up and he used bricks that had not had sufficient time to cool and set. As a result, in very short order they started to crumble and the members of the ***KALAMITY CLUB*** throughout the night could hear bricks falling from the walls, to the point where on one occasion so many fell that they couldn't get dressed in the morning without being seen from the street below.

CLEF CLUB...

Music has always played a significant role in Bracebridge society, no better exemplified than by the Bracebridge Citizens Band and the ***CLEF CLUB***, the two organizations with the greatest longevity of any musical organization in Bracebridge history. The ***CLEF CLUB*** was organized in 1908 under the leadership of Carrie Bowerman Thomson; the membership consisting of a group of young ladies studying piano music. Little did they know when they started what a great contribution the group would make to the people of Bracebridge and that it would flourish through the equivalent of three generations.

The membership of the Clef Club was comprised of the most talented singers and performers ever assembled in Bracebridge. The history of the Club is well documented by Patricia Boyer in her book ***LOOKING AT OUR CENTURY.*** They were in great demand and participated in as many as a dozen special presentations each year of their existence. The performances helped raise funds for many causes, including, the hospital (several times), British War Victims, the Citizens Band, Fire Department, and joined with the Women's Patriotic League to help in the purchase of an ambulance for war service. They held an annual banquet every year, the one in 1968 marked their 60th anniversary with three founding members present, Margaret Catherine Bird, Mary Bird and Eva Reid.

It was ironic that the Club ceased their operations in 1975, the same year as Bracebridge enthusiastically celebrated its 100th anniversary as a municipality.

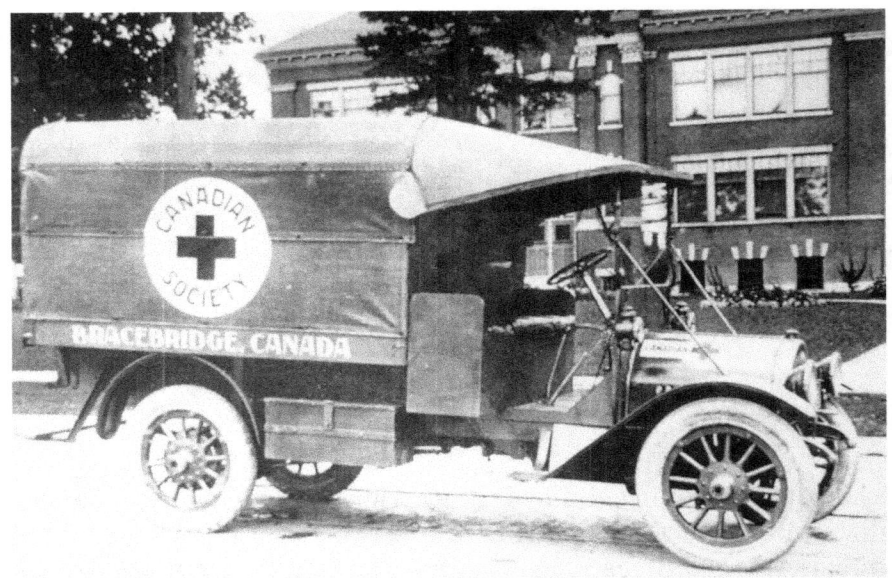

This is an example of the type of ambulance that would have been made available to Armed Service personnel through the efforts of the Women's Patriotic League.

BRACEBRIDGE CITIZENS BAND...

Although it was formed many years earlier, the history of the famous **BRACEBRIDGE CITIZENS BAND** organization closely parallels that of the Clef Club. Some of the greatest musicians in Bracebridge history comprised its membership and its excellent musical performances were in demand, not only in Bracebridge, but in many other venues across Ontario.

George W. Boyer, in **EARLY DAYS IN MUSKOKA** states that in 1888 the Band was engaged for the first time to play at the fall fair annual exhibition in Jubilee Park. There is little record of performances prior to that year but no doubt many months of preparation preceded any public appearance. A picture of the Band in the 1890s appeared in a 1974 edition of the Bracebridge Herald Gazette and listed the names of the musicians and, while W. S. Shaw (manager of the Anglo-Canadian Tannery) was not included, Redmond Thomas wrote in **REMINISCENCES** in 1970 that Shaw was a member of the Band and donated the original bandstand that stood in the park at the intersection of Dominion and Manitoba Streets before Memorial Park was created in 1900.

As with such operations, the Band struggled to pay its bills in the early years of its existence. In 1905 the Town Council stepped in to assist and, in exchange for getting ownership of the band instruments, paid the debt the Band had accumulated in the amount of $125.00. As a result the Town became *"owner"* of the Band and agreed to dedicate one mil in the annual tax levy to cover its costs resulting in Council having control and the right to set certain conditions governing its operations. Not knowing the total assessment that the one mil would have been applied against it is difficult to calculate what amount of money the one mil would have provided, but in later years Council put a cap on the levy at $1,300.00. The Band held concerts to raise money for itself and in 1924 reorganized its operations so that the only person to get paid for their work would be the bandmaster, concluding that the musicians should play for free ***"for the great privilege of being a member and a useful public member of the community."***

The **BRACEBRIDGE CITIZENS BAND** played in so many venues it would be impossible to list them all. It participated in parades of all kinds, exhibitions, sporting events, cruises, fund-raising events, regular concerts in Memorial Park, and even had a special platform provided in Dunn's Palace Rink where they provided music for public skating and figure skating carnivals. It provided the music for Sir John Thompson, Prime Minister of Canada on his visit to Bracebridge in 1894, the reading of the proclamation of King George V in 1910 and the benefit hockey game for Bracebridge's Ace Bailey in Maple Leaf Gardens in front of 15,000 fans. Many of its members were part of the Regimental Band of the 23rd Northern Pioneers Regiment in 1912. It won first place in a band competition in Barrie in 1911 and placed 6th in a competition in the Canadian National Exhibition in 1937.

No discussion about the **BRACEBRIDGE CITIZENS BAND** would be complete without mentioning John (Giovanna) Morra. An Italian emigrant, he arrived in Bracebridge in 1929 and was appointed bandmaster, a position he had held for 27 years when he retired in 1956. The Band was floundering when he came and through his talented efforts it was restored to its former glory. In 1940, when war with Germany gripped the world and Italy made the fateful decision to join on the side of the Germans, Morra was mortified that the place of his birth was at war with his newly adopted home. He was so despaired that the people of Bracebridge would think ill of him that he submitted his resignation as bandmaster rather than see his Band suffer because of his presence. He underestimated the understanding people of his new community and the affection they held for him. The Band president, J. W. Reid, refused to accept his resignation and instead assured him that Bracebridge had complete confidence in him as a leader and had no doubt about his loyalty to Canada.

John Morra was so much the glue that kept the Band together that when he retired it ceased operations. Many of the members joined with participants of Gravenhurst and Huntsville bands, who had also ceased to operate, and together formed the Muskoka District Band.

John Morra died in 1973 after a lifetime of service to music and the Bracebridge community that he loved.

BRACEBRIDGE CHORAL SOCIETY...

When Roxyna Phillips returned to her hometown of Bracebridge in 1945 from Edmonton, she was reported to have created the **BRACEBRIDGE CHORAL SOCIETY** and became the first president. However, what she created was actually a successor to the original society which was formed in 1922 under the leadership of President Mrs. H. Bird and conductor B.W. Tillson. According to the newspapers of that era others that were involved were J.W. Reid, Allan Hines and E.A.Whitten. Their second annual concert was held in 1923 with music provided by the Anglo-Canadian Orchestra and performances by Mrs. McGibbon, Mr. and Mrs. William Towns and Ernest A. Whitten.

Nevertheless the 1945 successor was a complete and successful rejuvenation of a wonderful musical heritage for Bracebridge. The Town Hall was their special place to perform and their headquarters where they stored all their sheet music, stage props and costumes; a situation which, due to a devastating fire a few years later, would lead to their demise. Their performances of the works of Gilbert and Sullivan were famous and they endeavoured to constantly introduce new players to their organization. Many worthy and needy causes benefited from their work, including the fundraising program for the Manitoba Flood Relief in the 1950s.

Patricia Boyer wrote a very interesting and informative chapter on the **BRACEBRIDGE CHORAL SOCIETY** in her book **LOOKING AT OUR CENTURY** and listed many of the talented individuals who participated. As Directors she noted Winnifred Anderson, Leslie Tennant and Glen Banks with music supplied by Marjorie (Quemby) Patterson, Arla Thomas, Gwen Vesey, Jean Greig, Dorothy Marrin and Winnifred Anderson. She listed the performers as Rev. Frank Nock, Leslie Tennant, Alma Peacock, Bill Patterson, Jean Rosewarne, Bob Boyer, Bill Towns, Stan Knowles and Glen Coates. A newspaper report of the day added Mayor Whitten, D. C. Thomas, Betty Higgins and Alma Peacock as officers.

As with many organizations that provided entertainment for the community, the Society suffered with the introduction of television in the 1950s. The final blow was its devastating loss of their music and equipment in the 1957 fire that destroyed the historic 1881 Bracebridge Municipal Building.

TOC-H...

The **TOC-H** movement, founded as a soldiers club in England with an oil lamp as a symbol, had a presence in Bracebridge following its formation in 1933 but there is little record of their activities. The only evidence of its commitment to build a better society and improve communities was its work in remodelling the 1904 stone *"lock-up"* behind the Town Office in 1935, which in that era was used more as an overnight lodging place for transients than for those incarcerated by the authorities.

CANADIAN CLUB OF BRACEBRIDGE...

The **CANADIAN CLUB OF BRACEBRIDGE** came into being in 1910 under the guidance of G.H.O. Thomas as President. It is not surprising that Thomas was involved in this worthy and credible organization; it is another indication of his leadership ability and dedication to Bracebridge and his country. The Club held seminars where they would invite speakers to address their membership on a variety of subjects, invariably relative to the welfare of Canada. Their guest speakers included the President of the University of Toronto, the Deputy Minister of Agriculture of Ontario and other university professors.

Others involved with the Club as officers were Samuel Shannon, H.C. Henry, W.I. Charles, M.P. McKay, Dr. McGibbon, G.W. Boyer, R. Lee and Henry Bird Jr. There is little reference to the Club after 1912 and no record of the reason for its modest longevity.

CANADIAN PATRIOTIC FUND...

Made more necessary due to the lack of Town Council support for the federal fund to provide for the families of Canadian soldiers at war, (Bracebridge was reported to have been one of only four towns of its size in Ontario to not contribute), a branch of the ***CANADIAN PATRIOTIC FUND*** was formed in 1915. The officers involved were the best of Bracebridge residents including doctors, lawyers, and business owners. A number of fundraising events was held and with the help of a very well received door-to-door campaign almost $4,000.00 was raised to support the cause.

WOMEN'S PATRIOTIC LEAGUE…

In further support of the war effort and the Canadian Patriotic Fund, the ***WOMEN'S PATRIOTIC LEAGUE*** was formed with Mrs. Kingsmill as President. They decided to partner with the *CLEF CLUB*, to raise enough money to purchase an ambulance. This joint effort resulted in a fully equipped, four-stretcher ambulance (as shown previously) manufactured by the McLaughlin Carriage Company being delivered to the Red Cross who immediately directed it to be placed in service overseas.

Through the efforts of the *MUSKOKA DISTRICT RECRUITING LEAGUE*, the Town did become involved in supporting the war effort and the ***WOMENS PATRIOTIC LEAGUE*** joined in to provide one field tent while others contributed to assist in the purchase of a field kitchen, mess supplies, etc. They also provided a club room for the soldiers of the 122nd Battalion in the Herald Hall on Ontario Street.

They did not stop there. In 1917 they arranged a farewell banquet for the soldiers of the 122nd Battalion and on their departure presented them with the Battalion ***"Colours"***. In 1918 they raised over $3,000.00 enabling them to ship 4,925 articles and 169 Christmas boxes to the Red Cross for distribution to the servicemen. One of their last acts was to provide a donation to the new Red Cross Hospital in 1932.

As a tribute to their efforts the League was presented with a flag showing the names of all those Bracebridge men who had served overseas during the war. They left it for public display with the Bracebridge Public Library.

EIGHTEEN KNITTING CLUB…

Not unlike the efforts of the WOMENS PATRIOTIC LEAGUE in World War 1, the ***EIGHTEEN KNITTING CLUB*** was formed as a support group for the war effort in World War 2. Eighteen participants, all wives and sisters of enlisted men, attended the inaugural meeting of the group and from that came the characteristic name, although others joined the group later. As the name implies, throughout the week the members ***"knitted furiously"***, according to Patricia Boyer in her fine book ***LOOKING AT OUR CENTURY,*** knitting socks which then became part of a parcel that was forwarded to each soldier from the Bracebridge area each weekend. The gathering had the additional benefit of providing moral support and friendship for the members during a time of great difficulty. The cost of the wool for the knitting projects was covered by the newly formed Bracebridge Rotary Club and their own fundraising efforts. At the end of the war the organization disbanded, their work done, and their excess funds were donated to the hospital.

KNIT KNUTS CLUB...

Although there is very little reference to the **KNIT KNUTS CLUB** in books on Bracebridge, they deserve to be remembered for their contribution and dedication to the community. Their function was very similar to that of the *EIGHTEEN KNITTING CLUB*, in that they knitted clothing for soldiers from Bracebridge serving with the armed forces overseas in World War 2. The main difference appears to be that this organization went beyond knitting socks; producing sweaters and like clothing, all of which was included in the packages that were sent abroad weekly. Long after the war ended, the contributors to this cause were fondly remembered by those soldiers fortunate enough to return from the misery of the bitter war with Germany.

BRACEBRIDGE CRICKET CLUB...

A number of references clearly confirm that baseball was the first team sport to be organized in this pioneer settlement. Bracebridge in those early days, as stated in a 1906 article in the Muskoka Herald, was *"... a sporting town."* and it was in 1879, not long after the 1872 organization of baseball, that the **BRACEBRIDGE CRICKET CLUB** came into being. There was an array of community leaders, names that are recognizable to this day, who participated in this sport that was obviously a heritage carried over from their British homeland. Prominent residents of the day like Topp, Daniels, Davidson, Jocques, Hunt, Hutchins, Bickmore, Binyon, Fenn, Mawdsley, Browning, Washburn, Prowse, Dill, Matthews, Davison and Boyer were the star players of the day.

It is recorded that in 1891 the club played 8 games. Although the competition was not identified, Bracebridge laid claim to winning 5 of those games. That successful record may have been the result of more intensive training following a drubbing the cricket players suffered in a challenge match they played with the Bracebridge baseball team a couple of years earlier which they lost by a score of 46 to 18.

The game of cricket experienced a short lived revival many years later in 1959. As a promotional event a dinner was held and George Boyer, who had participated in the original organization as a player in 1900, was the special guest.

98 CLUB...

There is little mention of the **98 CLUB** in Bracebridge; the only note being that of Robert J. Boyer in *A GOOD TOWN GREW HERE* where it mentions that in 1903 Dr. Francis Williams and his wife entertained the members of the club *"at their new and beautiful home, Carn Brae (at the foot of Manitoba Street)."* Boyer also notes that the club held a series of lectures at the Town Hall in aid of the V.O.N. There is no record of how long it remained active or reason for its demise.

BRACEBRIDGE CLUB...

It is mentioned briefly that in 1947 Gus Braida was elected President for the ensuing year. There is little information regarding the purpose of the organization, when it started or how long it stayed in existence.

MOTHERS PENSION BOARD...

This group was apparently given the responsibility of granting aid under the Mother Allowance Act and giving support to single mothers of orphans, wives whose husbands were disabled or in a hospital for the insane.

WOMENS INSTITUTE...

This organization blossomed and thrived in every small community in Muskoka but gradually faded away to the extent that only a few remain. Those that do continue to perform important functions in their communities.

LOYAL ORANGE LODGE...

One of the first fraternal associations in Bracebridge, the ***LOYAL ORANGE LODGE*** at one time dominated the social and fraternal activities of every community in Muskoka and to a limited extent is still recognized in some locations, Huntsville being one. Its affiliates or extended groups, often variously named in the different books on Bracebridge, among others were ***Knights of the Scarlet Garter, Royal Scarlet Chapter, Masonic Knights of the Scarlet Cord, Royal Scarlet Degree, Royal Scarlett Order, Royal Templars, Loyal True Blue Society, Ladies Orange Benevolent Society*** and university led ***Scarlet Knights,.***

CATHOLIC ORDER OF FORRESTERS...

...had a branch in Bracebridge according to Redmond Thomas in his column *"COMMENT"* in the Bracebridge Gazette of Feb. 15, 1945. As with many organizations, this localized group eventually evolved into the administration of their provincial or national leaders providing financial and social assistance to their members, in this case including a dedicated element of spiritual support.

SHEIKS...

This was a concordant body of the Independent Order of Odd Fellows until they were compelled to disband when their shenanigans became contrary to the IOOF principles.

GAME PROTECTION SOCIETY...

This was founded in 1932; its membership of 40 composed of people interested in the protection of game and fish. Axiel Milne (I believe this is a misspelling of his name; more likely it was the well-known and respected Alex Milne) was elected as its inaugural President.

CATHOLIC MENS SOCIETY...

This group was particularly active in 1914 and 1915 and is credited with organizing the Labour Day program during the era when that celebration included horse races and athletic events. It may well continue to exist under some other title but the reference on record is limited to those two years.

CHOSEN FRIENDS LODGE...

According to Redmond Thomas in his column **COMMENT** in the Bracebridge Gazette of Feb. 15, 1945 this group had a branch here. A **CHOSEN FRIENDS LODGE**, in present day terms, is a fraternal organization operating under the authority of *Prince Hall Freemasonry* and whose members are predominantly African-American. Prince Hall Freemasonry in Ontario, and certain States in the USA, is recognized as a legitimate organization by the Masonic Grand Lodge of Canada and a healthy relationship continues between the two jurisdictions.

The philosophy and membership requirements of Prince Hall Freemasonry may have changed over the last 50 or 60 years but it is highly unlikely; leading to the question of how there could have been such an organization in Bracebridge in the 1940s when there is little record of the existence of a sufficient population of African-American residents to support it. It could have been that there were those in the community that belonged to a **CHOSEN FRIENDS LODGE** elsewhere and made their membership known to the community, justifiably exhibiting their pride in being part of an organization that closely emulated that of the popular Muskoka Masonic Lodge which was formed in Bracebridge in 1877.

Redmond Thomas was not one to write carelessly about his community and there is no doubt that, odd as it may seem, there was a presence of this organization in some form in that era of Bracebridge history.

WOMENS CHRISTIAN TEMPERANCE UNION...

This organization was very active in the anti-liquor movement and donated the *"watering trough"* shown in **Chapter 14. PROHIBITION;** possibly as a consolation to the people following the success of a referendum that ended the sale of liquor in Bracebridge. In it its refurbished state it remains proudly on display in downtown Bracebridge.

BAND OF HOPE...

This group is referred to in *A Good Town Grew Here* where in 1897 it is said they met regularly and rented the Herald Hall for their meetings. It was a temperance organization focused on proper care of children, met once a week and heard lectures on the horrors of alcohol.

HARMONY CLUB...

This musical organization is also referenced in *A Good Town Grew Here* and met in the Herald Hall in the 1890s.

BRACEBRIDGE LITERACY SOCIETY...

Organized under the leadership of Mrs. Bettes in 1901 it perhaps provided the foundation of the *Bracebridge High School Literary Society* that was formed later in 1930. As the title indicates, it's obvious objective was to expand the reading, lecturing and debating skills of its members.

BRACEBRIDGE LADIES AID SOCIETY...

The original organization was born out of the appalling conditions experienced by the soldiers in the United States Civil War. Their objective was to improve conditions by introducing sanitary improvements wherever the need arose. The cause spread across North America, including Bracebridge, not for the improvement of situations of war but for housing conditions and education of the general public. Anne Adair, wife of John Adair the builder of the original stone building now the front part of the Inn at the Falls resort, played an important role as secretary of this society for a number of years.

BLUE GLASS CLUB...

While there is no written reference to this gathering of Bracebridge business and professional leaders, a senior citizen familiar with the group tells of how they assembled once a year for a day cruise and picnic on Muskoka Lake. Apparently there was always a good deal of refreshments available and no doubt it was a very enjoyable event. On one particular cruise however, things got a little carried away. During the festivities it became known that one of the participants had not been circumcised as a baby and, since another participant was a doctor, it was decided that they should remedy that situation.

Of course they didn't have the proper tools, but no matter, they went ahead anyway. One of their empty liquor bottles, which happened to be made of blue glass, was shattered on a rock and one of the razor sharp shards of glass then became their scalpel. They had lots of disinfectant (liquor), and lots pain suppressant (again, liquor), and proceeded merrily to perform the operation. There was no report on the final result, if in fact they proceeded with their idiotic plan, but if they did it would not hard to predict.

Likewise there was no report on the discomfort of the poor victim that made the mistake of revealing his secret to the world. The term **BLUE GLASS CLUB** was born.

367 CLUB...

Since the beginning there have been a number of organizations promoting business in Bracebridge; the *367 CLUB* is one of them. It was active in the first decade of the 1900s, but apparently faded away as World War 1 loomed on the horizon. It probably consisted of 15 or 20 of the top businessmen of the community who didn't do much except for chartering a steamboat once a year and touring Lakes Muskoka, Rosseau and Joseph. During that tour they would call at all the major points of interest on the lakes where they would dine, meet the people of that area and maybe stay for the night, all the while promoting business in Bracebridge to one and all.

A news article in a local newspaper showed an undated picture of those embarking on the cruise on an unidentified wharf and describes the efforts of the group. Robert J. Boyer, in *A Good Town Grew Here*, provides a more detailed description:

"The 367 Club was an informal organization of Bracebridge business-men who annually in the spring made a tour for a couple of days of the Muskoka Lakes ports."

Boyer goes on to list those who participated in the ninth such excursion on the steamer Nymoca in 1910 as follows:

"W.W. Kinsey, T.J. Woods, G.H.O. Thomas, James L. Fenn Jr., A.C. Salmon, William Kingsmill, James Thomson, Peter Hutchison, R.A. Lawson, W.C. Fryer, T.M. Morrow, John Code, P.A. Smith and Dr. McIlmoyle."

No doubt they did spread a lot of goodwill during their tour and enjoyed good fellowship at the same time. It was a positive move for them to make the effort meet the people in the various ports of call of the cruise because they knew they were the consumers they needed to support the businesses of Bracebridge.

There is nothing to suggest that the *Blue Glass Club* described above had any connection to the *367 Club,* but it isn't much of a stretch to link the two. Regardless, it clearly indicates that the Town and local businesses were very active in basic, on the ground promotion of the attributes of the community.

WINTER EVENING AMUSEMENT SOCIETY...

Mr. and Mrs. W.F. Burden founded the British Lion Hotel on the west side of Dominion Street in Bracebridge in 1872 -before Bracebridge was even known by that name. They came from Britain, which no doubt had a significant influence on the naming of their new establishment. They would have quickly recognized that the population of their new community was predominantly British and had every reason to believe that the flow of immigrants from that source would continue, and they were right.

They were skilled performers and it was through their efforts, assisted by W.E. Foot (who had moved to Bracebridge from Foote's Bay around the same time), that the **WINTER EVENING AMUSEMENT SOCIETY** (sometimes referred to as the *Winter Evening Entertainment Committee*) was created. Between them they drew people together, provided training and organized a number of performances (including some Shakespeare plays) to delighted audiences who were no doubt thrilled to have such professional entertainment in their pioneer community.

One interesting comment regarding a spring performance was that the attendance would have been a lot greater if the roads in Bracebridge had been more passable, noting that the mud on the main street was at least a foot deep. Some things never change; the condition of our roads was a common source of aggravation 130 years ago.

51. CHARACTERS WE HAVE KNOWN…

The various books, collections, and newspaper articles written on the evolution of Bracebridge often tell of individuals who, for one curious reason or another, catch our attention and occupy a special little place in our memory. They are not those who experienced great success in politics, business, or excelled in sports; those folks are well recognized for their achievement and are duly noted as pillars of the community.

This chapter is *not* about them. Generally speaking it is about others who stood out from the rest, were an important part of the community and unaware that their individual persona made any difference. As a result they were respected and remembered. Their names may not have appeared on many assessment rolls, voter's lists or graduation diplomas, but when historians wrote about the Bracebridge community their names were often mentioned, where thousands of the others were not.

Bracebridge has had many such characters. They have appeared in a number of references, often with humour and amazement and always with respect. Some lived in a world all their own that they rarely ventured from but within the community they did things that, in a way, defined the good character of the community.

They are among the people included here. No doubt there are some that have been missed, but if they were mentioned in the books and journals written on the history of Bracebridge by the remarkable authors we have known, or if I have encountered them in my way through life, then they are listed here. They may well be unfamiliar names to most residents of the 2013 Bracebridge community, nevertheless, they are people they *should* know about and remember because they are an integral part of our heritage.

JOHNNY MOON…

This could be a book all on its own and what is presented here is only a snapshot version of his life in Bracebridge. *Johnny Moon* was sent to Canada by Bernardo Homes, the famous agency founded by Dr. Thomas John Bernardo that rescued orphans and waifs from the streets of London England and shipped them to the **"colonies"** to, hopefully, give them a better life in a new world.

In December of 1897, Johnny, at the tender age of 15, was contracted to a farm owner in the Township of Draper, now Draper Ward of the Town of Bracebridge. The contract, as usual, required that he was to be provided a decent place to live and an education but in Johnny's opinion things didn't work out that way.

His stay on the farm in Draper did not last long. Moon must have had a very obstinate personality and character and as his story unfolds it gets more and more complicated. He bounced around from one place to another, including going back to England and to Toronto several times, but it seemed that he always ended up returning to Bracebridge. He just defied authority over him, perhaps because he had seen so much of it, perhaps he experienced a lot of abuse, perhaps he was lazy, but whatever the reason when it got too much to bear he always reacted the same way. He ran away.

Eventually he wound up living in town on a permanent basis. He worked for a while at the Bracebridge Library, for Dr. Williams or the Ecclestone families, but nowhere for an extended period. There is no question that ***Johnny Moon*** possessed a unique attraction to the people of the community. They wanted to help him but employers generally seemed to quickly wear on him, an insignificant dispute would arise between them, and he would leave.

An excellent example of that would be his employment with the Anglo-Canadian Leather Company tannery. During Moon's time in Bracebridge the tannery business was booming and hundreds worked there. Records show that he would be hired by them, work for a few weeks, then be **"*let go*"**, often a conflict with a foreman being the cause. However, for whatever reason, a few months later he would be hired back, work for a few weeks and again be "***let go***".

It was generally thought that Moon was well educated, but the records of the Bernardo organization in England said otherwise. They classified him as **"*dull*"**. A possible reason for the difference was that education in Muskoka in that era could not compare to the more highly developed education system in England, basic as Moons experience there may have been. Stella (Leeder) Hampson, born in Bracebridge in 1913, recalled that as a child her and her friends would avoid him when they saw him walking towards them down the street until one day he stopped and talked to them when he saw them playing in the yard. He told them exciting stories about crossing the Atlantic Ocean and what it was like in England. After that they looked forward to his visits.

Johnny Moon

He always dressed in the dark, tattered and shabby clothes of a vagrant, complete with a pole over his shoulder and a bag attached to the end of it. To say that he bounced around from ***"pillar to post"*** (his words), would be an understatement. He never seemed to have a permanent place to live until he discovered a washed out cavern among roots of the trees on the south side of the Muskoka River, just upstream from the Bracebridge main street, which he expanded and with some scraps of lumber built a front entrance. That became his permanent home. Doris (Leeder) Booth recalled that as a little girl she accompanied her father Art Leeder into his cave on one of Leeder's routine visits there; an indication of his concern about Moon's well-being.

As another example of what a fascination he was to the community, a number of men in Bracebridge, Art Leeder being one, decided that they should build him a better place to live. Just a few feet from his cave they constructed a rather neat shanty type building with proper doors and windows and Johnny Moon moved into it.

However, and this is another indication of his strange character, he only stayed there for a short time, He went to a local farmer and bought a flock of chickens, put them in the nice, new comfortable building and he moved back to his cave.

Another example how the public was fascinated by Moon. Why would anyone take a picture of his cave home? John Smith, a resident Springdale Park in Bracebridge did and proudly displayed it in the living room of his home.

Moon's last days are a mystery. It has been said that he took ill and entered a care facility in Peterborough, never saw Bracebridge again and his buildings crumbled to the ground. Another illustration of the regard the people of Bracebridge had for him occurred in recent years when the writer had a call from an individual who lived across the river from Johnny's home in the cave. The individual knew that I collected items of history for the Town archives and she said she had something to donate. When I asked what it was she replied, *"I have one of Johnny Moon's wine bottles."* I was speechless. I knew that he could have been categorized as a *"wino"* but why in the world would anyone row a boat across the river, search for his cave site and retrieve one of the many wine bottles that littered the area? I was happy to place it, along with its carefully handcrafted wooden case, in the Town archives. To my astonishment, since then another person proudly told me that he too had gotten one of Moon's wine bottles so that he would have a little something by which he could remember this odd character. Amazing.

James D. Lang served the Township of Draper and the Town of Bracebridge for 28 years as a member of the Municipal Council, 19 of them as Mayor. When he was a boy around 12 years of age, he and a friend were playing in the rubble of **Johnny Moon's** shack. He said a number of books littered the area and they each took one home. When Jim arrived home his mother looked at his prize, realized that it was special and placed it in her cupboard where it remained for many years. Upon her death, Jim came across the book and placed it in the Town archives. It was the story of Johnny Moon's life, handwritten by him, entitled, **"The Trail"**. The first line in the volume reads, **"This is the story of my life from 1882 to this day 1934."** It is a treasure of information describing the personal experience of a Bernardo Home Boy. It tells of the dread, fear, struggles, abuse, disappointments and despair of a child shoved into a scary new world of pioneers labouring desperately to settle this area of Muskoka.

Johnny Moon's bible, inside the front cover......

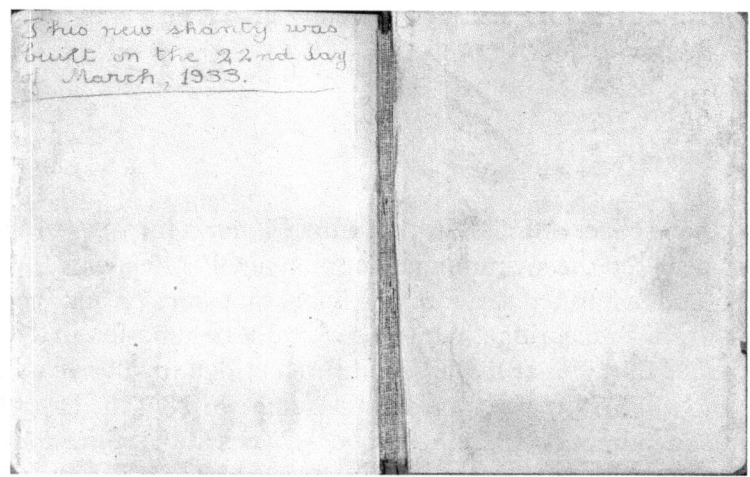
....and inside the back cover.

Jim's friend of the day, whose name he cannot recall, had also taken a book home that day. It was Johnny Moon's bible and is also in the archives. Aside from having been chewed by mice a little around the edges it shows little sign of being used, in spite of the fact that on Sunday mornings during the summer his neighbours could hear Johnny loudly preaching a sermon to the world while standing in the middle of Halstead's rapids near Bass Rock Park in the vicinity of his cave.

Strange, strange indeed.

OSCEOLA GLADIATOR…

An odd name to be sure and there is some doubt if it actually was this man's real name. He lived opposite the former Bracebridge and Muskoka Lakes Secondary School at the bottom of Rosemount Avenue, affectionately known as Tanbark Hill; in 2013 a part of Quebec Street. G.H.O. Thomas in his 1934 booklet ***Bracebridge Fifty Years Ago*** –which of course would make it 1884

—described him as a *"colored"* man although he was uncertain whether he was *"negro or Indian"*, and claimed that it was because of him living in that area of town that it became known by the very offensive name in our present day world, *"Nigger Hollow"*. As unacceptable as that reference is to us, to pretend it was not called that would be an attempt to change written history, something I will not condone. In assessment roles of the day he was shown as a *"labourer"* in one, a *"plasterer"* in another.

The reason for the recognition and respect that he enjoyed from the community, and why he is recorded in our history, was for one daring act that made him very popular. An unidentified resident, one generally considered to be nosey and a disturber repeatedly took it upon himself to appeal the property assessments of many residents of the community on the basis that they were assessed lower than the value of the property. This resulted, of course, in those residents paying higher taxes. While most residents affected felt awkward about taking this person to task for fear of retaliation, it would appear **Osceola Gladiator** decided that he had nothing to lose. Consequently, at the next opportunity he filed a lengthy appeal against the troublemaker's property assessment that proved successful, resulting in *him* receiving a greatly increased tax bill and the community celebrated **Osceola** (the) **Gladiator**.

CARL PILGER…

A 1941 Bracebridge newspaper article tells of a **Carl Pilger**, a member of the Royal Canadian Engineers, who was declared the swimming champion at CFB Petawawa. Quite an achievement considering the thousands of armed services personnel that were posted there in that era. Certainly that **Carl Pilger** was from Bracebridge, why else would it be reported in a local paper, but whether or not that was the same **Carl Pilger** that lived in Bracebridge in later years is unclear, although there is good reason to think they were one and the same. Firstly, the Bracebridge Carl would have been about the right age to be serving in the armed services at that time and secondly he was a renowned swimmer.

Stories abound about his swimming ability. More than once, while trying to illegally snatch spawning pickerel from the rapids at the bottom of Bracebridge Falls, Carl had to dive into the frigid, turbulent water of early spring and swim across the river to avoid detection by conservation officers. On another occasion, Carl was contacted by the operator of the Bracebridge Generating Station at Bracebridge Falls and asked if he could come to the wharf and help a tourist whose outboard motor had come loose from his boat transom at the dock and sank to the bottom of the river. Of course Carl responded, dove to the bottom of the river-some 12 to 14 feet, and in seconds carried the outboard to the surface and set it up on the wharf.

The tourist was delighted and asked Carl how much he owed him for his service to which Carl replied, five dollars. The tourist was taken aback and argued that it had only taken Carl less than a minute to retrieve the outboard and five dollars seemed like a lot of money for such a short period of time. Carl didn't bat an eye, he put his foot against the outboard and, in his usual stuttering voice said, **"Then you g-g-get the G-G-Goddamn thing."** With that he shoved the outboard back into the river and as it sank to the bottom Carl walked away.

Carl Pilger was tall, thin as a rail and could work like a horse although I don't recall him ever having a steady job; his ability was somewhat limited. Whenever someone had a physically difficult job they needed done they called Carl; sadly, some mean-spirited property owners would try to take advantage of him. He always seemed to enjoy life in spite of the fact that he stuttered badly when he talked. Often when he saw someone he knew walking on the far side of the street he would holler out, *"How's your w-wife and m-m-my kids?"*

Ironically, it was the water of the Muskoka River that took Carl's life. Although the facts were never made clear, it seems he was walking on the rocks in Hallstead's Rapids not far from where Johnny Moon preached his Sunday morning sermons just upstream from downtown Bracebridge, when he slipped, possibly hitting his head on a rock and he died there.

BILLY THE PIG…

Redmond Thomas, in **Reminiscences,** makes reference to a number of interesting characters that fit well into this chapter. *Billy the Pig* is one of them. William Gurrell was his name but more often expressed as *Billy Girl*, the way Billy Gurrell sounded when it was not pronounced correctly. But it was his appearance that gave him his nickname. He was short and fat with a round face that had a pig like appearance.

He was of English descent and worked at the Queens Hotel, always dressed in a neat blue uniform typical of the dignified doormen at quality hotels of the era, but his biggest contribution to the community was that he was skilled at organizing and detonating fireworks displays, which he conducted at the intersection of Taylor Road and Manitoba Street.   This organized display may well have been encouraged by the authorities because up to that point crowds of young men would line up on opposite side of Manitoba Street and hurl firecrackers at each other, hardly a healthy pastime.

Thomas reports that *Billy the Pig* left Bracebridge and moved to North Bay where he worked for a hotel in the same capacity as at the Queens, but misfortune struck and he was murdered, although the circumstances surrounding that event were not revealed.

"GATLIN GUN" SPENCER…

William H. Spencer was one of the earliest North Falls area residents. His contributions to Bracebridge and Muskoka are legendary as one of the first farmers, Monck Township Clerk and Police Magistrate for the Town of Bracebridge. Redmond Thomas, as a young law student, knew him personally and in his book ***Reminiscences*** provided an informative insight into Spencer's life. He noted that he was a witty Irishman and was a source of entertainment whenever he conducted his court proceedings. He actually arrived in Muskoka in 1861 in Macaulay Township, was Assistant Postmaster in 1864, moved to a farm in Monck Township and was appointed as Clerk there in 1870, a position he heard for 39 years. Spencer Street in Monck Ward of the Town of Bracebridge is named in his honour.

However, it is not as a result of his success in farming, legal matters or politics that he is included here -it is because of his curious nickname. Coupled with his characteristic Irish wit, it is noted in Bracebridge history that he talked very rapidly, never carelessly or frivolously and always with respect, but always fast. So fast in fact, that he acquired the nickname Gatlin Gun, after the innovative American Civil War weapon invented in 1861 capable of firing an unheard of two hundred rounds of per minute.

Little wonder that his courtroom hearings were well attended by local residents, more interested in listening to *"**Gatling Gun**" Spencer* dispense justice, than with the content of the case before him.

MORLEY CROCKFORD…

Morley Crockford was a very successful businessman, investor and considered by many as the best dentist in the country. Born in the village of Fraserburg in Draper Township, he was one of 6 children of William and Sadie Crockford and descendant of a fine pioneer family whose members were widely involved in business, politics and social life in Muskoka. Like Spencer, he is not included in this chapter because of his success, but because he was an interesting character that everyone seemed to like. Once met he was hard to forget.

Early in his career in dentistry, after acquiring his education at the University of Toronto under the tutelage of Professor Mark Boyes -oddly enough another Muskoka native having grown up in the not-to-distant village of Vankoughnet, Crockford established an extensive dental practice in Toronto. After a long career in Toronto he sold his operation and returned to Muskoka, established a practice in Bracebridge and built a new residence in Draper Ward. Co-incidentally, Mark Boyes around the same time returned to his homeland and lived out his retirement in Vankoughnet.

Morley Crockford didn't have the appearance of a rapscallion and made no attempt to try and be one, but he was just that. He knew what he liked and didn't mind spending his money to achieve what he felt were the finer things in life. He wasn't a practical joker by nature but he certainly was by default. The way he lived and some of the situations in which he found himself were classic; never intentional but almost always by his own making. Humorous and interesting stories are plentiful. When his neighbours on Fraserburg Road saw his luxurious Cadillac driving slowly along the road they all knew Morley was walking his dog; the unfortunate weimaraner *Wilhemenia* having to run alongside the car in the ditch to get its exercise. Who, other than Morley would mistake the alternating flashing red lights on top of a parked police cruiser for the wig-wag lights of a railway crossing? And who, other than Morley would use a pair of pliers to remove a painful, abscessed tooth from a carnival ride operator who insisted the extraction take place there in the middle of the Bracebridge Fall Fair Grounds so that he could continue to operate the ride and entertain the kids at the fair?

In ways that few ever realized, Morely was a generous and thoughtful person. He never talked about it but more than a few young people of Bracebridge seeking higher education were financially assisted by him. In 1970 when the Vietnamese *"Boat People"* refugees landed on Canadian shores, Morley was there to help in a significant way.

It was hard to get a *"one up"* on him because he really didn't care if you did, but in his own casual way he usually had the last laugh. There is no better example of this than the epitaph that he wrote for the headstone of his own grave in the Fraserburg United Church Cemetery. No doubt those who knew him would say, **"Yeah, that sounds like Morley"**.

Could a more appropriate epitaph exist for the gravestone of a dentist than "I FILLED MY LAST CAVITY"?

ALF "SHORTY" CONNERS…

Another person that does not appear in history books, **Alf "Shorty" Conners** was a fixture around the downtown area of Bracebridge for many years. He lived on Yonge Street and received his nickname Shorty because he was just that -short, well less than five feet in height. He was of English descent and was the main distributer of Irish Sweepstake tickets for the area. Selling them, maybe even buying one, was illegal because of Canada's archaic antigambling regulations of the time.

That didn't bother Shorty; he paraded up and down the street dropping into every friendly store with his little booklet selling tickets which were drawn at random later and tied to the performance of certain horses in the Irish Sweepstakes race. The success of the horse dictated the amount of money you would win. The profits from the draw were pledged to support Irish hospitals, but there were some who did not participate in the draw because they were not sure of its legitimacy. They might have been right because it was later revealed that the draw may have been run by a for-profit organization and that the proceeds did not always find their way to the hospitals.

Nevertheless, there were those in the area that profited nicely and Shorty was a hero. He always had willing buyers in Everett's Drugstore, one of them being the writer, who as a student worked there during the summer holidays and who never understood why the government of the day would stand in the way of the people having an opportunity to win a prize.

"RAS" JERMAN...

The Jermyn family has a long record of involvement with Muskoka, even as far back as the early 1900s. In fact, Charles Jermyn was one of only two members of Muskoka's 23rd Regiment Northern Pioneers chosen to serve at the coronation of King George V in 1911 and be presented with a Coronation Medal by His Majesty. Whether or not "Ras", (his given was Gordon although I do not recall him ever being called that, at least not on the street), was a descendant is unknown, but he may well have been somewhere down the line. Like Shorty Conners he was a familiar figure on Manitoba Street. Because he was medically handicapped and subject to epileptic seizures that would cause him to pass out, no matter where he happened to be, everyone was aware that he sometimes needed help. For a time he lived in a hut behind the Bracebridge Memorial Community Centre.

He had difficulty in speaking clearly which made those around him more observant in watching out for him. He would occasionally suffer one of his seizures while crossing busy Manitoba Street and store clerks and owners would be called on to stop traffic and get him to safety.

Few people knew that **"Ras"** had a very rare blood type and was often called on to go to the hospital to give blood. Noel *"Turk"* Lees told the writer that **"Ras"** saved the life of his mother Florence Lees by donating blood for her in a time of need. That was only one such instance; there were many others.

It was another example of how the people in small communities cared for each other.

CECIL MCNEICE...

The McNeice name has been a familiar one in business and political endeavours in Muskoka for generations and Cecil McNeice, who may or may not have been related to them, was another common figure in the Bracebridge business area. It was never known what his occupation was during his working years; certainly he did not work in the years that he visited the stores there. It was thought he had originally lived in Bala but in Bracebridge I think he lived in the Dill Street area.

He was partly crippled in that his neck was badly enlarged due to some kind of accident and he could not move his head without moving his entire upper body. That did not stop him from walking uptown every day, usually to get a newspaper at Everett's Drugstore where every day there was one saved for him with his name written in the margin.

TOM HOLIDAY...

Many in Bracebridge will have great memories of **Tom Holiday**, especially those involved with fastball. Tom was a fixture at Jubilee Ball Park when his favourite team, sponsored by Ecclestone Hardware, was playing. Tom was mentally challenged, but that didn't stop him from being an active, and respected, member of the community.

He took it upon himself to be the teams ball boy and what he didn't know about fastball, (he may have known more than he got credit for), he made up with enthusiasm. During a game his main job was retrieving the bat dropped by a batter after a hit and bringing it back to the bat rack in the dugout, all the while cheering his teammate's efforts with his characteristic husky voice and limited vocabulary.

He missed few games, until one day while sitting on the team bench during a game, he was hit in the head with a line drive foul ball, the last thing in the world he needed considering his handicapped condition. He was rushed to the hospital emergency room and transported to a hospital in Toronto where he had to undergo emergency neurosurgery.

Did that stop him from helping his ball team? Not at all. As soon he was able he was back doing his job, this time though, and from then on, he wore a helmet and facemask.

Tom Holiday, just like most would have known him, takes a break on a Memorial Park bench in downtown Bracebridge

FRED "BING" CROSBY...

Fred "Bing" Crosby; a fixture and reliable volunteer at hockey and baseball games in Bracebridge

For many years if there was a Bracebridge Minor Hockey or Bracebridge Minor Ball event going on you could bet on **"Bing"** (nicknamed that for the obvious reason) being there. In fact, he was a fixture at the arena no matter what was going on. So much so that there was a time when the manager of the arena, since **"Bing"** was forever around the place, hired him as one of the custodians of the building. Oddly enough, it didn't work out. He was more than willing to spend hour after hour there with the kids, coaches and fans for free, but when given a schedule to stick to things went to pieces, even though it provided some rare income for him. It wasn't that he didn't get his work done, it seemed the routine and responsibility inherent with employment was not for him. It interfered with his lifestyle of volunteering his time to help the kids of the community.

It was the same way at the ball park. He served as Manager for a number of travelling minor ball teams and delighted in repairing the webbing in baseball gloves for the players. He seldom had any money to spend on himself, (when he had money he usually spent it on the kids), so when he went to an out-of-town game others would have to buy his meals. No-one minded though, because everyone appreciated his help.

What most of his friends didn't know, because he did his best to not show or complain about it, was that he suffered from a serious health problem. He had a major diabetes affliction and a serious heart disease; knowing Bing, he probably never considered adjusting his lifestyle to accommodate his problems. It was diabetes that resulted in him having a leg amputated and it was his heart problem that took his life.

Bing lived life to the best of his ability as he knew it and a lot more could be written about his contribution to his community. After a hockey game at the local arena he and his friends would gather in the coaches' room and analyse the game; of course there was always a cocktail or two and Bing was a happy participant. He was one of the guys and proud of it. Whenever he entered the room his friends had a little routine that they knew he would enjoy. One would sing, in a melodious voice, *"Bing"*, the next would say *"Bing"* in higher note, the next would say *"Bing"* in a yet higher note, and so it would continue, emulating the ringing of a bell. Bing would grin from ear to ear. He knew he was home.

This is the headstone that marks his grave in the Bracebridge United Church Cemetery

As his sickness started to take a toll on his activities, his friends had a fundraising program to provide some financial aid and Dan Culos (Danny the Barber) and I were co-signers on an account set up in his name. He did not live to use all the money; he died suddenly one morning and the funds remaining were invested in a tombstone for his grave in the United Church Cemetery in Bracebridge. The usual information inscribed on such monuments in this case included something extraordinary- baseball bats and hockey sticks forming a cross - to remind those of us remaining of his dedication to the children of his favourite place, Bracebridge.

LARRY MAURO...

Afflicted with Downs Syndrome, **Larry Mauro** was a fixture on the main street of Bracebridge for many years in spite of his severe handicap. His well-known and respected family, to their credit, had provided him with sufficient training and gave him the freedom to walk there on his own and mingle with the shop owners and shoppers freely. Again, because of his disability people watched over him and seldom did he ever seem to be in an uncomfortable situation.

He always dressed in a jacket covered with patches and logos advertising one product or another and bottle caps. At that time, beer and pop bottle caps were manufactured with an inside cork lining that could be pried out and fastened to the jacket by putting the material between the two and forcing the cork lining back into place from the inside, thereby firmly affixing it in place. Many kids did the same thing but Larry did it a lot.

He also smoked and a cigarette, always in the middle of his lips sticking straight out, was one of his identities. Another was a cap pistol carried in a western cowboy style holster and belt, which every now and then he would pull out and point at a passerby on the street, often giving the object of his attention quite a shock. One time when he was being teased by another kid from the neighbourhood, he defended himself by pulling his gun and hitting his tormentor on the side of the head.

He also felt he had a job to do downtown every day. In that era many stores had day calendars in their window that, unlike present day digital models, needed to have the previous days date card placed at the back of the pile thereby revealing the correct date which appeared on the next card. Larry would faithfully come to each store that had such a calendar and change the date for the owner. The curious thing was that the store owners and staff trusted him to do that for them. It was never made clear whether or not Larry knew the proper date; it was more likely he knew he had to change a card every day.

Because of a death in the family, Larry went to a care facility and was not seen downtown thereafter. He was another Bracebridge favourite that gave the business community an opportunity to show its caring character.

BONEY…

He did not appear on any assessment role, he had no permanent residence, no-one knew where he came from, how he got to Bracebridge, and no-one seemed to know his proper name. Nevertheless, his lifestyle and bizarre conduct here in the 1890s rendered him worthy to be included in Redmond Thomas' excellent book *"Reminiscences"*, where he suggested that his first name might have been George, but he wasn't sure.

Thomas considered him to be impervious to cold and damp weather because in the spring, summer and fall he slept outside in the sawdust pile of the J. D. Shier sawmill. In winter he slept in one of the mill buildings. During the day he would walk the town and collect things, anything, that he could sell so he could have a few pennies to spend. He acquired the name ***Boney*** because he included bones in his search which he would sell, presumably to farmers and keepers of stock, which they would render into calcium-rich bone meal for fertilizer, feed and possibly human consumption as a dietary supplement.

Obviously he was unsavory in many ways but generally considered harmless, aside from the fact the children were afraid of him.

He eventually moved to North Bay where he became reacquainted with another former Bracebridge resident who related the story of ***Boney's*** experience there. He lived in a shack outside of town and one cold winter day his neighbour, noticing there was no smoke emanating from his rudimentary smokestack, investigated and saw ***Boney*** lying motionless on the floor. Presuming he was dead, the neighbour alerted the authorities and the local funeral director to make arrangements for his burial.

However, when they arrived at ***Boney's*** shack with a coffin on a horse drawn wagon and broke through the door, Boney suddenly jumped up and demanded to know what the heck was going on. Once the situation was explained and everyone had a laugh, Boney seized the opportunity to catch a ride into town with the undertaker. Instead of riding beside the driver though, Boney gleefully rode on top of the coffin like it was a horse, laughing and waving to those who watched this bizarre parade as it bounced along the street.

"MAW" FORTH...

It would be difficult to find a more hospitable lady in Bracebridge, in her own determined way, than *"Maw" Forth*. Her home on Woodchester Avenue for years was a welcome haven to many and what she had in her kitchen and refrigerator was there for the asking –for a price of course. The guests had darts, table-top hockey games, crokinole boards and card tables available for entertainment and it was a rare night that they were not all in use.

My first visit there was a memorable one. I was lead to her house by a friend who obviously was a frequent visitor because when she answered our knock on the door he was immediately called by name and waved inside. When I went to step across the threshold however a large arm was suddenly jammed across my path and in a demanding voice she said, *"And who are you?"* *"Maw" Forth* was a large woman, tough as they come and that arm looked to me to be a foot thick, perhaps it was. In a stumbling voice I stated my name and she replied, *"Are you related to Arnold Veitch?"* to which I replied yes, he is my father. Suddenly her voice softened and she immediately replied, *"Well, come on in then."* I guess my father was a frequent visitor as well.

That was my introduction to Maw Forth and I visited there a number of times after that. She was quite capable of maintaining law and order because those she welcomed into her home respected her and besides, she was bigger and tougher than most of them. Not once in my experience was there a raised voice in argument and I often thought that some of those guests were more behaved there that they would have been in a more public facility. Although they probably would deny even knowing her, a number of prominent business and professional residents of Bracebridge were among her clientele.

"LITTLE" JIMMY...

His name was James Macdonald but everyone in Bracebridge knew him as *"Little Jimmy"*. Like *"Shorty"* Conners, *"Little" Jimmy* was just that, little. No report gives any indication of his size but comparing him to the size of others he had to border on being a midget, a somewhat derogatory term that has given way over the years to *little* person; a condition caused by a genetic disorder often referred to as dwarfism.

"Little Jimmy", (James Macdonald) sits proudly amidst his friends in this picture taken on the main street of Bracebridge. Among those present are, Charles Lount, George Sibbett, A.E. Mawdsley, Robert Hutchison, John and Robert Leishman, J.H. Burton, Edward Prowse, William Simmons, Newton Langford, Herbert and J.J. Beaumont -the business and political leaders of Muskoka.

No matter, he was one of the boys on the main street of Bracebridge and it was a sad day when he died on March 12th, 1898. He was not a mover and shaker like many of his friends, he was never elected to anything, there is no record of him belonging to an organization, he never appeared on an assessment role and he seemed to have no family but his passing saddened of some of the most influential people in all of Muskoka.

52. STRANGE THINGS ARE DONE...

A number of interesting and curious experiences in the past have been recorded in the numerous books on Bracebridge. The fact that someone took the time to record them provides a certain degree of credibility and certainly qualifies them to be repeated here as *THINGS WE SHOULD REMEMBER*.

BLACK SQUIRRELS AND RACCOONS...

For example, in 1897 it was reported that a black squirrel had been seen in Muskoka. This was a rarity and its appearance no doubt created a lot of interest. Curious, to say the least that an animal so abundant in Muskoka in 2013 did not exist here 115 years ago.

Likewise, and also in 1897, the first sighting of a raccoon was recorded. Once again these animals were known to live further south, but in Muskoka? Never.

The oddest of all rare occurrences and the one that wins hands-down took place in 1938. On the *"Baysville Highway near the Pines"* (Taylor Road, presumably the area where the Pines Home for the Aged is located in 2013) there was a three feet long snake found that had *"short scaly legs"*. It is written in *A Good Town Grew Here* that, *"The monstrosity was thought to be from a freak show"*. Unfortunately it didn't say whether or not there had been a recent *"freak show"* or a circus exhibition nearby that it might have called home. Sadly, no additional information exists regarding the strange creature or whether any further attempt was made establish its identity.

TANNERIES AND THEIR EFFECT ON THE RIVER...

The importance of the Muskoka River in the development of Muskoka has been described earlier in this book. The fact is, it was not just important; it was vital to the logging industry, to industry for its hydraulic power and to visitors for its spectacular scenery; all of which brought people here from far and wide in pursuit of their particular interest in this land.

It is also a fact that it was used for purposes not quite so honourable. The old philosophy *"dilution is the solution to pollution"* was never more evident than the way the tanneries disposed of the waste from their tanning vats. No-one thought anything of it; that is what the river was there for they figured. Well, by 1900 it was becoming evident that the discharge was having a detrimental effect on the pristine waterway.

As early as 1901 consultants were recommending the installation of a sewage collection system for Bracebridge and the discharge from the tanneries was noted in their reports. Certain improvements were included, none of which suggested a complete ban on discharging waste from the tanks into the river. How could they, when the residential sewer lines proposed by the same consultant were designed to do the same thing?

Copies of the plan showing the Manitoba Street, Dominion Street and Kimberley Avenue collection pipes ending at the river's edge where it discharged the effluent into the river, duly stamped *"approved"* by governmental health agencies, existed in the town archives for years. The report stated that, *"...sewage purification works are not necessary immediately and when demanded they may be added at a comparatively small expenditure."*

In 1906 there was growing pressure on Council to increase the generation of electrical power, to further develop the supply of water from the town springs and to expand town services including *macadamized* (asphalt) streets. Into this mix the Bracebridge Board of Health pushed for the installation of that sewer system. To no avail, the provincial authorities agreed with the Board's proposal but included an unpopular recommendation for partial treatment of the effluent, including that of the tanneries. It was rejected and the system recommended in 1901 was eventually installed and served as a sewage system for years, thanks to the Muskoka River.

Reading between the lines of history, one can detect the attitude of the residents. Opposition to any kind of sewer system, on a number of fronts, abounded. They were generally against spending a lot of money, even though it was to be recovered by a levy only against the properties served. There was also determined opposition to having to treat the effluent from the collection lines. *Why not use the river? Surely such a small amount of effluent would have little effect on that huge body of water!* It was not until 1958, *52 years later*, that Council accepted a preliminary report to add 8.3 miles of sewage collection pipe and build a sewage treatment facility and not until 1971, 13 years after that, that a firm was hired to connect the rest of those original collection lines to the new system. They had been dumping raw sewage into the river all that time.

THE MUSKOKA GOLD RUSH...

Many thought it a fraud, but a claim that gold had been discovered in Muskoka sparked an incredible euphoria across the district. With the California gold rush still fresh in everyone's mind and rumours of big finds in the north rampant, visions of one in Muskoka no doubt raged in the minds of the people.

What made it more exciting was that there were a *number* of claims. In the book of early Muskoka documents and letters, **Muskoka and Haliburton 1615-1875** it is indicated that there was evidence of gold at Sparrow Lake and Skeleton Lake, while in **Remimisences,** Redmond Thomas quoted a 1945 article from the Bracebridge Gazette about gold having been discovered on a Kirk Line property in Macaulay Township. He also wrote about having heard of gold strikes in the community of Ziska in Monck Township, Township of Stephenson, Gravenhurst and Rosseau. The Gravenhurst claim of a gold discovery was given extensive coverage in the promotional book **Guide Book & Atlas of Muskoka and Parry Sound 1879.** An 1888 newspaper article said that gold–bearing rock had been found on Naismith's property in Macaulay Township and on a farm in Dunchurch.

Regardless of the claims of discovery and the resulting flurry of interest, no gold mine ever developed. The claims could have been fraudulent, a matter of inaccurate analysis of samples, wishful thinking on the part of the property owners, or whatever ore existed was of such limited quantity that a commercial operational was not viable. When asked about the Macaulay claim, an old-timer from that area suggested that the owner of the property *"...was just trying to raise the value of his farm so that he would get a little better price for it when it came time to sell".*

THE TEDDY BEAR...

A young 20 year old Seymour Eaton, a native of Euphrasia Township in western Ontario, just one year after receiving his teaching certificate arrived in Bracebridge in 1879 to assume the position of Principal of the Bracebridge Public School when it was located at the end of Robert Street. It was an interesting story told in great detail in the winter 2002/3 issue of *Vintage Muskoka* magazine which was based on a number of publications and thorough research by *Donna Ivey*.

He was related to the Wardell family who owned and operated businesses in Bracebridge, and later through marriage to the Adair family. No doubt Eaton chose to come to Bracebridge because he had relatives here. Unfortunately, although he visited later, he was not here as school principal very long having resigned as a result of his salary being reduced by the school board in reaction to unexplained complaints from a parent of one of his students.

While it would be a stretch for Bracebridge to call him a native son, it could be said that his brief presence here perhaps helped develop him as a person, a teacher, a businessman and the creator that he became. His long list of achievements in Canada and the USA is a clear indication that he was a brilliant entrepreneur, but his greatest success was a result of his literary creation of the adventures of two bears that he named Teddy-B and Teddy-G. The inspiration to create these rhymes of adventure came from a 1904 cartoon where President of the United States Teddy Roosevelt was portrayed as showing kindness to a bear cub while on a hunting trip.

The booklets, entitled *The Roosevelt Bears* (and resulting souvenirs), in short order became very popular and many leading newspapers in United States regularly serialized them in their publications. The circulation company that Eaton formed was hugely successful and had offices in many of the financial centres of the nation.

His portrayal of bears is said to have been the advent of the enormous **TEDDY BEAR** phenomena in children's toys and perhaps modified the thinking of millions of people on how they viewed wildlife. Robert Boyer in ***A Good Town Grew Here*** and G.H.O. Thomas in ***Bracebridge Fifty Years Ago*** cited Seymour Eaton as being the originator of this enduring and endearing child's toy. There may well be those who would argue against that being the case but it doesn't matter, we can believe it and celebrate the fact that this brilliant person was, for part of his life at least, one of us.

MUSKOKA LAMB...

Henry J. Bird chose *North Falls* as the location for his woollen mill in 1861 for two important reasons. One was the ready availability of hydraulic power produced by the waterfalls; the other was that in his opinion Muskoka would be a good sheep-raising district because the average rainfall (and perhaps colder weather) appeared to favour the growth of the sheep's wool. He chose wisely because he was right in both cases.

There is no record to indicate how much of his badly needed raw wool came from Muskoka farms, but it had to be a substantial amount. Aside from the industrial and retail businesses that appeared in the early days of the community, most of the free grant land settlers that arrived here were interested in creating the farm homestead of their dreams. As disappointed as some were with their allocated land, many took advantage of Bird Woollen Mill's ready market for sheep's wool. Henry

J. Bird knew what he was doing; he actively encouraged local farmers to raise sheep no doubt assuring them that he would be there to buy the resulting wool at shearing time.

The large number of sheep in the district gave rise to another product that became well known, -Muskoka lamb. It was a very popular menu item in restaurants and luxury resorts that populated the shore of the larger lakes of Muskoka. From there it developed an international reputation resulting in a much wider market and became especially popular in Toronto restaurants, no doubt abetted by the many visitors that considered Muskoka their summer home.

53. BUSINESS -THE FOUNDATION OF BRACEBRIDGE...

The Bird Woollen Mill is described in **Chapter 11** as the biggest and best early business, and it is that by a long shot. It could also have been identified as the business having the greatest longevity as a *family owned* business. While the Bird Woollen Mill is clearly in a class of its own there have been other *retail* and *service* businesses whose impressive longevity should be recognized.

Generally I have focused on those who were in business prior to 1950; if there is an exception to that it is because of the significant *impact* that particular business has made on our way of life.

Bracebridge from the beginning has been endowed with people blessed with a determined entrepreneurial spirit. Examples of that are abundantly evident in the many books, articles and documents we look to when we search for information on the history of this community. They did not hesitate to invest in their dreams, work unbearably long hours, sacrifice their personal interests for the good of their business and at the same time participate in social and political affairs for the benefit of Bracebridge. They deserve our most enthusiastic praise and appreciation. I have included here those who continue to be in business, although often under a different name, or have disappeared recently enough to be recalled by most people in the community.

Unquestionably there will be some I have missed, for that I apologize, but it was not until I got involved in writing this chapter that I realized what an incredible business heritage we have and the vast number of businesses that qualify as contributors to that heritage.

MUSKOKA PUBLISHING COMPANY...

For example, George W. Boyer started a lifelong and extended family career in the newspaper business when he started working with David Edgar Bastedo of the Muskoka Herald in 1903. He managed that company until he enlisted with the 122nd Muskoka Battalion, eventually serving with the Lord Strathcona Horse Regiment at the front in France in World War 1. When he returned to Bracebridge he created the *Muskoka Publishing Company*. His father, James Boyer, the first Clerk of the newly organized Township of Macaulay in 1871 (which included the community of *North Falls* and the new post office of *Bracebridge)* and the newly incorporated *Village* of Bracebridge in 1875, already had some experience in the newspaper business having had an association with the Northern Advocate. That involvement may have sparked the newspaper interest in his son George.

The rest is history. The *Muskoka Publishing Company* with its Muskoka Herald, later to become the Bracebridge Herald Gazette, is legendary. Its influence and dedicated devotion in reporting the affairs of Muskoka, and Bracebridge in particular, has provided us with a priceless asset. George's successor in the business, his son Robert J. Boyer, without a doubt has been the greatest contributor to our history through his numerous and excellent literary works. Will there ever be another like him? I doubt it.

MEDLEY BROS...

Tom and Perce Medley partnered in the *Medley Bothers* business in 1943 and from a modest beginning grew to be one of the premier aggregate businesses in Muskoka. Again, through reorganization, name changes and varying functions the company endures to this day and continues to serve the public.

Eventually developing into P. Medley & Sons Ltd., like many others it has survived through difficult times, the stress of changes in the economy and ever-changing governmental regulations. Tom and Perce laid the foundation for the company and family members still own and operate it in 2013.

NORTHERN PLANING MILLS...

George Tennant and his partner picked an ideal time to get into the lumber business when he fired up his sawmill in 1925. Operating later from the remnants of the abandoned Furniture Factory building there is no doubt he laboured endlessly to build his reputation and to create a company on which the people of Muskoka could rely for their wood products. Many name changes and family members became involved over the years, including Les Tennant, Ted Reid and son George Reid under the name of *Northern Planing Mills* and in later years Northern Buildal.

WAITE'S BAKERY...

Arthur Thomas Waite and his wife Edie May came to Bracebridge in 1927 and bought the small bakery of Bill Leece operating from a small building on Manitoba Street. From that modest start *Waite's Bakery* became a trademark of Bracebridge; people came from afar to purchase their quality baked goods and the chelsea buns were everyone's favourite. For example, a president of an international manufacturing corporation visited Bracebridge as part of their consideration of the area as a location for a production plant and nearing the conclusion of the deliberations with municipal representatives he directed one of his associates to leave the meeting and purchase a package of *Waite's Bakery* Chelsea buns. We were stunned that he even knew about them. The last view we had of the delegation was them boarding their Lear Jet at the Muskoka Airport, each carrying a bag from *Waite's Bakery*. Amazing. We wondered afterwards if that may have been the reason they visited Bracebridge in the first place because nothing resulted from their visit to the area.

Geoff Waite had assumed the bakery operation from his father years before, eventually moving the bakery to a new building on the south side of Ontario Street while his sister Joan continued to operate a very successful and delightful tearoom on Manitoba Street. Sadly the bakery closed in 1989 after attempts to sell the business, and its recipes, failed. For many years Geoff, like his father, had started his day's work at 4 o'clock in the morning and it just became too much.

Chelsea buns have never been the same since.

WES FINCH & SONS EXCAVATING LTD...

Little did Walter Finch know when he started his business in 1929 that the Finch name would be thriving in the industry in 2013. It was not unlike all those who took up the challenge of a new adventure and worked long hours to realize their dream. They didn't necessarily do it to create an enduring, family empire; they did it to make a living. Considering the difficult decade dominated by the woes of the great depression it is to the credit of all those who started businesses in that era that they survived those struggling years. Many didn't survive, but those that did grew because of the hardships they endured, stronger because of the determination of their founders.

Walter's sons Murray and Wes came into the business at an early age and learned the business from the ground up working with their dad, and they learned it well. Following Walter's death in 1967, Murray continued his father's company and Wes formed **Wes Finch & Sons Excavating Ltd.**; in 2013 celebrating 83 years in the industry after Walter fired up the engine of his first truck in 1929.

MacNAUGHTAN HARDWARE...

Three generations of the MacNaughtan family have steered this busy retail hardware operation from its beginning in 1946 to recent times and its ultimate sale as a continuing hardware business in Bracebridge.

Peter MacNaughtan, already experienced in retail trade, set up his own store in a small building on Manitoba Street where it stayed for 31 years. Many will recall the incredibly cramped quarters, narrow aisles and stuffed shelves of the old store and puzzled how the staff could ever find anything. But find it they did; their personal service was impeccable and long term employee Don Pickles was considered the paint expert of all time. He was also the guru of all things hardware and could cut glass for a window pane like magic. What he didn't know, *you didn't need*.

The business finally relocated in 1977, under the leadership of son Jim and grandson George MacNaughtan, to the much, much larger building formerly occupied by the Dominion Food Store at the north end of Manitoba Street. I am sure they wondered how they would manage in such a large facility but they stuck to being a good *hardware* store and did just fine, in spite of stiff competition and the threat of the new fad *big box* stores.

The business was sold from the family name in more recent years; the new ownership continuing to operate under the dealer owned banner *Home Hardware,* (of which Jim MacNaughtan was a charter member in 1964), in still larger premises; the size of which would have flabbergasted founder Peter.

ECCLESTONE HARDWARE/ECCLESTONE & BATES...

The Ecclestone family name in Bracebridge is so weaved into the fabric of the community it is almost impossible to follow it all. George W. Ecclestone came to Muskoka in 1878 where he found employment in a retail hardware store in Huntsville. In 1894 he moved to Bracebridge and went into partnership with Milton Ramsay in a hardware store proudly identified with their names, Ecclestone and Ramsay. Five years later he took over from his partner and created **Ecclestone Hardware** with himself as President.

He was a key figure in the community, serving on the Municipal Council, Water, Light and Power Commission, as Mayor and later as the Member of Provincial Parliament; winning re-election several times. His son George N. Ecclestone, already well trained in the business, assumed the Presidency in 1939. Like his father, he was also active in the community, serving on the Municipal Council, the Curling Club executive, the Red Cross Society and Rotary Club. In 1963, George R. (Butch) Ecclestone took over the President's position; thereby joining a very exclusive group where three generations in succession operated a family business. Butch was an active supporter of winter sports, a member of the Bracebridge High School Slater Cup hockey championship team and the Provincial champion Bracebridge Bears Intermediate hockey club. They served the hardware needs of Bracebridge for close to 100 years.

George W. Ecclestone's other son Albert E., partnered with Arthur S. Bates and George James Fenn in 1909 and took over the plumbing business of the hardware store. For many years **Ecclestone and Bates** was dominant in that business in Bracebridge and was considered one of the best in Muskoka. They installed the plumbing in many of the grand old resorts and summer mansions on the lakes. Albert also served as Chief of the Bracebridge Fire Department for close to 40 years and was renowned for his insistence on proper training for the firefighters. It was because of his work in this respect that the Bracebridge department was often victorious in competitions with other departments in the region. **Ecclestone & Bates** closed their business in the late 1960s after more than 50 years serving Muskoka. It was here where the principals of many of the plumbing companies that appeared later in Bracebridge received their training.

In 1963 Ecclestone's sold off another part of their business, that being the appliance division, to one of their employees -a very young Jim French who, assisted by his father Charles, formed French's Appliances. It was sold in 1992 to Al Davey.

The Ecclestone name disappeared from the hardware business when **Ecclestone Hardware** was sold to new owners in the 1970s. They had served the people of Muskoka well for 75 years.

HAMMOND TRANSPORTATION/MUSKOKA TRANSPORT...

Orvil Hammond in 1944 at the age of 15 started a taxi business, teaming up shortly after with George Parlett as a partner in Park Taxi. Parlett, at about the same age already had a licence (the issuer said *"I may as well give you a licence, I see you driving all over town anyhow!"*), but Hammond's licence was restricted by the condition that he could drive for only one company, and it was not *his* company. Apparently Orv had acquired a taxi licence at age 14, indicating that a *drivers* licence was not a prerequisite to getting a *taxi* licence. Strange. Although both would probably deny any suggestion that their driving habits left a lot to be desired, it is a fact that their business had the rather suggestive nickname **"Pearly Gates Taxi"**. It has also been suggested that some girls in town were forbidden to ride with George and it was often said that both he and Orv **"drove like hell"**.

Nevertheless, the two partners went on to great entrepreneurial business careers whose businesses stretched far beyond the narrow limits of Muskoka; but their hearts and their dedication remained with Bracebridge. After the partnership ended, Parlett went on to develop successful companies involved with long haul transportation and an automotive dealership while Orv proceeded to expand to **Hammond Transportation** including Hammond Taxi and Hammond Ambulance Service.

In time, Orv sold off parts of his business venture. The ambulance business to long time employee Ivan Beasley, the taxis were split off to others and, in 1971, sold the transportation business to his brother Paul Hammond who established *Muskoka Transport Ltd*. Always the opportunist, Orv was forever making deals and as an indication of his foresight, in spite of having sold his taxi business long before, still maintained *one* town taxi cab licence. Clearly he knew, that if all else failed, he could always go back to where he started. He had not forgotten where he came from; something we all should think about.

The involvement of Orv and wife Fran's family added to the success of their bus business, including son Greg, in 2013 thriving in in spite of active competition. Likewise, Paul's *Muskoka Transport Ltd.*, again with the assistance of family members and Paul's son Darcy in 2013, developed into an international shipping and haulage business and continues to this day. Although other jurisdictions have lured them to locate elsewhere, to their credit, and to the benefit of everyone, their roots have remained firmly planted in Bracebridge and Muskoka.

MUSKOKA GARAGE...

His nickname was *"Teddy bear"*, understandable considering that his initials were T. B.. Thomas B. Rosewarne and his wife were married in Lambton, Ontario and migrated to Muskoka in 1901 taking up residence on the Kirk Line in Macaulay Township. It is reported that he came as a school teacher but quickly turned to farming where he excelled with his strawberry farm, producing *"6000 boxes"* in 1922. That sounds impossible, but that is what was reported. He was active in municipal affairs and for a while served as Township Clerk.

Their sons Earl and Les must have inherited their father's business acumen because it was at a young age they started their own successful careers.

Earl Rosewarne, upon return from service with the Canadian Armed Services in World War 1, didn't take long to get into business in Bracebridge. It was in 1921 that he bought *Muskoka Garage* from Lou Pelletier and from that modest start an enormous business base in the automotive industry evolved. He started his first garage during the *"Model T"* days on the property where in 2013 the Woodchester Parking Lot is located on Entrance Drive in Bracebridge.

In an era when automobiles were becoming popular, he sold a number of different vehicles bearing names that most have long forgot, like Durant, Star and Rugby trucks, proceeding later to dealerships with Chrysler in 1933 and General Motors in 1947. He branched out to operate service stations in Powassan, Haileybury, Englehart and Kirkland Lake and founded Muskoka Garage Transport to distribute gasoline supplies. In 1953 his son Gord bought Sutcliffe motors and in the early 1960s, when General Motors decided to split model dealerships, partnered to start Gordon Motor Sales Chevrolet Oldsmobile and an Esso service station. In 1965, his son Norm took over the Muskoka Garage Pontiac Buick dealership, keeping it in the Rosewarne name until 1978.

In the meantime, Les Rosewarne was busy founding the Bracebridge Garage Ford dealership and service station beside the Bracebridge Public Library on property later occupied by the Federal Building and Post Office. This was also part of the property previously used for circus performances affectionately recalled by Redmond Thomas in his booklet *Reminiscences*. He expanded his building in 1934, was proud to announce his *"new English Ford"* cars for sale in 1949 and expanded again in 1954 to house body shop equipment he bought from Aubrey White. He relocated his business in the mid-1950s to the former Arnott's Nursing Hospital building at the corner of Manitoba and MacDonald Streets; a property occupied in 2013 by Kentucky Fried Chicken.

Like the rest of the family, Les was dedicated to community service, receiving a life membership from the Bracebridge Rotary Club in 1988.

An item of particular interest exemplifies the creativity and entrepreneurship of the Rosewarne family. Earl Rosewarne, way ahead of his time, in 1928 stripped a Rugby truck down to its bare chassis and with the help of Northern Planning Mills built a structure on it that could easily be described as the first RV motorhome ever. It was a marvel to all, especially when Earl and his wife loaded their family into it and drove to Florida for a holiday. Considering the condition of the roads in that era, that has to be hailed as quite a challenge, to say the least.

For over 70 years the Rosewarne family was an intricate part of the Bracebridge automotive business community; the term early retirement didn't seem to be part of their vocabulary.

P.J. MARRIN WHOLESALERS...

Phillip J. Marrin came to Bracebridge in 1898 to work with Joseph Caisse as an apprentice barber. It was not long before he branched out on his own, creating his own barbershop on Manitoba Street in 1906, but his entrepreneurial spirit did not stop there. He recognized an opportunity when he saw one and in 1919 took over the grocery store business of M.C. Lacey in a building previously occupied by the Hunt's Bank. Along with his retail grocery store he developed a wholesale tobacco distribution system and in 1942 it became the central focus of his affairs. It was to his distinct advantage that his was one of few such distributers between Toronto and North Bay and business grew rapidly.

In 1950 his son Morley took over the business and in 1974, in a challenging move, relocated operations from the downtown area to Highway 118 west, one of the first businesses to dare move from the hallowed area of Manitoba Street. With a greatly enlarged warehouse it worked well. When Morley retired in 1995, after an incredible *70 years* in the family business, sons Jerry, Jim and Michael took charge, making it one of the select few companies that enjoyed three generations in the operation of a Bracebridge business.

The business was closed in 2007 after a 101 year reign of family operation Bracebridge.

H.J. BROOKS & SONS...

George E. Brooks came with his parents to Ryde Township in Muskoka in the 1880s at the age of 18 years. His father was a lumberman and he chose the perfect time to be in that business in Muskoka. Young George was not about to stay in the lumbering business with his father, moving to Bracebridge in 1890 where he took up the carpentry trade. His son Herman, like his father, chose not to continue in the same line of work as *his* father, instead working with Ecclestone's Hardware for a number of years before buying the storefront of Armstrong's Butcher Shop on Chancery Lane in 1945.

In 1946, Herman converted the shop into an electric supply and appliance store and with the assistance of his two sons, George S. and Jerry, the firm of **H.J. Brooks and Sons** was born. It was a business that would survive and thrive in that retail trade, albeit with a name change in later years, for three generations. I can recall as a youngster growing up in the small community of Ufford my family buying appliances from Herman Brooks and when a delivery was required (as it always was -my family didn't have a vehicle), it was Herman and his son George that always appeared at the door. The success of the business necessitated a move from the small shop on Chancery Lane to a bright new Manitoba Street location in 1959. On Herman's retirement, George S. took over the store while Jerry focused on the electrical supply division, later going into real estate sales.

When George S. semi-retired, his sons Alex and David continued in the business and entered into a franchise agreement with Leon's Furniture. This progressive move resulted in the need to build another much larger show room and retail outlet away from the congested area of Manitoba Street. From there additional outlets were created in Huntsville and Orillia. In 2013 the legacy of **H.J. Brooks and Sons** continues under the leadership of Andy Brooks.

Not to be forgotten however is that his father George S. Brooks, at the age of 89 after 66 years in the business, is still active in selling appliances just like he did as a young man in 1946 when he worked with his father Herman after returning from service in World War 2.

Herman, in spite of his diminutive stature, had founded an empire.

THE THOMAS COMPANY...

Little did George Henry Oakwood Thomas know when he stepped off the steamboat the *Kenozha* at the Bracebridge Wharf in 1884 and climbed the steep hill at the end of Dominion Street on his way to the British Lion Hotel that he would become such an integral part of his chosen community. His marvelous legacy and that of his subsequent family, in business, the arts, service to Bracebridge, politics and enthusiasm for life is unmatched and could be the standard by which all should be measured.

He came to Bracebridge as a teacher, probably not expecting to become involved in the myriad of things that would unfold in his future, but his determined entrepreneurial spirit took over his life very quickly. A description of all of his achievements would fill a book, a very interesting book, but for the purpose of *this* book the focus is on his founding of *The Thomas Company*.

He became involved in the retail trade while still teaching school when he bought the William Colville *"stationery and fancy goods"* store in 1889, according to his obituary in the May 18th, 1939 edition of *The Bracebridge Gazette*, which carried a sad headline *"G. H. O. T. IS DEAD"*. In *A Good Town Continues* it is reported that in Bracebridge's Centennial year of 1975 The Thomas Company announced that they had been in business for 94 years which would mean it started in 1881. That indicates that they included the Colville store in the tenure of their business (even though it was not in their ownership) because in Thomas' own words he did not arrive in Bracebridge until 1884. Whether it was 1881 or 1889 makes little difference.

In short order he bought the Ball Bros. *"jewelry and confectionery"* store and merged the two although no confirmation is made as to what the business was called. He then partnered with Harry Booth, an expert jeweller, to form the Thomas and Booth firm, an agreement that probably included his merged store, and opened a store in Huntsville. It wasn't long before the partnership was dissolved and Booth stayed in Huntsville while Thomas remained in Bracebridge, expanded his business to include his brother Noah's stationery store in North Bay, and named it all ***The Thomas Company***.

Later still, he partnered with his brother Philip in a drug and stationery store in Sturgeon Falls and in 1900 left his position of school principal to focus on his business ventures. ***The Thomas Company*** evolved over the years to include the Thomas Tea Room and his *son* Philip became involved with the store with his optometry clinic. In 1906, Thomas ventured into a totally new enterprise when he partnered with Harry Linney to purchase The Bracebridge Gazette.

G.H.O. Thomas' legacy in Bracebridge includes many things including serving as a municipal councillor, mayor, working to create Memorial Park, the present day public wharf in Bracebridge Bay, arranging for the first paved road, the first cement sidewalk, a written record of Bracebridge in 1884 and many other remarkable achievements. For the purpose of this chapter, his greatest contribution to the *retail* history of Bracebridge was ***The Thomas Company*** which was eventually sold to Paul and Doris Smellie in 1980 and out of family ownership.

It is an incredible record of achievement that deserves to be included in ***"…and things we should remember!"***

ELLIOTTS 5 TO $1.00 STORE...

J. Hilliard Elliott was a graduate optician but when he decided to open his store on the west side of Manitoba Street in 1910 he knew that he would have to have more of a drawing card than that to attract customers. As a result, he added jewellery and watchmaker to his *"shingle"* hoping the demand for those services would add to his business. He was absolutely right. Optometry, as it is known in 2013, is an important and thriving occupation, but in 1910, not so much. Pioneers were not an affluent bunch and as their vision dimmed magnifying glasses were the norm; trying to read by the light of kerosene lanterns in pioneer shacks no doubt aggravated the condition severely.

His successful business allowed him the time to be an active member of the community and he spent it wisely. He spent a number of years on the Board of Education and Board of Trade and was highly respected for his dedication and contribution.

His business survived through the struggles of the *Great War* of 1914 but it was the *great depression* that challenged the business. Being the entrepreneur that he was, he came up with a brilliant business plan that clearly shows he was way ahead of his time. Modern retail ventures have produced outlets like Dollar Stores, Dollar Giant and Buy Smart that focus on selling items generally for a dollar, or less, yet J. H. Elliott saw the benefit of that sales strategy in the *"dirty thirties"* when a lot of businesses were struggling to stay afloat and many didn't make it. His timing was perfect when he created *Elliott's 5¢ to a $1.00 Store*; it was an immediate success.

He didn't abandon his old business plan though and in 1941 he opened a watch and jewellery store down the street. When his son Bill returned from serving with Canadian armed services in World War 2 the ownership of *Elliott's 5c to $1.00 Store* became his. In Bracebridge's Centennial Year of 1975, it was celebrated that the Elliott store had been in business for 65 years. It was sold out of family ownership when Ted Williamson bought the business in 1979.

STONE'S MENS AND LADIES WEAR...

Although it didn't travel between family members, *Stone's Men's and Ladies' Wear* deserves recognition when it comes to the longevity of service to the people of Bracebridge. Founded by Phillip Stone in 1938 after moving to Bracebridge from Orillia, it celebrated its 37th anniversary in business in 1975 and was eventually purchased by Merv and Betty Speck in 1977. The business was closed in 1999, a serious blow to shoppers who appreciated the high quality of work clothing the store had provided for years.

MUSKOKA TRADING COMPANY...

Most of Muskoka's early settlers, especially those who came to take advantage of the Free Grant Land and Homestead Act's offer of large tracts of land, began their existence by trying to create farms. After all, it was suggested that success was almost guaranteed because the land was covered with lush growth and the soil fertile. At one time there was a large number of operating farms in the District, albeit small, -far more than the handful we see in present day.

As a result, there were a number of grain grinding, cleaning and feed store businesses in Bracebridge. When Harold Clarence Frowe started his business the *Muskoka Trading Company* in 1933, he did so in a building that had previously been used for the same purpose and he continued to provide that service well into modern days; adding groceries and specialty items as time went by. The service provided to the customers was superb and many relied on their grocery delivery service.

It had been in business for 40 years when Don and Betty Speck took ownership in 1973. In *A Good Town Continues* it explains that the business moved into larger premises in 1989 but due to reasons beyond control of the owners, including a devastating robbery in 1991, the business closed -to the dismay of those dedicated supporters who appreciated the quality of the personal service they provided.

UPTOWN SERVICE STATION...

In **Chapter 43. AN INTERESTING INTERSECTION –DOMINION AND MANITOBA**, there is mention made of a service station being built in 1929 by J. Hudson Burton and that it was operated by his son Douglas, as referenced in ***BRACEBRIDGE AROUND 1930*** and ***A GOOD TOWN CONTINUES***. In 1975, Bracebridge's centennial year, it was celebrated that the property had continued in that use for 46 years.

It had a number of different owners but it was when it came under the ownership of a local entrepreneurial and talented business family, Fenton, Bill and Ernie Patterson and later Ted Smith, that it became known as *Uptown Service Station*.

It continued to serve the community until 1980 when the property was sold and the building converted to a restaurant; a use that continues in 2013 as the Old Station.

RIDLEY CLEANERS...

After 14 years in the business of dry cleaning fabric in Goderich, William Snazel moved his company to Bracebridge and opened under the name *Ridley Cleaners* in 1934. There seems to be no written explanation of the reason for selecting that name; maybe it just sounded good. He set up business in a former grocery store building on Manitoba Street that in 2013 adjoins the Thirsty Judge.

Following the end of World War 2, Jack Fawcett and Doug Kirkness purchased the business and after the death of Fawcett, Kirkness continued on his own for 25 years, celebrating its 40th anniversary in 1975. Doug Kirkness was very involved with Bracebridge, playing on the 1933 High School hockey team, serving with the Royal Canadian Legion, the pipe band and Independent Order of Oddfellows. In the armed service he attained the rank of Flying Officer.

Regardless of all that, however, he will be remembered best by the sports fans of Bracebridge for another accomplishment. When the Bracebridge Memorial Community Centre was completed in 1949, it was in a hockey game that was part of its official opening ceremony that the first *recorded* goal was scored in the new arena. It was Doug Kirkness that scored the goal.

Ridley Cleaners was sold to Jim and Mary Bradbury in 1974 who continued operations, adding related businesses in later years.

SHIER'S INSURANCE...

Wilfred Andrew (Biff) Shier was a barber by trade, buying the shop of Fred Bradshaw on Manitoba Street in 1927. He must have been successful because he opened an additional shop in Nobel in 1941 and hired a manager for his existing operation.

As it turned out though, cutting hair was not to remain in his future. In 1943 he started what would be a long-lasting family business that continues to serve Bracebridge 69 years later.

Like most companies of extended tenure, *Shier's Insurance* changed over the years, in this case to include a real estate and brokerage identity, but the insurance aspect of the operation is the one that remains in most memories. When Biff's son Wilf Jr. returned from armed service following World War 2 Biff gradually eased away from active involvement and Wilf Jr. and his wife Shirley (and husband Joe Gauley following Wilf Jr.'s death) played an increasingly large part in the company; in the late 1970s their son John continued the family ownership.

As with all companies, there were many challenges, both internally and externally, that had to be overcome over the years and in 2012, then involving Adam Shier -the 4th generation of the family, the company remains active. Other partners and an excellent staff over the years played an integral part in its ongoing success but for the purpose of this document it is the continued participation of the family of W.A. (Biff) Shier that is the emphasis of this chapter.

Biff died in 1969 following a lifetime of service to his community including being a founding member of the Bracebridge Kinsmen Club, years of involvement with the Minor Hockey Association, municipal council, Police Boys Club and the Lions Club, among others.

Quite a legacy for his successors to emulate.

DOWNTOWN GARAGE...

It was in 1933, when gasoline was selling for 2 to 3 cents a gallon, that Seth Hillman started *Downtown Garage* in a building that had previously housed a livery stable. In fact, 1933 was not that far removed from the era of the horse and that location would have been an active corner for that trade -near two active hotels (the Albion and the Queens), and on the road leading to the eastern and northern areas of Muskoka.

Seth must have had a keen eye for choosing people to work for him because he had some of the most personable and well liked individuals in Bracebridge on his staff. Ernie Coulson, Jim Hillman, Fred Forrester and Bud Hampson were among those he hired and in 1948 Harold Blanchard started and stayed until 1972. In 1935, Seth's brother-in-law Art Crockford joined him as a partner, a relationship that would endure for 40 years until they sold the property in 1975.

Downtown Garage, in a personal and personable way, had served the motoring public of Bracebridge for 42 years.

MUSKOKA FOUNDRY...

Muskoka Foundry had an enormous and continuing impact on Bracebridge. It, its founder Mungo Park McKay and subsequent family, left this community a legacy that will remain forever; their achievements, accomplishments and contributions are carefully detailed in a number of books, especially those of Robert J. Boyer.

It is a lengthy story but for the purpose of this chapter it can only be dealt with as it relates to the longevity of the business and its impact on Bracebridge. Suffice it to say that Mungo Park McKay, (his given names acknowledged Mungo Park, a famous Christian missionary), and his family were active in community politics, athletics, the founding of the Kelvin Grove section of Bracebridge Bay Park, the original motor car club, Masonic Lodge, and business support groups; the list is endless.

His family was from Gravenhurst, having emigrated from Scotland, and it was there where he got his training in foundry work. In 1902 he and various partners F.M. Johnson, John Robertson and

George Mahaffy established a foundry operation on the north side of Ecclestone Drive that is presently the sight of a housing development beside Kelvin Grove Park. It was an immediate success and flourished, prompting it to relocate to the abandoned Dominion Linen Mills building near Muskoka Road (later to front on Entrance Drive) around 1917.

He was succeeded in the business by his two sons Park and Ronald after his retirement and death in 1941. The property and business was sold in 1964 to G.W. Wilson, later to Northern Ontario Castings and the foundry use eventually ceased. In 2013 the building has experienced a dramatic shift in use, being converted to the delightful retail outlet Simply Cottage.

At each main entrance to Bracebridge this sign welcomed visitors in the late 1920s.

It was cast at Mungo Park McKay's **Muskoka Foundry** and was recovered from their discard pile by Arena Manager Tom Robinson and the writer in the 1970s. It is on display in the Muskoka Pioneer Power collection in Bracebridge.

On the reverse side those leaving Bracebridge received this
message of sadness at their leaving and hope for their return.

J.D.SHIER LUMBER...

The Mickle Dyment lumber company and **J.D. Shier Lumber** are recognized in many publications as being by far the largest companies in that industry to have used the Muskoka River to transport logs to their sawmills. The Mickle Dyment mill was on the shore of Muskoka Lake in Gravenhurst Bay but Shier's was at the confluence of the two branches of the river in Bracebridge, saving him the time consuming process of having to drag booms of logs the length of Muskoka Lake.

James Dawson Shier was born in Brock Township and farmed there for 25 years before coming to Muskoka, arriving in Bracebridge in 1882. He learned the lumber business working in a lumber camp and eventually partnered with Singleton Brown in the purchase of an existing shingle mill. The mill burned in 1898 and they went their separate ways; Brown continuing to make shingles in a mill in Bracebridge Bay while Shier rebuilt his operation and continued to produce lumber, this time in a much bigger way.

What a success in was! It is stated that he installed a **"double-cutting"** (teeth on both sides of the blade) band saw, the first in Canada, that cut logs into lumber in his two storey building on carriages that moved in opposite directions on different floors. A picture of the staff at the mill in the 1920s submitted by Mrs. Milton K. Shier and printed in the ***Bracebridge Herald Gazette*** in 1974 includes 57 people but it is unclear whether or not this included the staff in his three winter logging camps. It was in those camps where the work started -and was the hardest. Men laboured felling trees from dawn to dusk, six days a week under difficult, cold and dangerous conditions. It was tough but necessary work; it kept the sawmill busy the rest of the year.

A humorous incident cited by Redmond Thomas in ***Reminiscences*** tells of a gentleman by the name of Matthews who had a painting contract on a property on the South Branch of the Muskoka River upstream from the mill. On his way there by rowboat he found that his path was blocked by a raft of logs above a chained log boom that stretched from shore to shore. He complained to Mr. Shier and received the explanation that his company had the legal right to block the river in this way and there was not much they could do about it at that time. Matthews, however, had other plans. The next day it was reported to Shier that the boom in question had broken and great effort was expended to strengthen the boom at the mill so that it could hold the weight of the additional logs that were charging downstream.

It was established that the boom chain that held the logs in place had been tampered with and Shier was understandably furious, immediately offering up a substantial reward to anyone who could identify the culprit. Within a few days, Mr. Matthews appeared at his door and stated that he knew who had done the dirty deed. Shier was delighted and appealed to him to state the name but Matthews said he wanted the reward first and then he would tell him. Shier happily gave him the money and Matthews said, **"Thank you. It was me"**.

There is nothing written regarding later legal action taken against Matthews for his little vengeful deed.

J.D. Shier died in 1915. He was active in local politics, served as a councillor and Mayor and was instrumental in supporting the new concept of electrical energy produced by hydraulic power.

The business continued under the leadership of son Ken until his death in 1938, grandson Aubrey and nephew Roy in various years until the business was sold; later discontinuing operations.

NORWOOD THEATRE...

The film entertainment business runs deep in the Giaschi family heritage. Guiseppe (Joseph) Giaschi, who died in 1952, founded a chain of theatres that operated in Huntsville, Bracebridge and Port Colbourne in an era when such entertainment was moving from silent movies to the thrilling new concept of *talking* pictures. He had moved to Huntsville in 1915 to work at the tannery there, at the amazing wage of $1.75 per day; what sparked his interest in the theatre business is not recorded.

His son Andrew, already well trained in the business, moved to Bracebridge in 1936 to manage a theatre owned by Sherman Kirby who had built his first theatre here, called the Princess Theatre, in 1922. Giaschi's management skills were needed because the theatre was being totally remodeled and was to re-open under the name of the Strand Theatre; the transition from silent to talking movies may also have been a factor. The Strand was located near the top of the **"Queens Hill"** on the east side of Manitoba Street.

Sometime after moving to Bracebridge Andrew acquired ownership of the business and in 1948 built the ***Norwood Theatre*** that proudly stands in the same location in 2013, albeit with a number of expansions and modifications.

Following Andrew Giaschi's death in 1964, his son Larry and wife Marion assumed operation of the theatre. In 2001 when Larry died suddenly the business passed into the hands of his daughter Gina Giaschi-Mitchell. Seventy-six years and counting in Bracebridge, the 4th generation of the Giaschi family in 2013 continues to bring movie entertainment to Muskoka.

The Giaschi's were excellent operators, innovators and survivors in movie entertainment. Their hard work, determination and dedication resulted in great success in every aspect of their business. This writer, during his tenure as CAO of the Town of Bracebridge, was often given the responsibility of negotiating with Larry Giaschi on issues that rose from time to time involving his numerous projects. On reporting back to Council on a satisfactory result of our discussions I was often asked, ***"Did you get that in writing?"*** My answer was always the same; it was unnecessary. I knew who I was dealing with.

REYNOLDS FUNERAL HOME...

Life in a frontier community must have been something to behold. As set out earlier in this book, records show that the average age of the settlers was remarkably low, probably in the twenties or early thirties, no doubt reflecting the stamina and strength required to eke out a living in the dense Muskoka wilderness. Survival was first and foremost in everyone's mind and caution was often disregarded.

The long hours of hard labour, the danger inherent with clearing the land of trees, the treacherous task of running logs down the Muskoka River combined with the limited medical care available must have created a very short life expectancy in the community. It did not take long for graveyards and undertakers to become a necessity.

In a list of businesses contained in an 1891 edition of the Muskoka Herald, W.J.White is shown as an undertaker and W.W.Kinsey as a saddler and harness maker. In another location however, Kinsey is also identified as a funeral director as well as a seller of pianos, organs and agricultural implements. He was covering all the bases when it came to funeral arrangements. As was the custom in that era funeral services were often associated with furniture makers, no doubt because of their ability to build the necessary coffins, and these two pioneer funeral businesses were no exception.

Kinsey had the additional advantage of having a licensed embalmer, Joshua L. Yeoman, a graduate of the Chicago College of Embalming, on his staff. His competitor White had to bring an embalmer in from Gravenhurst when such services were required. A chapter in ***Reminiscences*** by Redmond Thomas provides an incredibly good description of ***"Old Style Funerals"*** and it would seem that embalmers were not found to be necessary in every case. It is also made clear that the process of preparing the deceased in whatever way found to be necessary was never done in the undertaker's place of business; it was always done at the residence of the deceased. When there was no place of residence or a co-operative family member, a temporary storage area -probably a ramshackle shed behind their storefront shop, served the purpose. It is also clear that before White and Kinsey started their businesses, and even after in some cases, no-one bothered with undertakers. There have been many reports of human remains being found; some in the vicinity of Muskoka Road near the Royal Canadian Legion, in Fraserburg and on the Morley farm in Ufford.

This is one of the doors of the horse drawn hearse used in the funeral business of George C. Marshal and previous owners W.J.White and W.W.White. The four doors were saved from the scrap bin and placed on display in the Muskoka Pioneer Power collection in Bracebridge.

What happened to Kinsey's business is not clear but the W.J. White funeral director business has endured under other names and owners to this day. His son W.W. White assumed the business from his father and sold it to George C. Marshall who is shown in a 1930 advertisement as ***"funeral director"***.

Walter Reynolds, after returning from service in World War 2 in 1946, purchased the business from Marshall. The sale and building of furniture ceased, the focus became a quality funeral service, and the name promptly became the ***Reynolds Funeral Home***; still existing after being sold to Murray and Joan Dauphin in 1967 and new owners Bruce and Kathy Turner in 1994.

THE BIG BUSY STORE (T.J. ANDERSON AND SONS)

Few would recognize *The Big Busy Store* as having one of the longest tenures in Bracebridge history. That really wasn't the name of the store; it was more of a localized nickname given to a retail operation that started out as Topp and Anderson. T. James Anderson had come to Bracebridge in 1871 and teamed up with Dr. J.W.B. Topp, an established dentist, to open the store in 1891. In 1896 Dr. Topp sold his interest to James L. Fenn Sr., the store name was changed to Fenn, Anderson and Company and it was at this point, it would seem, that the moniker *The Big Busy Store* came into being.

That partnership lasted until Fenn's death in 1935. At that point T.J. Anderson purchased sole ownership with the commitment that *The Big Busy Store* would continue its retail operation but it was then that the nickname started to slip away. Again the name changed, this time to *T.J. Anderson and Sons*, the sons being Wilbur and Fred. They, along with their father who remained a silent partner until his death in 1951 at age 84, continued operations as an active, integral part of the retail business community of Bracebridge until it closed in 1966 after 82 years of family ownership serving the consumers of the area. It is still remembered by some as one of the few places in Ontario that sold Hudson Bay blankets and coats, a very popular item especially with American tourists who usually bought out the entire stock in the summer months.

An interesting feature of the store was a spring activated tube system that carried cash in a small round container from the checkout counter to a central cashier. Here, the amount was checked and the appropriate change, if any, was sent back to the checkout counter through the same tube system and presented to the customer. It sounds like an awkward and slow way to pay for a purchase but in fact it was fast, accurate and capable of handling more than one customer at a time. In reality, it was possibly *less* awkward than the debit card system of present day where pin numbers and a card reader machine (that sometimes refuses to work) consume so much of a sales clerks time.

In the category of *what goes around comes around* it is interesting to see that the modern big box store Home Depot has a very similar system of transporting cash; in their case using a vacuum system for propelling a tube container to a central location.

FOWLER CONSTRUCTION COMPANY LTD...

Fowler Construction, founded in 1950 by partners Glen Coates, Ralph Boothby and Archie Fowler, has consistently provided employment, albeit during construction season, for as many as 400 people each year. Glen had the business acumen, Ralph knew the work and Archie had the equipment. It was a good partnership. Tragically, shortly after the firm started business, Fowler died in an automobile accident and the remaining partners decided to name the company *Fowler Construction* in his memory.

Fowler Construction has put Bracebridge on the map in many ways. They were successful right from the start. The partners knew Muskoka well, they knew the business well and their positive approach in dealing with people resulted in the company growing rapidly. It has always been a major employer in Muskoka and deeply involved in supporting the community in a variety of ways.

Many such new ventures struggle and flounder amidst severe competition; **Fowler Construction** on the other hand, has developed into one of Ontario's premier construction companies, still in business and thriving in 2013.

MUSKOKA CONTAINERIZED SERVICES...

Muskoka Containerized Services (MCS) was founded by Don Coates in the early 1960s; it was an opportune time to get involved in the garbage business. There is no other word to describe the function; it was the collection and disposal of garbage. New terms refer to it as waste management, environmental services, waste disposal, waste sanitation and others but it was and still is all about garbage and waste in whatever forms it takes. Coates facetiously referred to himself as the local ***"garbologist"***.

It was a time when there were 26 municipalities in Muskoka. Each had their *dumps* and although they would never admit it, they knew it had to end sometime as their populations grew and the provincial authorities started asking questions. For the most part they had no idea what they would do next. Into that quandary came the saviour *MCS* with its roll off garbage containers in transfer stations and a ready solution to their problems, it provided them with a simple and convenient way out of their dilemma.

After successfully bidding on an important contract Don Coates received this picture bearing the caption, "We knew MCS was good, but this is incredible!"

As society grew to recognize the importance of proper disposal of waste and the new concept of recycling, so did **Muskoka Containerized Services** grow into one of Ontario's leading collection and disposal companies; continuing in 2013 under a new name and ownership, it is still on the leading edge in that industry.

BB AUTO AND SPORTS SUPPLY…

Lorne Shier's **BB Auto and Sports Supply** store on Manitoba Street was something to behold. Those who shopped there would never forget it. The store, where Blackbird Vintage Gallery is in 2012, was just 10 feet wide and not very long but the walls were lined from floor to ceiling with shelves. It must have had more product per square foot than any retail store before or since and Lorne Shier knew exactly where everything was located. It was the only place in town that sold Dinky Toys, a very popular item in that era.

He opened the store shortly after World War 2 and finally closed the doors in 1976 to everyone's dismay. Every visit there was a pleasant experience.

W.J. LANG AND SONS…

Walter Lang started **W.J. Lang and Sons** in 1947 and for over 20 years provided furnace fuel and propane to residents, cottages and businesses throughout Muskoka. No area was beyond their reach and nothing prevented them from servicing their customers. Tales of difficult situations like dragging propane tanks over the ice of some remote lake to rescue some cottager from freezing, abound. James Lang often said he rarely enjoyed a Christmas eve or Christmas day at home with his family; invariably a customer, and they could be from any place in Muskoka, would call in a panic because their furnace had failed, often because they had neglected to buy fuel, and Jim would be on his way.

James and Joe Lang, the *"sons"* in **W.J. Lang and Sons** took over the business when their father passed away and continued the faithful service until 1979 when the business was sold and eventually phased out of operation.

HOLIDAY HOUSE…

John Adair would have had no idea when he built the original stone structure at 1 Dominion Street in 1875 that it would wind up being one of Muskoka's top tourism destinations. He was just making a living and it is a marvel how he was able to work those massive blocks of stone into a two story structure that looks as solid in 2013 as when it was built.

The property was purchased in 1877 by William Cosby Mahaffy, a young lawyer who had just set up a practice in Bracebridge and who would be destined in 1888 to become the first Judge for the District of Muskoka. Following his death it went through a number of owners and uses but its destiny changed in 1943 when the rather run down structure was purchased by Ernest and Marion Allchin.

They went at the restoration of the property with a vengeance; Ernie could take on the most difficult task as a handyman, (as well as serving as bartender and cook), and Marion, (she soon became known as "Timmy" –no explanation why), was an astute business manager. In 1944 they opened their sparkling new restaurant and hotel **Holiday House,** a name borrowed from a favourite Bing Crosby movie of that era.

Timmy was a tower of strength for Bracebridge. She supported and got involved in many things including the Chamber of Commerce, Business and Professional Women's Club, a key figure in starting the first Santa Claus Parade, one of the founding members of Santa's Village and made *Holiday House* the town's favourite gathering place.

Timmy died in 1973 and in 1974 Ernest sold the property to Jim and Jacqueline Niven. In 1983 Arthur and Sylvia Richardson took ownership, changed the name to Holiday House Inn, and in 1986 Peter and Jan Rickard continued to expand its fine hospitality. In 1999 it was purchased by Trillium Leisure Corporation and still serves as one of the premier tourism features in Muskoka, maintaining, as all previous owners have, the intriguing history of strange apparitions that have appeared there over the years.

CATHCART'S GARAGE…

What was later to become *Cathcart's Garage* started out as Stuthers Garage when Nelson Stuthers opened its doors some time after his return from service in World War 1. It was obviously in the very early days of the automobile and there is no doubt that a lot of the work at the time would have been repairing farm wagons and carriages. It would have been very interesting watching the transition from horse drawn power to gasoline engines. One of a select few, he made it through the great depression successfully and expanded into a larger operation as the automotive trade developed in the 1930s and 1940s.

It was in 1949 that Lyle Cathcart bought the business, changed the name to *Cathcart's Garage* and grew it into a much larger operation including an International Truck franchise, an American Motors dealership and tow-truck agency. Lyle and wife Margaret continued the business until its sale in 1977 to Doug Duff and Ron Hicks.

Part and parcel of *Cathcart's Garage* success was the dedicated involvement of Lyle in the community. As a member of municipal council, community centre board, community policing or the Bracebridge Bears Intermediate Hockey team, Lyle's involvement went far beyond the call of duty. Joining the Bracebridge Lions Club in 1951, Lyle has now celebrated his 62nd anniversary as a member, 61 of those years with perfect attendance. Anyone who has attended an outdoor steak barbeque in Bracebridge will surely have noticed that the master chef behind the barbeque was Lyle. This writer recalls, as a teenager, attending a Lions Club *"mammoth"* bingo (which Lyle founded) in the Bracebridge arena having a smartly dressed Lions member efficiently doling out bingo cards and wearing an apron full of cash. It was not until years later that I realized that it was Lyle Cathcart that I saw in the arena on that occasion.

It must have been the excitement of driving the constantly improving new cars that, in the same era Orv Hammond and George Parlett's Park Taxi acquired the nickname *"Pearly Gates Taxi"*, Lyle developed the nickname *"Crash"*. However, it was not quite the same; that moniker came from a mishap that occurred when Lyle and Margaret borrowed Lyle's father's car and left to celebrate their honeymoon. Due to reasons that have not yet been (and may never be) revealed, Lyle wound up off the road in Algonquin Park, damaging the car beyond repair. The honeymoon ended not quite as enthusiastically as it had begun because the bride and groom, battered and bruised, rode home to Bracebridge in the cab of a rattling, noisy wrecker.

NEWARK BOAT FENDERS...

One of the most inconspicuous and least known manufacturing companies in our history has to be ***Newark Boat Fenders.*** Many had no idea it even existed in spite of the fact that it was in business for 5 decades on the north-east corner of McDonald and Hiram Streets in a building that also served as John Newark's home for 75 of the 81 years of his life. Previously, the property was the location of the Barber Tannery, one of four such businesses in earlier times.

The name of the business fairly accurately described his end product but the process to manufacture it was a work of art; an intricate weaving of marine rope, delicately intertwined to form a tubular cushion that was placed over the side of a boat to prevent the finish from being damaged by the often crude wooden wharfs that lined the lakes of Muskoka.

John Newark was born in Bracebridge in 1903 and started his business in 1922 at the young age of 19 years. He stayed in that business for 58 years, retiring in 1980. His products were tried and true, evidenced by the lengthy tenure of his manufacturing operation; no doubt new materials and modern production methods employed by his competitors plus his advanced age played a role in his decision to bring his business to a close.

There is no indication that he manufactured anything other than his famous boat fenders, odd as that may be, but a contributing factor may have been the limited mobility he experienced due to being physically disadvantaged. One who knew him well suggested that his handicap was the result of being afflicted with polio at a young age.

Nevertheless, he made a good living for his family and was proud of his work even though the only people that appreciated it (even knew about it) were those who used his respected product.

SANTA'S VILLAGE...

There are few companies in Bracebridge, past or present that have had the impact on *tourism* like ***Santa's Village.*** No other recreational feature in Muskoka can compare to the throngs of enthusiastic visitors, often in excess of 100,000 per year all jammed within a span of 2 or 3 months, that walk through the gates of *The Village*. It has also been, and still is, a major provider of summer jobs for youth of the area. Bracebridge is known as the home of ***Santa's Village*** in some of the strangest and most remote places in the country.

It all started modestly with a discussion among a handful of business owners and friends musing about what could be done to improve the economy of the area. Highway #11 had just been relocated from the main street of Bracebridge to a new corridor on the north-east side of downtown and paranoia was rampant among business owners as they pondered what they considered to be a bleak future. How could they ever exist, they thought, without that highway traffic in front of their stores. There is no indication that the idea of a ***Santa's Village*** here was prompted by the successful operation of a theme park by the same name in New Hampshire (it opened for business in 1953), but what is clear is that there was an ingenious vision that Bracebridge's geographic location on the 45th parallel of latitude (half way between the equator and the North Pole), made it a perfect place for Santa's *summer home*.

So they went to work. They raised money by selling shares of a proposed new company and, strengthened by strong support from the people of Bracebridge, took a daring leap of faith by making application to charter a new company for the purpose of building *Santa's Village*. The application was signed by Roy Garwood (clothing store), Douglas Wells (motel), Marion Allchin (Holiday House), Clarence Green (variety store) and Robert J. Boyer (publisher). No doubt many others were involved but it would appear that these were the leaders in the project.

They built *Santa's Village* on an 11 acre property on the north bank of the Muskoka River in Monck Township; most of the original buildings remain, they obviously built them to last. The official opening took place in 1955 with Premier of Ontario Leslie Frost and renowned marathon swimmer Marilyn Bell cutting the ribbon. It is written in *A Good Town Continues* that by 1956 a total of 207,468 people had visited the Village and they celebrated the one millionth visitor in 1965. The record one day attendance was set on July 25th, 1977 when 2,581 excited patrons walked through the gates. The guest register for that same year indicated there were visitors from 22 European countries, United Kingdom, Australia, New Zealand, Israel, India, Mexico, 14 U.S. states and every province in Canada.

The recreation experience has been enhanced significantly by expansion of the Village and the introduction of special features to the original favourites *"Kris Kringle"* cruise boat and *"Candy Cane Express"* train. Well managed and maintained, *Santa's Village* continues in present day to provide first class entertainment to the world. It is yet another example of the vision and dedication of entrepreneurs with which Bracebridge has been blessed since its beginning in 1859.

Nelson Goltz, manager of Santa's Village, drives the Candy Cane Express, one of the Village's favourite attractions.

DAWSON'S ELECTRIC...

The Dawson family of **Dawson's Electric** had their roots in the Windermere area of Muskoka. Abram, one of 12 children of George and Edith Dawson, like many other young Muskoka men in the tough years of the 1930s, decided that his future lay in the West and spent 5 hard years in Saskatchewan labouring on the massive farms that dominated that province. He even tried to develop his own farm there but it was not to be; he returned to his native Muskoka and by 1939 had started an electrical contracting business, a trade that no doubt came easily to him because of his previous qualification as a 4th class Stationary Engineer.

Any business starting in the era of the 1930s encountered significant trials and difficulties. Success was only achieved as a result of long hours of hard work, but for Abram (who became known by a number of endearing nicknames, Albert, Abe and Ab among them), the hard work was nothing compared to what he had endured in the west. As a result, his business survived and grew.

Twenty-five years later, his son Harold, having become a certified electrician in his own right working with his father, entered into an agreement to purchase the business. In order to do so however, Harold had to come up with a sufficient amount of cash to finalize the transaction –which he didn't have. However, he had a plan. He went to his mother Marion and borrowed $800.00 which he then gave to his father, and the deal was complete. Whether or not his father knew about the mother/son deal that made the change of ownership possible was never made clear; or else it didn't matter to Abram.

Harold's involvement in the community went beyond that of doing business. He spent many years serving the public on the fire department rising to the rank of Fire Chief, as a town councillor and 30 years as a member of the Water Light and Power Commission. His favourite recollection of his firefighting experience was the first alarm he received which happened to be for the Town Hall fire of December 13, 1957. His wife Pauline had supper all prepared when the call came in and Harold had to quickly don his attire and leave the house, noting as he did so that he would probably be back shortly to join her for the family meal. But that is not the way it turned out. It was four and a half *days* later that he finally returned after fighting one of Bracebridge's most devastating fire disasters that not only consumed the municipal office and police headquarters but the Town's own fire hall as well.

In 2013 **Dawson's Electric** is one of Muskoka's premier electrical contracting companies, now involving Harold's son Mike, a certified Electrical Technologist and his grandson Jeff, an Electrical Engineer, making it one of very few businesses in Bracebridge history to be able to claim a continuing operation involving four generations. A remarkable achievement to be sure.

KNOWLES PLUMBING...

After having served in the Canadian Army Corp of Engineering during World War 2, it was in 1947 that Stan Knowles started his career in the plumbing trade, a lifelong interest that grew into a thriving and popular Muskoka-wide operation as **Knowles Plumbing.** He learned his trade well under the tutelage of Ecclestone & Bates (who are described in a previous chapter) and Jack Olimer before developing the courage to step out on his own and establish his own company in 1958; continuing under the ownership of his son David and son-in-law Mike Clipsham in more recent years.

Good leadership always results in good employees and the **Knowles Plumbing** staff is no exception, evidenced by their willing participation in community projects. The company maintains a business profile that closely emulates the popularity of Stan's tutors Albert Ecclestone and Arthur S. Bates, the founders of the company where he began his career.

Stan Knowles was born on a farm in Ufford, not far from the birthplace of this writer. Stan and his brother Allan were greatly admired for their skiing ability which they demonstrated on some of the heavily treed and rocky hills in Ufford, sometimes at night using coal-oil lamps hung on tree limbs as their only source of light. Stan's entrepreneurial spirit and working career did not interfere with his love of skiing, and he went on to be one of the top ski instructors, designers of commercial ski resort facilities and coaches in Canada.

Stan was deservedly inducted into the Canadian Ski Instructors Association Hall of Fame in 2004, served on the Board of Directors of the Canadian Ski Instructors Alliance for a number of years and was appointed a member of the Canadian Ski Coaches Alliance. His achievements, like the company he founded, brought distinction to all of Muskoka and Bracebridge in particular.

54. HOW HOT IS HOT?...

The adage *"there is no news in good news"* is never more evident than in the information we receive from the media almost every day regarding our climate. Our lakes are going to dry up, our trees are going to die and we are facing a dismal, bleak future. It's as if wild fluctuations in our weather are a new phenomenon. It would be nice if those making such dire predictions about our future could be held accountable so that if the future proves them to be inaccurate, appropriate penalties could be applied.

There is no doubt that this earth of ours is changing, it always has been and will continue to do so. Clearly our winters aren't what they used to be. I recall stepping out of the front door of our log cabin home in Ufford in 1953 to start my quarter-mile walk to public school and the thermometer that was attached to the outside of the door frame read minus 50 degrees Fahrenheit. It was one of those extremes that you tend to remember; it may well have been a perfectly normal temperature the next day, but that would not have been remembered. A glance at a topographical map of Muskoka will show many marshy wetlands with a small bay of water in the centre; clearly the wetland was a lake a few hundred years ago, slowly filling up with decaying leaves and aquatic vegetation.

While it is a long term view of the evolution of our earth, National Geographic in the promotional material for their very interesting *Genographic Project* explain how North America became populated by migrants crossing the *"Bering Land Bridge"* between Asia and North America at a time when it was a *"launching pad"* created by lower sea levels during the Last Glacial Maximum - between 15,000 and 20,000 years ago. It goes on to explain that they were stranded there for years because they were cut off by *"vast sheets of ice covering the entire Northern Hemisphere from Alaska to Newfoundland"*. Imagine! All that happened at a time when there was little, if any, mankind created carbon footprint! Maybe the *"everlasting ice"* isn't so everlasting. The 20 year *"comprehensive satellite study"* quoted on the Deutsche Welle website claimed that the polar ice caps are melting *"faster in the last 20 years than in the last 10,000"*. Maybe they are right, although I wonder how they can be so sure of what was taking place 10,000 years ago in work that has only been done in the last 20 years -in spite of satellite technology. Certainly we are told they are often enough, but is it so absolute that they can to make such an alarming, influential statement?

Perhaps those who believe that extremes in temperature and weather have never happened before should have been around in 1881 when, according to newspaper reports, Muskoka recorded a heat wave and the temperature lingered at 97 degrees (36c), or when official observer John Hollingworth of Beatrice, just north of Bracebridge recorded temperatures of 92 (33c)degrees in 1897. The recent winter of 2011/2012 was so mild that the main sections of Muskoka, Joseph and Rosseau Lakes didn't completely freeze over -but that is little different than the way it was in 1906, *107 years ago.* That year, it is written in *A Good Town Grew Here,* those same lakes didn't freeze over until late January and even then there was such little frost that a number of teams of horses drowned when they plunged through the resulting thin ice. Log and tanbark stockpiles were stranded in the bush because the winter roads to provide access to them could not be built due to the lack of frost. Likewise, in 1932 geese were flying north in February and the winter was considered *"snowless"* until March 21st when a snowfall was finally received.

On the contrary, the more recent winter of 1983 was so bitterly cold that the lakes of Muskoka froze over by the end of November and stayed that way right through to mid-April. Southern Ontario municipal water systems had buried mains frozen solid, a very rare occurrence, and in Bracebridge there were dozens of temporary lines running to residences, bypassing frozen pipes deep underground.

A headline in a recent local newspaper, following three days of presentations by environmental *"experts"*, read ***"Biodiversity Summit Warns of Doom"***. Doom? Really? Pretty scary stuff, dripping with sensationalism and exaggeration. While conference organizers later claimed they intended the message to be positive, the fact remains that the headline was accurate. That is the way many of those in attendance interpreted the message; the presenters were not there to bring *good* news. Had that been the case I wonder if they would have been invited.

It was interesting to read that one of the world's leading scientists on climate change and a founder in that environmental movement, James Lovelock *"the godfather of global warming"*, in an article by Lorrie Goldstein /QMI Agency in 2012 quoting a UK's Guardian newspaper and msnbc.com interview with him, acknowledged publicly that he had been unduly *"alarmist"* about climate change. It was said the temperatures have not changed the way computer based climate models predicted 20 years ago and *it is not known what the climate is doing*. It also said that it is now clear that the doomsday predictions, his own and those of Al Gore, were incorrect. The interview went on to criticize the fact that the green movement has now taken over from religion in the use of *guilt* as a weapon against all those who dare argue against their alarmist views. Those who make a living lecturing on the horrors of climate change (almost always supported by the public purse) must have had a fit.

We have had similar alarming messages for a number of years going back as far as the *"acid rain"* days when it was predicted that our hardwood trees were dying from the top down and *"experts"* wrote at length about, *horror of horrors*, a lot of branches lying on the forest floor -all faithfully reported by the media, often in bold headlines. I received a copy of an editorial that appeared in an Alberta daily newspaper in the 1980s that told in great detail how hardwood trees in Muskoka were dead or dying and maple syrup production would be a thing of the past. I can remember wondering as I read the article how a responsible newspaper editor could write with such authority on the subject without making sufficient enquiries of Muskoka people to establish whether or not this situation actually existed.

In the midst of the acid rain debate a forester employed by the Provincial Ministry of Natural Resources, with whom I worked as a volunteer with a forestry committee, told me that it never ceased to amaze him how people worried unnecessarily about our forests dying because of acid rain. He quoted a number of incidences where he had attended public gatherings and cottage association annual meetings to which he had been invited as a guest speaker to discuss forest health. No matter what he presented all they wanted to hear about was acid rain. He could not get the message across that there were a number of things far more damaging to the forests of Muskoka than acid rain, like caterpillars, droughts, a variety of tree diseases and unsustainable forestry practices. When he mentioned those topics his audience would immediately bring the discussion back to acid rain.

In that same era, I planted spruce, red oak, white oak, beech, maple, apple, hawthorn, high-bush cranberry, ash, elm, white birch, cedar, and butternut trees at my new residence in Bracebridge and they have absolutely flourished. I recall wondering as I was doing so, based on the predictions of the day, if I was wasting my time. The water level of the small lake where I have a cottage has not changed since 1973 and the view from my back yard, where at one time I could easily see my neighbour's house across a huge ravine, now is totally obscured by a blossoming native Muskoka forest.

We are all affected to some extent by our environment and it is important to do what we can to protect the world around us. Some things are within our control but the greater power is not one of them. Scientists suggest a massive volcano is way overdue to erupt in Yellowstone National Park, predicted to be several times more powerful than that of Mt. St. Helens. Will the resulting massive plume of ash in the atmosphere have an effect on our climate? *Absolutely.*

There is one thing for certain. When a weather event occurs, even a minor one, *anywhere* on this earth, we will hear about it within minutes thanks to our modern highly developed communications and social networking systems. A few decades ago it would have taken months, maybe years, for us to hear about such things; or we might not have heard about it at all. Is this making a difference in the way we view our environment? Is it fuelling the fire of the experts?

Since the beginning, whenever that was, such events have formed this earth and will continue to do so. In spite of how smart we think we are there is little or nothing we can do to prevent them.

55. THE LAST WORD...

There is so much more to be told about the Bracebridge experience. As I have said many times during presentations on Bracebridge history -*write down your life story*. It may not seem of much importance to you right now but a hundred years those reading it will gain an insight into our world and marvel at how it differs from theirs. We have a number of good examples of that, and its importance, in the memoirs of Anne (Mrs. John) Adair, Johnny Moon and the authors of the various books on our colourful past.

There are many individuals in Bracebridge that I turn to when faced with a question that I cannot answer from my own experience or from the *Veitch Index*. I value the advantage of having them assist me in my endeavour to keep our history alive. I greatly appreciate their assistance and friendship.

INDEX	PAGE
Abandoned baby in BB	145
Adair , m/m John -her diary, opinion of settlers plight	51,52
Adair, John -Beardmore tannery site	107
Adair, John -built Inn At the Falls	206
Adamson, Will -reovated original auditorium	139
Agricultural Society	76
Albion Hotel -owner bought a cadilac	58
Alcohol approved for sale with meals 1962	58
Alexander Murray	16
Alexander, David W. tannery	109
Algonguin Park	15
Algonquin Dome	15
Allchin, Ernest & Marion (Timmy)	51,206
Allchin, Marion -foundedSantas Village	209
Alley Way/Alleyway -Chancery Lane	81
Alport, A J -getting railway	33
Ambulance purchased by Womens Patriotic League	px160
Ancient Order of Workmen	158
Anderson, Alex -cheese factory	85
Anderson, T J & Sons	204
Anderson, T J -Brilliant Light Co	73
Anderson, T J/Wilbur/Fred	204
Anderson, Winnifred -Choral Society	162
Anglo-Canadia Leather Co	107
Anglo-Canadian Band	110
Anglo-Canadian Leather Co -Moon worked there	170
Annie Williams memorial Pk	98,120
Apple Tree Park,-water fountain	43,px56,px57
Arena history	87
Armstrong, Allan Silver Bridge lights	67
Armstrong, Butcher Shop -Brooks bought	195
Armstrong, Sam -Flora Barnes lawsuit	95,100
Arnott, Fanny (Hare)	144
Arnott, Mary Ann (Rutherford) -nursing home	143
Arnstrong, Sam -opposed buying powerhouse land	111
Aubrey Street- description/history	127
Austrian prisoners of war -working at tannery	109
Baddeley, F. H.	17
Baddeley, Frederick	16

Bailey Grist Mill	px40
Bailey, Ace -benefit game in Maple Leaf Gardens	161
Bailey, Ace -skating in Dunns rink	88
Bailey, Alex -hired White	101
Bailey, Alexander -grist mill	23,24,px25,50
Bailey, Alexander -hired White	127
Bailey, Bert tannery accident	111
Bailey, owned Victoria Hotel	27
Baileys Grist Mill	23
Baker, John -built stome jail	100
Ball -Aubrey St	128
Band of Hope	167
Bandsaw -double cutting -Shiers	201
Bandstand in Mem Pk	px92
Banks, Glen -Choral Society	162
Banting, Dr wanted Caisse to work with	105
Barber Tannery -location of Newark	208
Barber, David -tannery	108
Barnes, Capt Thomas	95
Barron Springs	40
Baseball -1st in BB	72
Baseball -Crosby helped	180,181
Bass Rock Park Rapids	62,65
Bastedo, A F -helped Rene Caisse	105
Bates, Arthur S.	192,211
BB Auto & Sports	206
BB Dairy Bar -part of old Dominion Hotel	26
Beal, John 1st settler, climbed difficult terrain	19,21,125
Bealey, Ivan -Hammond Ambulance	192
Beardmore Tannery	107
Beardmore Tannery -bought Adair property	52
Beardmore, A W -prisoners at tannery	109
Beaumont, Herbert/J J	px183
Beaver Temple IOGT	53
Bell, Harold (Ding)	129
Bell, Marilyn -cut ribbon at Santas Village	209
Bell, Robert recommended town site	118
Beverly, Al -Queens Hotel	46
Bickmore -Bracebridge Cricket Club	164
Big Busy Store (T J Anderson & Sons)	204
Billy the Pig	175

Binyon -Bracebridge Cricket Club	164
Binyon, Ed -hockey	88
Binyon, Gustavus Adolphis -barber	67
Bird Grove road thru to north/east	27
Bird House on Free Methodist Hill	27
Bird Mill Mews -Dr Williams home location	121
Bird Mill pumphouse	115
Bird Mill warehouse	116
Bird Woolen Mill	50
Bird Woolen Mill -history/products	39,px40,41
Bird, Henry J - mill and residence	115
Bird, Henry J -opposed buying powerhouse land	111
Bird, Henry J. Woolen mill	26,27
Bird, Henry J. Sr Woolen mill/Jr./Thomas/John/Peter	39,41
Bird, Henry Jr -Canadian Club of BB	162
Bird, Margaret Catherine/Mary Clef Club	159
Bird, Mrs H -original Choral Soc	161
Bird's Bridge	26
Black Hand	156
Black River	15
Black River -blackish and bitter water	51
Black Squirrels and raccoons	185
Blackbird Vintage Gallery -former BB Auto	206
Blanchard, Harold -worked at Downtown Garage	199
Blind pigs -bootleggers	57
Blue Glass Club	167
Boake property -Aubrey St	128
Boney	182
Booth, Doris (Leeder) -visited Moons cave	171
Booth, Harry -partnered with Thomas	196
Boothby, Ralph -Fowler Construction Co	204
Bowman, Jonas -tannery	108
Boyer -Bracebridge Cricket Club	164
Boyer, Bob -Choral Society	162
Boyer, G W -Canadian Club of BB	162
Boyer, George, James, Robert - Musk Publishing	189
Boyer, Henry, Harry, Sam	73,74
Boyer, James -disputes over Town Hall construction	137,138
Boyer, Robert J -foundedSantas Village	209
Boyer, Ted -Aubrey St	129,130
Boyes, Graydon/Mark -Richardson	147

Boyes, Mark -taught dentistry	176
Bracebridge Acetylene Co	73
Bracebridge Bay Park waterwheel emulating original	24
Bracebridge Bay -route of explorers	16
Bracebridge Bears	134
Bracebridge Bowling Alley	123
Bracebridge Cheese Factory -started	85
Bracebridge Choral Society -lost music etc in '57 fire	161
Bracebridge Citizens Band -history	160
Bracebridge Citizens Band -Shaw	111
Bracebridge Club	165
Bracebridge Cricket Club	164
Bracebridge Falls -description	114
Bracebridge Falls-1st recorded visit	16
Bracebridge Garage -Les Rosewarne	193
Bracebridge High School Literacy Society	167
Bracebridge ladies Aid	167
Bracebridge Library -Moon worked there	170
Bracebridge Liquor company	29,79
Bracebridge Literacy Society	167
Bracebridge Memorial Community Centre ist face-off	87,px89
Bracebridge -part of United Townships, naming	22
Bracebridge Public LibraryéSenior Centre	125
Bradbury, Jim & Mary -bought Ridleys	198
Bradshaw, Fred -bought by Shier	198
Braida, Gus -Bracebridge Club 1947	165
Brazier, Bill and Agnes/Buster (Bus)	152
Brazier, Bus	89
Brazier, Charles, Robert, George, Victor, Percy, Edward	152
Brewers warehouse & liquor store approved	58
Brick Block -McMurray	38,px39,158
Bridge at Wilsons Falls	62
Bridge over falls, pine tree, drunk saved by branch	20
Bridge Street	62
Bridges in BB	61to65
Bridgland, Emily Agnes/Mary -married White	102
Bridgland, J W -dismal view of Muskoka	51
Briilliant Light Company	73
British Lion Hotel	44
British Lion Hotel -prisoners escaped to	97
British lion Hotel -Sibbett	79

British Lion Hotel -used by Rene Caisse	105
British Military	15
Brooks, Alex/David/Andy	195
Brooks, George E./Herman/George S/Jerry	194,195
Brooks, H J & Sons	194
Brown, Singleton -opposed buying powerhouse land	111
Brown, Singleton -partner with Shier	201
Brown, Singleton Shingle Mill in BB Bay	114
Browning -Bracebridge Cricket Club	164
Browning, Robert M. -funeral service	126
Buckerfield -Brilliant Light Co	73
Burton, Bob -maintaining old post office	124
Burton, Hudson -service stn	125
Burton, J Hudson/Douglas	px183,197
Business The Foundation of Bracebridge	189
Byers, Dr J N -Adair	52
Caisse, Joseph -Marrin started there	194
Caisse, Rene Cancer clinic -in Br Lion Hotel	44
Caisse, Rene M history of Essiac	105,px106
Caldwell, John A -Ancient Order of Workmen	158
Canada Day fireworks on Aubrey St	128
Canada Packers bought tanneries	112
Canada Wood Specialties -tannery site	107
Canadian Club of BB	162
Canadian Patriotic Fund	162
Canal system -Geo Bay to Ottawa R	16
Cancer Nurse, The -Rene Caisse	106
Candy Cane Express -Santas train	209
Cannons in Mem Pk	94
Carn Brae -Dr Williams home	121
Carthew, John	16,17
Cathcart, Lyle (Crash) & Margaret -bought Stuthers	207
Cathcart, Lyle Town Hall fire 1957	140
Cathcarts Garage	207
Catholic Mens Society	166
Catholic Order of Forresters	165
Champlain, Samuel	15
Chancery Lane -the alleyway, lawyers offices	81
Chapel Gallery -built to emulate 1st Church	65
Chapel Gallery -former site of Prsbyterian Church	53

Characters We Have Known	169
Charles St	127
Charles W I -Canadian Club of BB	162
Cheese factory Corner	85
Cheese Factory Hill	86
Childrens Aid Society -abandoned baby	145
Childrens Aid Society -Dr Williams	120
Chosen Friends Lodge	166
Circuses to BB	px35,87,125
Clarridge, Mrs Earl -Aubrey St	128
Clef Club	159
Clef Club -ambulance for WW 1	163
Climate Change	213
Clipsham, Mike -Knowles Plumbing	210
CNR -protect from things off trains on walkway	116
Coates, Don Kinsmen fireworks for Canada Day	129
Coates, Glen -Fowler Construction Co	204
Coates, Don -Muskoka Containerized Services	205
Coates, Glen -Choral Society	162
Cockburn, A P M.P.P. post office for BB	22
Cockburn, A P M.P.P., Railway	29,33
Cockburn, A P -hired White	102
Cockburn, W P -wharf negotiation	69
Code, John -367 Club 1910	168
Colville, William -Thomas bought	195
Commandant -Aubrey St	128
Committee of 100	53
Confederation Day -naming streets	29
Conners, Alf (Shorty)	177
Conway, Abbott -tannery	110
Conway, C W -control of tannery	112
Cook, Gerald -Pawson harness	123
Coombs, A B -Ancient Order of Workmen	158
Cooper family/Musk Rd	31
Cooper Hotel	25
Cooper St	127
Cooper, Alex, Andrew, Arthur, Edward	19
Cooper, Ernest, George, Gordon, Harold, Bob	19
Cooper, Hugh, Robert, John, Thomas	19
Cooper, Joseph letter re bridges	64
Cooper, Joseph, James 1st bridge	19
Cooper, Roy hockey	88

Coopers Rapids	62
Coper, Joseph -Aubrey St plan	127
Coulson, Ernie -worked at Downtown Garage	199
Court system 1868, other Towns upset 1888	22
Courtney, David bought Northern Advocate	37
Cox, Brenda and Art -restored Memorial Pk fountain	93
Crockford, Art -worked at Downtown Garage	199
Crockford, Arthur	75
Crockford, Morley/William and Sadie	176,px177
Crompton, Thomas -store	77
Crosby, Fred (Bing)	px180,181
Crystal Palace Jubilee Pk named after London Eng	83,px84
Crystal Theatre	123
Culos, Dan	181
Currie, Don -retored fountain Memorial Pk	93
Cutler, Percy -reception with Vincent	152
Dale, Joseph -dismal opinioon of Muskoka	49,50
Daniels -Bracebridge Cricket Club	164
Dauphin, Murray & Joan -Funeral Home	203
Davey, Al	192
David Thompson	16
Davidson -Bracebridge Cricket Club	164
Davis, John Kinsmen fireworks for Canada Day	129
Davison -Bracebridge Cricket Club	164
Dawson, George & Edith/Abram/Albert/Abe/Ab	210
Dawson, Harold & Pauline/Mike/Jeff	210
Dawson's Electric	210
Dee Bank River	16
Dennis, J S survey line	19
Diaper Row -Aubrey St	128
Different points of view on early BB	47
Diggle, Charles W Dep. Registrar	127
Dill -Bracebridge Cricket Club	164
District Exchange of Teviotdale	29,px30,50
Dobbin, John -town pump	81px83
Dobbins Gardens -Dominion St	82
Dodge, A P C0 -White worked for	102
Dods, Dr R J Town Hall fire 1957	140
Dominion Hotel/House	26,27,43
Dominion Linen Mills -McKay bought	200
Dominsalo, Raphael -murdered	156

Dowler Match Factory	71
Dowler, George/Joseph	71,72
Downey -Aubrey St	128
Downey, Ken -Aubrey St	128
Downtown Garage	199
Dufferin Hall	75
Dufferin, Lady -view of Muskoka	50
Dufferin,Lord and Lady visit 1874	75
Duffus, William designed original Town Hall	137
Dunn, John E built skating rinks	87,px88
Early days in business	21,23
Eaton, Seymour -The Teddy Bear	187
Ecclestone and Bates/Albert E.	192
Ecclestone Drive-part of Hawkins line	17
Ecclestone Harware/Ecclestone & Bates	191
Ecclestone, Albert	211
Ecclestone, family -Moon worked there	170
Ecclestone, George W -bandstand	92
Ecclestone, George W/George N/George R (Butch)	191,192
Eighteen Knitting Club -for war effort	163
Electrical generating station -Shaw Town bought	110,111
Electrical generating stn at High Falls	117
Electrical generating stn at Wilsons Falls	116
Electricity -concern about using it	73
Elephants to BB for circus, died on street	px35,36
Elliott, J H-clock in Post office, described	124
Elliott, J Hilliard/Bill	196
Elliotts 5 to $1.00 Store	196
Everett, Bob -Aubrey St	128
Ewing, m/m Gordon	69
Explorers	15
Fairy Lake	16
Falls -importance to development	23
Falls on Muskoka River	23
Farmers Market on Kimberley	85
Farms -too positve, million acres	16
Fawcett, Jack -partnered with Kirkness	198
Fenn -Bracebridge Cricket Club	164
Fenn -Brilliant Light Co	73
Fenn, Anderson & Co	204
Fenn, George James partner in Eccleston & Bates	192

Fenn, James L Jr -367 Club 1910	168
Fenn, James L Jr -store	204
Ferguson Hwy -building	121
Ferguson, W S -Ancient Order of Workmen	158
Finch Gravel pit-Musk Rd	31
Finch, Walter/Murray/Wes	190,191
Findlay, James Mem Pk honour plaque	px91
First Jail -log, still around on Santas Village Rd	98
First municipality in Canada to own a generating stn	111
First Nations	16
Flaxman, E -Ancient Order of Workmen	158
Flora Barnes (boat) history, lawsuit	76,95
Flynns Rapids	62
Foot, W E	169
Foote's Bay	169
Forgione lumber mill -tannery site	107
Forrester, Fred -worked at Downtown Garage	199
Forth, Maw	183
Fountain, Boer memorial by GHO Thomas	93
Fountain, for public drinking water	px56,px57
Fourth Ward -annexed area	110
Fowler Construction Co	204
Fowler, Archie -Fowler Construction Co	204
Fox, Gerry -Musk Rd	31
Francois Joseph Bressani	15
Fraser, Duffy -Aubrey St	129
Free Grant Gazette	37
Free Grant Land and Homestead Act	15
Free grant Land and Homestead Act	26
Free Methodist Hill	65
Free Methodist Hill pt of Musk Rd	32
Free Methodist Hill/church hotels located on	27
French, Charles/Jim -French's Appliances	192
French's Appliances	192
Frowe, Harold Clarence	197
Fryer, W C -367 Club 1910	168
Funeral for Browning-coffin slid out of wagon	126
Fur traders	16
Furniture Factory -Tennant smill	190
Gallanger -Aubrey St	128
Game Protection Society	166

Garden Café restaurant	125
Garrett, E -tannery	108
Garwood, Roy -foundedSantas Village	209
Gauley, Joe & Shirley (Shier)	198
Geological Survey of Canada	16
Giaschi Bldg -former Ecclestone/Teviotdales	29
Giaschi, Guiseppe (Joseph)/Andrew/Larry & Marion/Gina	201,202
Giaschi-Mitchell, Gina	202
Gladiator, Osceola	173
Glennie, Bill recipe for Essiac	105
Glover, John waggon shop 1878	79
Gods, The -Town Hall seating	138
Goggin, William/Private hospital	143
Gold Rush in Muskoka	186
Golden Beaver statue	px77
Goltz, Nelson -Manager of Santas Village	px209
Gordon Motor Sales	193
Gow, m/m George F -Adairs	51
Graffe & Co. newspaper 1878	37
Grand Falls -Muskoka Falls	118
Gravenhurst opposed court to BB 1888	22
Gravenhurst, new road to	31,34
Great Falls -Muskoka Falls	118
Green, Clarence -foundedSantas Village	209
Greig, Jean -Choral Society	162
Grist Mill -farmers coming in from Ufford	24
Grove, The -McMurray home/high school	38
Gurrell, William -Billy the Pig	175
Hallsteads Rapids	62
Halstead and McNicol sawmill	62
Hamilton, W E-BB 60 % good land in Muskoka	48
Hamilton, W E-BB in 1861	21
Hammond, Greg/Paul/Darcy	193
Hammond, Orv -partnered with Parlett-Park Taxi	192
Hammonds Transportation/Muskoka Transport	192
Hampson, Bud -worked at Downtown Garage	199
Hampson, Charles	88
Hampson, Stella (Leeder) -knew Johnny Moon	170
Hanna Chute	118
Hare, Fanny (Arnott)	144
Harmony Club	167

Harper, Richard	114
Hart, Harold and Peggy -Aubrey St	128
Hart, Les -Bernado Home, worked for Williams	121
Harvie Line of Stages -Adair	51
Harvie Stage Co -in Mem Pk	31,93
Hawkins Line -set Township lines	17
Hearse -picture of door	px203
Heart of Muskoka-naming	18
Henry, H C -Canadian Club of BB	162
Her Majesty`s Old Reliable Shaving Saloon	67
Herald Hall	167
Herald Newspaper 1878	37
Higgins Hotel (Queens)	44,45
Higgins, Betty -Choral Society	162
Higgins, John -Ancient Order of Workmen	158
High Falls -description	117
Hillman, Jim -worked at Downtown Garage	199
Hillman, Seth	75
Hillman, Seth -worked at Downtown Garage	199
Hines, Allan -Choral Society	161
Hockey 1st telvised hockey game in Canada	90
Hogson, D T -Ancient Order of Workmen	158
Holditch, William history/2 horse power boat	69
Holditch, William married Willson	116
Holditch, William -naming streets	29
Holditch, William -part with Willson	62
Holiday House	206
Holiday, Tom	178,px179
Hotels in BB, after earliest	43
Hotels in earl BB	25
Hotels, Early	25
House of Commerce	71
How Hot is Hot	213
Hudson Bay Company	16
Huggard, Viola (MacMillan) life story	141
Humphries, Jame P -store	71
Hunt -Bracebridge Cricket Club	164
Hunt, Alfred sold land for powerhouse	111
Hunt, Alfred/Bank	34
Hunt, Ed built service stn	125
Hunter Bros -store	77

Hunt's Bank, Alfred	71,73
Hunts Hill	65
Hunts Hill bridge	62,63,64
Huntsville and Bracebridge Tannery Co	110
Huntsville opposed court to BB 1888	22
Hurst, Mayor Roland -Lincoln Eng opened visitor centre	116
Hutchins -Bracebridge Cricket Club	164
Hutchison, Peter -367 Club 1910	168
Hutchison, Robert	px183
In at the Falls ground sinking in parking lot	43
Independent Order of Forresters	157
Independent Order of Good Templars	53,58
Independent Order of Oddfellows	76,79
Independent Order of Oddfellows	121
Inn at the Falls -formerly Holiday House	206
Introduction	13
Ivey, Donna -Researched Eaton	187
Jail -1st one then brick one/fenced enclosure	98,px99
Jails -Stone cottage etc	97,px98,px101,px99,100
Jamieson, Clarence Louis (Dutch or Moose) hockey	88
Jamot, Right Rev. Monseignor street named after	28
Jerman, Gordon (Ras)/Charles	178
Jocques -Bracebridge Cricket Club	164
Johnson, F M Musk Foundry	199
Johnson, Tom -Brilliant Light Co	73
Jubilee Pk fo annual fair	34
Jubilee Rink	87,px88
Kalamity Club	38,158
Keith Road -part of Hawkins line	17
Kelvin Grove Pk- named in deed	114
Kenoza boat, Thomas arrived on	195
Kentucky Fried Chicken -location of Arnott hospital	143
Kentucky Fried Chicken -location of Rosewarne dealer	194
Kettle -Aubrey St	128
Kimberly Ave -naming	93
Kingsmill, Mrs -Patriotic League	163
Kingsmill, William -367 Club 1910	168
Kinsey, W W -Funeral Home	202
Kinsey, W W -funeral service for Browning	123,125
Kinsey, W W-367 Club 1910	168

Kinsmen Club	67
Kinsmen Club took over fireworks	129
Kirby, Sherman	202
Kirk, William -Brilliant Light Co	73
Kirkness, Doug -partnered with Fawcett	198
Knit Knuts Club -for war effort	164
Knowles Plumbing	210
Knowles, Stan & Doris/David	210
Knowles, Stan -Choral Society	162
Kris Kringle -Santas boat	209
Lacey, M C -Marrin bought shop	194
Lake of Bays	16
Lakes Muskoka, Rosseau and Joseph	16
Lakes of Muskoka Cottage Brerwery	60,123
Lang, James D -found Moon's diary/bible	172,px173
Lang, W J & Sons	206
Lang, Walter/James/Joe	206
Langford, Newton	px183
Laquer -Aubrey St	128
Last Word, The	217
Lawson, R A -367 Club 1910	168
Lee Roche & Kelly -former Br Lion Hotel	44
Lee, R -Canadian Club of BB	162
Leece, Bill -Waite bought his bakery	190
Leeder, Art -helped Johnny Moon/chickens in new house	171
Leeder, Stella (Hampson), Doris (Booth) -knew Moon	171
Lees, Noel (Turk)	130
Lefebvre, Gord Aubrey St	137
Leishman, John/Robert	px183
Leith, David early settler	19,21
Leons Furniture -formerly Brooks	195
Lidstone, Harry and Doris -Aubrey St	128,129,130
Lieutenant Briscoe	15
Lighting the lights	67
Little , John -descendant of Adair	52
Little Jimmy -James MacDonald	px183
Livingston, Neil -completed work on original Town Hall	137
Local option vote	53,79
Loftus, Jane -descendant of Adair	52
Log Jail	px98
Lomas -Aubrey St	128

Lount Charles	px183
Lount, George Crown Land Agent	102
Loyal Orange Lodge	165
Loyal Orange Lodge bldg 1871	37
Mac Millan, Viola (Huggard) life story	141
MacDonald, Hiram -developed subdivision/street names	27
MacDonald, Hiram James -Adairs	51
MacDonald, Hiram -tavern and store	21,26
MacDonald, James -Little Jimmy	px183
MacIver -Aubrey St	128
MacMillan Grocery store/ Norman J	121
MacMillan, Norman J -born in BB,President of CNR	114
MacNaughtan Hardware/Peter/Jim/George	191
Madawaska River	16,17
Magee -Aubrey St	128
Magee, Thomas waggon shop 1878	79
Mahaffy, Arthur A -Judge	39
Mahaffy, Arthur A/Bros 1st car in BB	121
Mahaffy, George Musk Foundry	199
Mahaffy, Judge W C -Ancient Order of Workmen	158
Mahaffy, William Cosby -bought Adair house	51,206
Manitoba Street -part of Hawkins line	17
Marble and Granite Works	73
Market St -changed to Kimberley	93
Marrin, Dorothy -Choral Society	162
Marrin, P J Bldg	71
Marrin, P J Wholesalers	194
Marrin, Phillip J./Morley/Jerry/Jim/Michael	194
Marshal, Charles -describing North Falls 1870	26
Marshal, Gerge C. -Funeral Home	203
Marskell -Bracebridge Acetylene Co	73
Mary Lake	16
Masonic Lodge -in Brick Block	39
Matthews -Bracebridge Cricket Club	164
Matthews -cut Shiers log boom loose	201
Maude, Col. -Prospect Lake	71
Mauro, Larry	181
Mawdsley -Bracebridge Cricket Club	164
Mawdsley, A E	px183
McConnell, Police Chief	109
McDonald, Duncan jailer	98,99,100,101

McDonald, Hiram -see MacDonald	26
McGibbon, Dr -Canadian Club of BB	162
McGibbon, Dr Peter	119
McGibbon, Mrs -Choral Soc	161
McIlmoyle, Dr -367 Club 1910	168
McKay M.P. -Canadian Club of BB	162
McKay, Mungo Park	34
McKay, Mungo Park sold Kelvin Gr Pk to Town	114
McKay, Mungo Park/Park/Ronald-Musk Foundry	199
McLaren, Mrs Forbes -letter confirming street naming	69
McMurray, Thomas -Brick Block	158
McMurray, Thomas promotor of Muskoka	30,37
McNeice, Cecil	178
McPherson, Mary -friend of Caisse/recipe for Essiac	105
McVittie, Jack/Don -protecting red pine plantation	120
Medley Bros	189
Medley, Tom/Perce	189
Memorial Park history	91
Memorial Pk	87
Methodist Church construction	71
Methodist Episcopal Church -Willson	62
Methodist Episcopal minister -Willson/Williams	116,120
Mill Street to grist mill site	24,115
Mills, Richard jailer	98
Milne, Axiel (Alex)	166
Miners, Norm and Dolly -Aubrey St	128,129
Minett Shields Co -boatbuilders	114
Minett, Bert -boat builder	114
Moon, Johnny -Bernardo Home, worked for Williams	121
Moon, Johnny -his story in BB	169
Moore -Aubrey St	128
Morley, Mr -Dr Williams talked to him	121
Morra, John BB Citizens Band	91,161
Morrison -Aubrey St	128
Morrow, T M -367 Club 1910	168
Mosbaugh, F R -control of tannery	112
Mothers Pension Board	165
Muskoka Canyon	116
Muskoka Colonization Rd, location/difficulties/losing	31
Muskoka Containerized Services	205
Muskoka Falls -description	118

Muskoka Falls log slide building	118,px119
Muskoka Foundry	34,199
Muskoka Garage -Rosewarne	193
Muskoka Gold Rush	186
Muskoka Lamb	187
Muskoka Linen Mill on former fairgrounds	34
Muskoka Navigation Co	33
Muskoka Navigation Co hired White	102
Muskoka Publishing Co	189
Muskoka Rd construction -Coopers	20
Muskoka River dispute logs vs Navigation	103
Muskoka River -its importance to BB & Muskoka	23,113
Muskoka terrain described -good and bad	48,49,50,51
Muskoka Trading Co	197
Muskoka Trading Store	123
Muskoka, conflicting views	49
Muskoka, describing its attributes for settlers	48,49
Muskokaville -site recommended by Bell	118
Musquash River	16
Myers, Mr -owned building	77
Myers, Thomas -street named after	82
National Bank	87
Native population	15
Nelan, Andy recipe for Essiac	105
Nelson, Mr -service stn	125
New York Horse Shoeing Emporium	75
Newark Boat Fenders	208
Newark, John	208
Ney, John W -store	77
NHL 1st oldtimers game	89
Niagara of the North -High Falls	117
Nick's Family Restaurant -former Thomas house	93
Ninety 8 Club	164
Niven, Jim & Jacqueline -bought Holiday House	207
Nock, Rev Frank -Choral Society	162
Norsemen	15
North American Hotel	43
North Falls	16
North West Company	16
Northern Advocate BB 1870/McMurray	26,37
Northern Ont Castings	200

Northern Planing Mills/Buildal	190
Northern Railway -rock cut	115
Norwood Mills -Willson/Holditch	62,69,116
Norwood Theatre	87,201
Nymoca -boat -367 Club 1910	168
Olan, Ron and Jean -Aubrey St	128
Old Established Waggon Shop	79
Old Station Restaurant	125,198
Old timers hocke 1st NHL game in BB	89
One hundred mile cruise	155
Order of the Knights of the Macabees	157
Organizations we have known	153
Oxtongue River	16
Palace Rink burned 1931	87,px88
Palace Rink -special platform for Band	161
Park Taxi -Hammond & Parlett (Pearly Gates Taxi)	192
Parlett, George -partnered with Hammond-Park Taxi	192
Patterson -Aubrey St	128
Patterson Bros. -Queens Hotel	45
Patterson, Bill -Choral Society	162
Patterson, Ernie, Fenton	125
Patterson, Fenton/Ernie/Bill	125,198
Patterson, Marjorie (Quemby) -Choral Society	162
Pawson Harness Shop/Richard (Dick), Jack, fire	123
Peacock, Alma -Choral Society	162
Pearly Gates Taxi -Park Taxi	192
Pelletier, Lou -sold garage to Rosewarne	193
Pelletier, Mrs-fire destroyed Warlow house	26
Peninsula Lake	16
Perry & Myers -bought Teviotdale store	29,px30,50
Petry -Aubrey St	128
Philips, Roxyna -created Choral Soc.	161
Pickles, Don	191
Pilger, Carl	174
Pine Tree bridge over BB Falls, drunk saved by branch	20
Pisanis, Joseph -charged with murder	156
Pope, Robert T -surveyor	127
Post Office	87
Post Office -naming by LaSuer	22
Post Office -old, building, 1915, campaigning for	123
Prentiss, James tannery accident	111

Presbyterian church 1st church bldg	27
Presbyterian Church -location of Chapel Gallery	53
Presbyterian Church -road to Hunts Hill passed	65
Prince Hall Freemasonry	166
Princess Theatre	202
Prisoners excaped to hotel/whitewash clothes	97,99
Prohibition	53
Prowse -Bracebridge Cricket Club	164
Prowse. Edward	px183
Queens Hotel	44,px45,123
Queens Hotel -Billy the Pig	175
Raeburn, Jim and B -Aubrey St	128
Railway companies -clarification of those to BB	34
Railway -good so people can't see area south of Grav.	33
Railway Hotel (Albion)	44
Railway -negotiation to get it here,describing Muskoka	33
Rama Township	17
Ramsay, Milton -partnered with MacNaughtan	191
Recollet missionaries	15
Red Cross Hospital	143
Reid -Aubrey St	128
Reid, Eva Clef Club	159
Reid, J W -refused Morra's resignation/Band	161
Reid, Stu -1st face off in new arena	89
Reid, Ted/George	190
Reid, Wellington/Ruth (Reid) -Silver Bridge lighting	66
Relighting the lights ceremony	67
Rene Caisse Lane named	94
Reynolds Funeral Home	20
Richardson, Arthur & Sylvia -bought Holiday House	207
Rickard, Peter & Jan -bought Holiday House	207
Riddle, Justice	156
Ridley Cleaners	198
Road from Muskoka Rd to east/north through Bird Grove	27
Robert Bell -set Township lines	17
Robert Dolphin -heart of Muskoka	18
Robertson, John Musk Foundry	199
Robinson, Bud opened visitor centre	116
Robinson, Tom Aubrey St	131
Robinson, Tom -welcome to BB sign	200
Roche, Nick recipe for Essiac	105

Rock Cut -bridge over	35,px36
Rogers Insurance	125
Rogers Pump Works	125
Rombos Pizza -Town bought property	116
Roosevelt Bears -by Seymour Eaton	187
Rosewarne, Earl	125
Rosewarne, Gord -Gordon Motor Sales	193
Rosewarne, Jean -Choral Society	162
Rosewarne, Thomas B./Earl/Les/Gord/Norm	193
Rosewarnes, Les garage -location of Arnotts hospital	143
Ross, Mr. operated hotels	26
Rowe, Wally Aubrey St	137
Royal Canadian Legion -Musk Rd/hospital founding	31,92
Royal Engineers	16
Royal Hotel	26
Rusk, James	85
Rutherford, Mary Ann (Arnott)	143
Rutledge -Aubrey St	128
Salmon, A C -367 Club 1910	168
Salmon, Russ Service Stn	116
Salvadore, Sam -charged with murder	156
Salvation Army bought Dufferin Hall	75
Samuel Richardson	17
Sander, Fred -Ancient Order of Workmen	158
Santas Village	208
Sault du Sauvage -Muskoka Falls	118
Schools in BB-1870	22
Scows, serving as a bridge in winter	66
Sedgwick -Aubrey St	128
Settlers -difficult times, developing of Muskoka	47
Settlers Friend -Dobbins	82
Sewers -evolution of their installation	185
Shannon, Samuel -Canadian Club of BB	162
Sharpes Creek -Musk Rd	31
Shaw Bros W.S. /C.O.	110
Shaw Cassels Co -tannery	110
Shaw, W S -donated bandstand	92
Shea, Bert Ufford book	24
Shieks	165
Shier, J D Lumber	200
Shier, J D Lumber Boney slept in sawdust pile	182

Shier, J D Lumber rail siding	108
Shier, James Dawson/Ken/Roy	201
Shier, Lorne -BB Auto & Sports	206
Shier, Mrs Milton K	201
Shier, Wilf and Shirley -Aubrey St	128
Shier, Wilfred Andrew (Biff)/Wilf Jr./Shirley/John/Adam	198
Shiers Bridge	px32
Shier's Insurance	198
Shirreff family	15
Short, Gerry -Aubrey St	129
Sibbett, George W	px183
Sibbett, George W -liquor manufacturer	54,79,px80
Silver bridge construction/lighting	66,px67
Simmons, Bab -Jail worker	97
Simmons, William	px183
Simple Cottage -old foundry	200
Simple Cottage-former foundry	34
Sinclair, Gordon 1st NHL old timers game	89
Singleton Brown Shingle Mill	110
Skating rinks 1st	87
Skeleton Lake	16
Skinner, Don & Jen -Queens Hotel, 2 suspected spies	46
Smellie, Paul & Doris -bought Thomas Co	196
Smith, John -picture of Moon's shack	px172
Smith, P A -367 Club 1910	168
Smith, Peter A -tannery	109
Smith, Ted	125,198
Snake with legs found	185
Snazel, William -Ridley Cleaners	198
Sons of England	153
Sons of Scotland -Scotsman Days	154
South Falls -Muskoka Falls	118
Specht, Lou -Aubrey St	128
Speck, Don & Betty bought Musk Trading	197
Speck, Merv & Betty -bought Stones	197
Spence, Bob Kinsmen fireworks for Canada Day	129
Spencer, Gattlin Gun (William H.)	100,101,176
St Thomas Ang Church McMurray bldg	38,39,158
Stephenson, E F -Gazette 1872	37
Stewart, Margaret	27
Stone, Phillip	197

Stone's Mens and Ladies Wear	197
Storey, Charles -original Town Hall	137
Story, waggon shop 1878	79
Strand Theatre	202
Strange Things Are Done	185
Street naming -Confederation day, McLaren letter re	69
Street naming -Holditch	29
Stuthers Garage bought by Cathcart	207
Stuthers, Nelson	207
Sugg, H E S (Bert) -bought stone jail	100,px101
Survey of Hawkins/Bell meet in BB	17
surveyors	17
Surveyors	17
Sutcliffe Motors -bought by Gord Rosewarne	193
Suter, Frank	89
Swain, Richard Horse shoeing	75
Tange -Aubrey St	128
Tanneries and their effect on the river	185
Tanneries history	107
Tanneries -prisoners of war proposed to work there	109
Taplin -Aubrey St	128
Teddy Bear, The -Eaton	187
Tennant, George/Les	190
Tennant, Leslie -Choral Society	162
Teviotdale, John/Ann	29
Teviotdales District Exchange	29,71
Teviotdales Spring	29,80
Theatres	202
Thomas and Booth store	196
Thomas Company	195
Thomas Tea Room	196
Thomas, Arla -Choral Society	162
Thomas, D C -Choral Society	162
Thomas, G H O -367 Club 1910	168
Thomas, G H O -Kalamity Club	158
Thomas, George Oakwood/Noah/Philip	195,196
Thomas, GHO	54
Thomas, GHO -Canadian Club of BB	162
Thomson, Carrie Bowerman Clef Club	159
Thomson, David opinion of Muskoka	51
Thomson, James -367 Club 1910	168

Thomson, m/m John Queens Hotel	45
Three 67 Club 1910	168
Three Mile Lake	16
Three Mile Lake Wolves -to grist mill	24
Thur, Don and Carol Aubrey St	135
Tillson, B W -Choral Society	161
Tillson, Charles W -tannery	108
Toc-H -remodeled the stone jail	162
Tombstone factory	73
Topp and Anderson	204
Topp -Bracebridge Cricket Club	164
Topp, Dr J W B	204
Toronto, Simcoe & Musk. Junction Rwy Co -forming	33
Toronto-Bracebridge Old Boys & Old Girls Assoc	155
Town Hall -1881	137,px138
Town Hall -auditorium 1881/1908/performances	138,139
Town Hall fire 1957	px139
Towns, m/m William -Choral Society	161,162
Townsend -Aubrey St	128
Township lines -Hawkins - Bell	17
Trading Lake	16
Trading Posts	16
Trillium Leisure Corp -bought Holiday House	207
Trimble, Herbert hockey	88
Trustrom, Vic -Aubrey St	128
Turner, Bruce & Kathy -Funeral Home	203
Twenty Third Regiment Canadian volunteers	123
Ufford	14
United States -territorial expansion	17
Uptown Service Stn	125,197
Veitch, Elijah -told of Dr Williams and Morley	121
Vesey, Gwen -Choral Society	162
Victoria Hotel	26,27
Vincent, Howard	149,px150
Vincent, Howard (DCM)/medals	px151,152
Vincent, Mr -Adairs helped	52
Vincent, Thomas Ray and Suzan (Emerick)	149
W. B. Marlow	15
W. M. Smith	15
Waites Bakery/Arthur Thomas & Edie May/Geoff/Joan	190
Walker, Earl (Squirrely) hockey	88

Walkway uner CNR track -protect from things off trains	115
Wardell family Eaton related to	187
Warlow, M/M John fire child died 1904	26
Warner, waggon shop 1878	79
Wartime Housing Ltd -Aubrey St	128
Wasdell, Fred -Mem Pk honour plaque	px91
Washburn -Bracebridge Cricket Club	164
Waste land	17
Waterfalls -22 in BB	113
Waterfalls importance to BB	23
Waterways condominium -former tannery	52
Waterwheel of Bailey, one built to emulate	25
Weather fluctuations	213
Wellington Street -part of Hawkins line	17
Wells, Douglas -foundedSantas Village	209
Wes Finch & Sons Excavating	190
Wharf 1st for steamships	24
Wharfs 4 in BB history	114
White, Aubrey -cairn at High Falls	px104,117
White, Aubrey -coming to BB/history	101
White, Aubrey -Rosewarne bought body shop	193
White, W J/W W -Funeral Home	202
White, Warden -Town jail	97
Whitten Hardware Store -post office built there	124
Whitten, Ernest A -Choral Society	161
Whitten, James -Ancient Order of Workmen	158
Wild Falls -Muskoka Falls	118
William Hawkins	17
Williams, Dr Francis -98 Club	164
Williams, Dr James Francis/Annie (Bird) -history	119,px120
Williams, Dr. -Moon worked there	170
Willis, Dr Eugene -1st NHL televised hockey	90
Willson, Gilman -sawmill	69
Willson, Gilman -store sold to Teviotdale	29
Willson, Gilman/Elizabeth -sawmill	62,69
Willson, Gilmore/Elizabeth	116
Wilson, G W -Foundry	200
Wilson, Susan -found McMurray cornerstone	39
Wilson's Falls bridge removed by Twp	62
Wilsons Falls -description	116
Winonah landed at 1st dock in BB	24

Winter Evening Amusement (Entertainment) Society	168
Women`s Institute	165
Women`s Patriotic League -ambulance for WW1	163
Women's Christian Temperance Union	53,166
Woodchester -Bird home	px41
Woods, T J-367 Club 1910	168
Woods, Thomas J -Queens Hotel	45
Wright, Fred -reception with Vincent	152
Yearley, George arena	89
Yeoman, Joshua L -embalmer	203
Young, Ralph and Ida Aubrey St	137